UNM-GALLUP
ZOLLINGER LIBRARY
200 COLLEGE ROAD
GALLUP, NEW MEXICO   87301

1. Books may be kept two weeks and may be renewed once for the same period.

2. A fine is charged for each day a book is not returned according to the above rule. No book will be issued to any person incurring such a fine until it has been paid.

3. All injuries to books beyond reasonable wear and all losses shall be made good to the satisfaction of the Librarian.

4. Each borrower is held responsible for all books charged on his card and for all fines accruing on the same.

Handbook of Walkthroughs, Inspections, and Technical Reviews

Little, Brown Computer Systems Series

Gerald M. Weinberg, *Editor*

Basso, David T., and Ronald D. Schwartz
Programming with FORTRAN/WATFOR/WATFIV

Chattergy, Rahul, and Udo W. Pooch
Top-down, Modular Programming in FORTRAN with WATFIV

Coats, R.B., and A. Parkin
Computer Models in the Social Sciences

Conway, Richard, and David Gries
An Introduction to Programming: A Structured Approach Using PL/1 and PL/C

Conway, Richard, and David Gries
Primer on Structured Programming: Using PL/1, PL/C, and PL/CT

Conway, Richard, David Gries, and E. Carl Zimmerman
A Primer on Pascal, Second Edition

Cripps, Martin
An Introduction to Computer Hardware

Easley, Grady M.
Primer for Small Systems Management

Finkenaur, Robert G.
COBOL for Students: A Programming Primer

Freedman, Daniel P., and Gerald M. Weinberg
Handbook of Walkthroughs, Inspections, and Technical Reviews: Evaluating Programs, Projects, and Products

Graybeal, Wayne, and Udo W. Pooch
Simulation: Principles and Methods

Greenfield, S.E.
The Architecture of Microcomputers

Greenwood, Frank
Profitable Small Business Computing

Healy, Martin, and David Hebditch
The Microcomputer in On-Line Systems: Small Computers in Terminal-Based Systems and Distributed Processing Networks

Lias, Edward J.
Future Mind: The Microcomputer — New Medium, New Mental Environment

Lines, M. Vardell, and Boeing Computer Services Company
Minicomputer Systems

Mills, Harlan D.
Software Productivity

Daniel P. Freedman
Gerald M. Weinberg

Handbook of Walkthroughs, Inspections, and Technical Reviews

Evaluating Programs, Projects, and Products

THIRD EDITION

Little, Brown and Company
Boston   Toronto

Library of Congress Catalog Card No. 81-12977

ISBN 0-316-292826

9 8 7 6 5 4 3 2 1

ALP

Published simultaneously in Canada
by Little, Brown & Company (Canada) Limited

Printed in the United States of America

Acknowledgments

Article on pages 46–54 reprinted, by permission of the publisher, from
Management Review, June 1973. © 1973 by AMACOM, a division of
American Management Associations. All rights reserved.

Material on pages 294–95 and pages 313–15 courtesy of Boeing Computer
Services Company.

Material on page 316 and pages 339–44 reprinted courtesy of IBM
Corporation.

Material on pages 345–47 copyright Bell Telephone Laboratories, Inc.,
1974. Reprinted by permission.

Material on pages 371–74 reprinted with permission of *Datamation* ®
Magazine, copyright 1977 by Technical Publishing Company, a Dun &
Bradstreet company—All rights reserved.

Material on pages 423–24 from personal letter to author from Gary Shelly,
1977. Used by permission.

Article on pages 425–34 from *The Compiler*, fall 1977. © Anaheim Publishing Company. Used by permission.

Contents

PART A

Introduction

About This Handbook

Why Are You Publishing This Handbook?

Over several years of conducting formal technical reviews, our associates have accumulated an impressive store of information on what to do and what not to do. As we visited client after client, we kept wishing there were some easier way to transmit the bulk of this information than by trial and (costly) error.

A number of our clients have attempted to put together formal manuals describing formal technical reviews. We've reviewed these manuals in our classes and in our clients' offices. For the most part, they don't do the job we want—they concentrate on the *how* but neglect the *why*. This handbook is our attempt to do the job as we think it should be done.

How Was the Handbook Developed?

Acting on the ideas of students and clients, we assembled "notes and queries on formal reviews," patterned somewhat on the famous anthropological fieldwork guide, *Notes and Queries*. As we heard the same questions repeatedly, we would put them into the notebook along with informal but informative replies. Then we'd review these answers and revise them to increase their interest and information content. These reviews often generated further questions and further answers to be reviewed.

For a while, we thought the process would never end, but eventually we began to see a decline in previously unseen questions. We then gathered the questions and answers and spent a long time arranging and rearranging them until a meaningful structure emerged. At that point, we decided to assemble them for distribution to our clients, students, and other interested parties.

Why Have You Changed the Name for the Third Edition?

As the audience for the handbook grew, we received many comments to the effect, "We wish we'd heard of this sooner." The former title emphasized the source of the material, but wasn't as descriptive of the contents. Also, because of the wide use of the first two editions, our sources of review experiences have grown, so a broader title is more appropriate. Finally, there is about 25 percent new material added to the second edition and about 50 percent added to the first, so a new title may appropriately describe the situation.

Doesn't the Question and Answer Format Lead to Redundancy?

Yes. Our hope is that this redundancy will increase the probability of each user finding the answer to every question, even though the question may be posed in different manners by different people. We've also added an index to help in this search for answers, so the redundancy doesn't hide information by its very bulk.

But What About Those of Us Who Want to Read the Entire Handbook?

The question and answer format was chosen to provide lots of interest, as well as information. Our trials have shown that as long as the questions and answers are sufficiently interesting, the redundancy doesn't bother anybody. Besides, it doesn't hurt if you learn an important point twice, but it may kill you if you don't learn it even once. In fact, that's one of the deep philosophies behind the entire formal technical review movement:

**Better to find an error twice
than never to find it at all.**

Glancing at the Table of Contents, I Don't See Very Many Pages Devoted to the Inspection Method (or Walkthrough Method, or Whatever) Which Is Our Primary Interest. Why Are You Ignoring This Important Method?

We are not ignoring it. You are simply being misled by the organization of the handbook. Information about the inspection method is scattered throughout the book because inspections share much with other methods. The section on inspections deals only with ideas peculiar to inspections in general. In other sections, you will find extensive checklists which can be used in inspections, plus information on the conduct of *any* type of review. By using this format, we are able to cover many formal review methods in a relatively small amount of space. We are also able to show you how much the various methods have in common, rather than emphasizing their differences, as their avid supporters are inclined to do. If you are to make intelligent choices among methods, and to adapt "pure" methods to your own day-to-day realities, you will find our organization essential.

Even if you have someone else's inspection manual (or walkthrough manual, or whatever), you will find this handbook an essential aid in really *doing* formal reviews.

How Can We Contribute New Questions, New Answers, or Corrections to the Handbook?

Please write to us at:

Daniel P. Freedman
110 Moore Avenue
Binghamton, N.Y. 13903

How Can We Find Out More About the Training and Consulting You Offer on the Subject of Technical Reviews?

Write to us at the above address.

What Is a Formal
Technical Review?

Why Do We Have Technical Reviews?

Technical work needs reviewing for the same reason that pencils need erasers:

To err is human

The second reason we need technical reviews is that although people are good at catching some of their own errors, large classes of errors escape the originator more easily than they escape anyone else. The review process is, therefore, the answer to the prayer of Robert Burns:

**O wad some power the giftie gie us
to see oursels as ithers see us**

A review—any review—is a way of using the diversity and power of a group of people to:

1. Point out needed improvements in a product of a single person or team;
2. Confirm those parts of a product in which improvement is either not desired or not needed;

7

3. Achieve technical work of more *uniform,* or at least more *predictable,* quality than can be achieved without reviews, in order to make technical work *more manageable.*

Aren't Reviews for Communication?

Even if technical products were free of errors, reviews would probably be justified solely on their *educational* value for the participants. Without reviews, communication in a large technical institution is slow and unreliable. As a rule of thumb, a programmer who regularly participates in formal and informal reviews—of his or her own work and the work of others—gains experience at a rate perhaps three times as great as a programmer working in solitude.

Reviews also serve to communicate technical information widely in a large project, supplementing or replacing formal written communication.

Then Why Are Reviews Different from the Budgetary and Scheduling Reviews Our Management Now Conducts?

When we speak of *technical* reviews, we are speaking of the *content* of technical material in a project, not the *context* of that material in the business environment, such as schedules and budgets. The question to be answered in a *technical* review is this:

Will this product do the job it's supposed to do?

Of course, if it costs too much or isn't on time, then it won't do its job; but on the other hand, if it doesn't do its job, *no schedule is on time and no cost is cheap enough.*

Questions of schedule and cost are management questions, not technical questions. There may be a technical *component* to schedule and cost questions—in programming, there almost always is. The *formal* technical review provides management information bearing on cost, schedule, manpower, and other management concerns. Without the information provided by *reliable formal technical reviews,* management is managing from a base of quicksand.

Is There Any Difference Between These Formal Technical Reviews and the Progress Reports We Now Use?

The analogy between formal technical reviews and progress reports is a good one. Formal technical reviews can be thought of as a *kind* of progress reporting system—one that contains checks and balances that *ensure the reliability* of the progress information.

Many systems exist for reporting "progress" in programming projects. Some report on how many hours have been spent on a particular project segment. Others report on the number of lines of code produced or pages of documentation written. These components of "progress" are then charted against master schedules and resource allocations to inform management of potential trouble areas. Such systems can be very effective *if the progress they report is true progress.*

Without checks and balances, however, there is no way of ensuring that 1,000 lines of code represent any useful work at all. The programming business is all too familiar with "progress" reports of 99 percent completion when the project in question isn't even 10 percent finished. Why? Because the 1,000 lines of code may be completely wrong, or partly wrong, or wrong in just one or two tiny places—places that may take 2,000 man-hours of work to correct.

A system of formal technical reviews is needed to give *meaning* to the marks on the progress reporting charts. Without *quality* measures—as provided by the formal technical reviews—quantity measures are likely to be *more dangerous than no measures at all.*

Why Do You Call Them Formal Technical Reviews? Is There an Informal Review?

Informal technical reviews take place all the time. They are an essential part of the real world of programming work. A team member passes a diagram to a teammate for an opinion on how to represent a particular situation. Someone asks help from someone else in finding a bug. A set of test cases is passed around to see if anyone can think of something that's been overlooked. One person reads another's user document to see if it's understandable. Without a constant flow of such informal review of one another's work, programming any meaningful project would be impossible.

Formal reviewing, on the other hand, is not *essential* to programming, and many small projects are accomplished without formal reviewing. As projects grow larger and more complex, however, the work of many people must be coordinated over a long period of time. Such coordination requires *management,* and such management requires *reliable* information. Formal reviews, remember, are designed to provide reliable information about technical matters.

What makes a review *formal* is a combination of "medically proven ingredients":

1. A *written* report on the status of the product reviewed—a report that is available to *everyone* involved in the project, including management;
2. Active and open participation of everyone in the review group, following some traditions, customs, and written rules as to how such a review is to be conducted;
3. Full responsibility of all participants for the *quality of*

the review—that is, for the quality of the information in the written report.

Can You Clarify the Responsibilities of the Review Group?

Notice that we said

> **The review group is responsible for the quality of the information in the written report.**

Obviously, the review group cannot and must not be held responsible for a bad product. If management punishes a review group for reporting that a product is bad, then future reviewers will be reluctant to report that products are bad. Then the quality of review information will deteriorate, and the review will become a kind of institutionalized yes-group.

On the other hand, if the review says a product is *good*, then the group does, in effect, become responsible for that product being good. If the product later proves to be of poor quality, contrary to the assurances of the review group, management will be well advised to attribute a generous share of the blame to the review group and not wholly blame the producers. Nobody can reliably evaluate the quality of their own work, so each producer must be able to depend on a high-class professional job of reviewing its formal reviews.

If a product is *bad*, then the review group has the responsibility for giving an *accurate* appraisal of that badness. Criticisms must be reported accurately and specifically. If a review group is overly or unjustly critical, it is also failing in its function.

In short, the review group is responsible for giving an accurate message to management, to the producers, and to all other parties that are concerned with the technical quality of a product.

But What If the Review Group Fails to Do This Job?

Then it is the responsibility of management to find out why and to take appropriate action. If, for instance, the review falls apart due to dissension or noncooperation, it is the review leader's responsibility to report to management *why* the group was unable to produce an accurate appraisal message. If the review leader is the source of the trouble, the group members have the obligation to report to management. But don't worry too much about failure of the reviews. Although initiating the reviews may prove a challenging management problem, once they've become part of the installation's routine, they seldom go awry. If you follow the guidance in the rest of this handbook, you shouldn't have any problems you can't handle.

Just How Effective Are Reviews?

It's difficult to give a simple number or short answer to this essential question, so we've provided a lot more detailed data later on. Still, it's a fair question to ask before you embark on an ambitious program of reviews, so we'll try to give an overall impression of our experience. In the case of ordinary application programs, such as extracting a report from an existing data base, even semiformal reviewing has almost entirely eliminated other forms of program testing. That is, clients report that the *majority* of such programs run correctly the first time they ever touch a computer—provided they have been previously reviewed. This result contrasts with an average of ten to fifty runs for "debugging" under the previous practices.

In larger systems, where accurate records have been kept, projects with a full system of reviews report a *ten times* reduction in the number of errors reaching each stage of testing. The concomitant *cost* reduction for testing efforts runs between 50 and 80 percent, even when the cost of reviewing is added to testing costs.

Reviews also have a very favorable effect on *maintenance* costs. A typical program that has been thoroughly reviewed during development and for which maintenance changes are also reviewed shows a five to one reduction in maintenance costs.

In the long run, reviews have a remarkable effect on staff competence, a difficult effect to quantify. In general, we see increased morale and professional attitude, reduced turnover, more reliable estimating and scheduling, and better appreciation of the management role in project success. At the same time, reviews provide management with a better appreciation for staff competence, both individually and collectively.

As consultants, we visit dozens of installations every year. The best way to summarize the effects of properly instituted reviews is to report that after five minutes in an installation, we can tell—without asking directly—to what extent there is an effective review practice. How do we tell? Metaphorically, we tell in the same way an FDA inspector tells about a food-processing plant—by the way it smells. It's hard to describe, but when you smell the difference, you know it!

The Level of Formality You Propose Is, I Believe, Unproductive. Formality Can Become a Crutch for Ineffective Management, and the Type of Control System That You Propose Lends Itself Very Well to Management Focusing on Paperwork and Appearances Rather Than Results or the Final Product. Don't You Agree with This Danger?

In our opinion, the best attitude to take about formal procedures is: Use them as little as possible, but use them when necessary. It seems particularly important for people starting the system of reviews to have the support of formality to get them over some of the interpersonal difficulties. As they mature in the use of reviews, a lot of the formality can drop by the wayside.

Certain things that may seem to be formality and paperwork, however, are absolutely essential. The review reports represent a distilled minimum output from the reviews. Without these reports, we believe, it would be impossible to manage software development at all. That doesn't mean you can't be successful without them, it just means you can't consistently get successful development without them in a large organization. In a small organization where there is not a lot going on at any one time, informal, verbal reports on issues raised in less formal reviews may be quite adequate.

In other words, if you feel you can succeed with reviews without this much formality, by all means do so. If you fail, however, don't blame it on the reviews. Maybe it would be better to start using the system as we propose it and then drop off the formality a piece at a time, according to what you find most offensive.

The Review Process Appears to Reinforce the Tendency of Technicians to Want to Work in a Vacuum, in the Backroom, Behind Closed Doors. Does It Work That Way?

On the contrary, the review process forces everybody to do their work out in the open, whether they like it or not. If they want to hide, they can hide up to the formal review, but not after. Usually though, once people understand that their work will be reviewed, they tend to bring it out for public scrutiny earlier and earlier in the process. This is often true in informal reviews among friends, which is perfectly all right as a technique and tends to make the formal reviews even more effective. We've certainly never observed the tendency of reviews to hide people's work.

Rather Than Adopt Consensus, Why Can't Each
Individual Reviewer Sign Off on the Product Subject to the
Exception of Their Comments, Which Are Attached to the
Report?

The principal problem with this approach is that the comments can grow to a level where their mass of paper is greater than the mass of the report. Such comments won't be read. Such comments are not very meaningful for management. Such comments are an outlet that permits the review group members to avoid actually facing the issue and taking responsibility.

Read the material on the review reports and see if you wouldn't find that total approach better, both for management and for technical workers.

PART B

The Review Environment

Selecting Reviewers

How Many People Should Attend a Formal Review?

Validated scientific studies (whose references we've unfortunately lost) have proved that the optimum number of people at a formal review is 3.1415926.... Like most theoretical studies, this one's result isn't very practical as a guideline, since few installations can manage for exactly that number of programmers to be present at the same time. In fact, the only way to achieve this number exactly is to have three programmers and one eleven-and-a-half-week old German Shepherd puppy. Therefore, most installations must find some way of approximating the optimum or perhaps stop thinking in terms of "optimum" and start thinking in terms of "good" and "adequate."

The first principle of formal review composition is this:

Select the reviewers to ensure that the material is adequately covered.

One consequence of this principle is that there is *no* fixed optimum size of a review group. The size of the group depends on the material to be covered and on the skills and review experience of the potential participants.

For instance, if we are reviewing some material that depends heavily upon the behavior of a special piece of hardware, we may need to add a person to the group merely to obtain the needed expertise in that hardware item, for otherwise the material will not be adequately covered. On the other hand, if one of the available people happens to have experience in that hardware in addition to experience in other areas important for the reviewed material, then an extra person will not be needed.

Is There Some Maximum Number of Attendees?

We always want to assure that the review is concentrating on the material at hand, rather than on managing the review itself. That's one reason we keep the reviews relatively formal in procedure, so each participant knows what's to be done without a lot of discussion. By keeping the review small, we minimize the management, or "overhead," required to keep it on track. Obviously, at a certain size, you begin to need *Robert's Rules of Order* to keep it going. If that happens, you know the review is too large.

To a great extent, the maximum size depends on the skill of the review leader. An experienced leader of moderate talent can usually keep a group of seven (including the leader and the representative of the inventor or creator, if present) close to the task at hand. If the leader is less experienced or skilled, the group should be kept smaller—perhaps by including more broadly experienced people who can handle several aspects of the material.

If the leader is inexperienced, but there seems to be no way to cover the material with fewer than six or seven people, then *choose a different leader.*

If no experienced leader is available, then *break down the material to be reviewed.* For instance, have a special review for conformity to standards, if this would eliminate the need for two standards specialists in the review and thus reduce the group to four or five, rather than six or seven.

Since no leader in the world is skilled and experienced enough to consistently conduct successful reviews with groups larger than seven, break down the review any time you think you need more than seven people or more than two hours.

It Seems Wrong to Say That Size Depends on Leader Ability, Not on the Needs of Material Reviewed, Especially Since Reviewers Are Professional People. Any Comment?

We agree that in an ideal world, all professional people would be equally qualified to participate in or lead a review, so that this statement would be false. On the other hand, in an ideal world, we wouldn't even need a special review leader. In many ways, the review leader's job is to ensure that a close to ideal review is obtained, even though the review must be staffed with far from ideal people. For further insight into the review leader's role, see the section in Part C on the review leader.

Is There a Minimum Number of People in a Review?

Because the review must be *public,* in the sense of representing openly expressed points of view, there must obviously be at least two people. Why must it be public? Because if one person "reviews" something, there is absolutely no check, at the time, on whether that person has actually gotten into the material. In an open review, other people can spot the person who hasn't actually looked at the material, or who hasn't understood it, or who doesn't care about it. The open nature *ensures the quality* of the review. Of course there can be quality reviews with a single person—often a single person will do *better* than a review group that is not well prepared or well led. But with the private review, there is no way of *telling* a good review from a poor one—each one merely has a signature and a list of comments of unknown value.

If a public review is bad, at least two people will know it's bad. In practice, that's not safe enough, so the minimum review group should have three people—and not all good buddies. If the inventor or creator is present, it may be advisable to raise the number to four, especially if this person is known to be good at laying down smokescreens.

If the Minimum Is Three or Four and the Maximum Is Seven, Why Not Just Pick Some Number, Like Five, and Decree That This Will Be the Size for All Reviews? Wouldn't That Save a Lot of Discussion?

Why do we want to save discussion? In most reviews, the most important discussion takes place *before* the meeting—in selecting the people to perform the review. Once you get the right group together in the right physical setting looking at the proper material from the correct points of view, you're pretty sure of getting a good review. That's why we do reviews—so we can have *confidence* in their conclusions.

Everyone wants to have some magic formula by which they can know that a program or other piece of work is good or bad. In their dreams, they see a software solution to the problem, but when awake, they only dare go as far as imagining that they could use an automatic, unthinking procedure to achieve the result. Wouldn't it be nice to know that if you stick an arbitrary five people in an arbitrary setting with an arbitrary piece of work for exactly two hours you would get a reliable evaluation of that work?

Unfortunately, it doesn't happen that way, so you have to think about how that review is put together in order to make it succeed. That's where the talent comes in, which is why managers get paid those fabulous salaries. The manager who knows when to put that extra person in the review, or when to insist that a certain extra person stays out, or how to recognize that there is too much to be reviewed at one sitting—that's the manager who's doing a real management job and who will get useful results from reviews, rather than a false sense of security.

Is It Management's Responsibility to Select Review Group Members?

The primary function of the review is to provide management with reliable information about the quality of technical work. Therefore, the manager receiving the review reports will want to have confidence in the people whose signatures are on the report. This means the *ultimate* responsibility for selecting review group members belongs to the manager who is responsible for the piece of work being reviewed. But the manager at *which level?* As with all responsibilities, this one is delegated down from the top to some level that works effectively.

Sometimes top management sets up a special staff team to conduct reviews and choose members—an audit or quality assurance function. This relieves the first-level manager from the contradictory task of choosing people to review work for which that manager is immediately responsible. But it also can create a problem if that manager doesn't want to believe the reports of that review group. Such problems, if they arise, have to be resolved at the level of the manager to whom audit or quality assurance reports.

At the other extreme, the immediate manager chooses the review group for each product under management. This eliminates the problem of that manager's belief in the review reports, but creates several other potential problems, such as:

1. obtaining a broad enough view by including people outside that manager's span of control;

2. obtaining an unbiased view that upper management will believe.

But all these problems are only *potential* problems. We don't want to make selection of reviewers sound terribly hard. Instead, what we mean to say is that there are *many* ways, in practice, by which reviewers actually get chosen. Reviewers may be:

1. Specialists in reviewing (quality assurance or audit),
2. People under same management as product,
3. People invited by the producers because of their known quality as reviewers,
4. People who "invited themselves" because of significant interest in the product,
5. Visitors who have something to contribute, or
6. People invited from organizationally remote functions.

Usually, a system of reviews involves a mixture of these approaches, which is very healthy because of the variety of viewpoints it introduces.

I Can See the Value of Inviting People Who Are Organizationally Remote, but Since They Are Under Different Management, How Can We Get Them to Attend?

You have to establish the idea that it is important for the whole organization for them to attend. The "top-down" approach is to sell this idea to the manager at a sufficiently high level to embrace these people under one span of control.

But even if upper management is "sold," you won't be very happy with results if people are "ordered" to come to reviews that they really don't want to attend, so you must also work on convincing people that it is in *their* interest to attend. Some of the advantages to them are:

1. Reciprocal reviewing by your group for *their* products,
2. Learning about new techniques, and
3. Broader understanding of the organization's total mission.

Why Is It So Important to Us to Have These "Outsiders"?

There are many reasons:

1. You learn from them;
2. You get less biased evaluation from them;
3. You have a better chance of discovering problems of an organizationwide nature, such as improper interfacing;
4. Your reviews will be more lively and interesting, which will make your own people more eager to participate;
5. Your people will behave better in the presence of "outsiders," to show them "how good *our* reviews are."

The important thing is not to get your reviews in a rut, or their quality will deteriorate. If they become too predictable, they may not be serving their function.

What Are Some Other Ways to Break Down a Review That Is Too Big or Too Long?

There seem to be at least two general approaches to breaking down a review that threatens to be beyond the reviewing capacity of an organization—by its form and by its function.

Breaking down the review by function is the easiest to understand. If a program is too big to review at one sitting, the program should be decomposed into modules that can be reviewed. If those modules are not actually modules in the program, then perhaps the program needs to be redesigned! A document can be reviewed chapter by chapter or paragraph by paragraph or diagram by diagram. If such a decomposition doesn't correspond to functional divisions, then the document needs to be redesigned! (Unless, of course, it's organized like this silly document.)

Breaking down by form is not always so obvious. In essence, we seek *different points of view* on the same material. For instance:

1. Standards can be reviewed separately from conformity to specifications;
2. Code and other documentation can sometimes be reviewed separately;
3. Efficiency can be reviewed separately from other specifications;
4. User interface can be reviewed separately;
5. Maintainability can be reviewed separately from conformity to functional specifications;
6. Operating convenience may be a separable review item.

For more information on this subject, see Parts E and F.

All Our Experience Indicates That Two Hours Is Too
Short a Limit for a Serious Job of Reviewing. How Can
Anything Useful Be Done in That Short a Time?

The two-hour limit is really built into human beings. Five-year-olds have an attention span of perhaps five minutes; ten-year-olds, perhaps twenty minutes; adults, generally, no more than two hours. This is a simple psychological fact about human beings in our culture, not an arbitrary limit imposed by us. In fact, even the two hours should be broken by a ten-minute break in the middle, so people can get their second wind.

But I Can Concentrate for Much More Than Two Hours,
If I'm Really Committed to the Task. What's Wrong with
People in These Reviews? Aren't They Committed? Aren't
They True Professionals?

Most professionals can, on occasion, concentrate on a task
for much more than two hours, but this isn't an ability
that we can count on five or seven people to produce on
demand or on a regular basis. Moreover, if you do this
kind of extended concentration, how can you be sure
you're actually performing to the level of accuracy that's
required in a review? Haven't you ever gone through one
of these extended "productive" periods only to find that
you had been completely on a wrong track or producing
errors at the rate of one every ten minutes?

From time to time, in a great emergency, we may
have to call upon people to spend longer than two hours
in a review, and many times they will succeed in that
environment. People are not easily boxed into neat little
psychological categories, but respond with amazing abilities in times of need. On the other hand, we don't want
to *plan* to run our projects on the basis of an endless
succession of emergencies or of spectacular performances.
We want to be able to work with ordinary exceptional
professional people working in a mostly calm environment—so we'll have a reservoir to tap when we really do
need a superhuman effort once in a while.

In Going Through the Handbook, I Didn't See Any
Mechanism to Buy the User in. You Can't Possibly Have a
Successful Product Without User Participation and
Commitment. The User Must Be As Responsible for the
Success of the Product As Any of the D.P. Staff. Where Do
Users Fit Into Your Scheme of Formal Reviews?

We certainly never meant to exclude the user from reviews, because we feel that in those products that the user
has a hand in, user participation in reviewing is essential.

Perhaps we didn't give sufficient emphasis to the user role in the first edition. If not, let's emphasize it again right here. Any product that users will interact with must have users involved in its review. This would seem to always include specifications and things like user manuals, error messages, operating procedures, and test criteria. Depending on the nature of the user and the user's sophistication, there could be user involvement in any formal review, even of designs and code.

Support Groups (e.g., Systems Testing) Send People to Reviews for Training and Can Easily Cause the Limit of Seven to be Exceeded, Although They Don't Really Participate. Should These People Be Counted in the Limit?

They needn't be counted if they actually don't participate, especially if your physical setup allows for spectators who can't participate, as in the operating theater of a hospital, where medical students can sit in a glass-enclosed balcony. There are ways of accommodating educational needs like this without excessively disturbing the review—see Part E.

Is There a Tendency for Companies to Use Outside Consultants for Reviewing, Rather Than Their Own People?

If you mean a tendency to have reviewing done completely by outsiders—the way an audit is done, for example—then we don't know of any cases even close to this situation.

But some of our small clients are calling regularly on local consultants to come in periodically and sit in on their reviews. This adds some new viewpoints and perhaps new technical information. Also, of course, we get called in frequently to consult on how the review process is going. Part of that consultation is inevitably sitting in on some reviews, which is why we know so much about reviews!

But we feel that turning over the complete review job to a consultant, or a team of consultants, would be a big mistake. Among other things, you lose the educational factor, which in the end may be the most important reason for doing reviews.

Does the Size of the Review Team Vary Significantly with the Product You Are Reviewing? For Example, If You Are Reviewing a Specification as Opposed to Reviewing a Module of Code, How Significantly Should the Size of the Review Team Vary?

For a long time, specification "reviews" in industry and government frequently involved dozens or even hundreds of people, which is probably why the large audience review techniques were developed. This need for large numbers of people makes sense in the specification stage, because there may be large numbers of people whose interests might be affected by the system being developed. But one of the objects of a well-controlled development life cycle is to eliminate the need for communicating with large numbers of people once the specification stage has been completed, because it's not practical to work with such large numbers: It's costly; it's inconvenient getting them all together; and it's unlikely to produce a good product.

In other words, it takes a large and discerning clientele (specifiers) to make a good restaurant, but too many cooks (designers) spoil the broth. By the design stage, the job should be reduced to comparing reviewed specifications with projected designs, and this job shouldn't take large numbers of people on the review team, any more than it takes a large number of designers on any one module. Indeed, the major problem in the size of design and coding reviews may be the tendency to make them too small. You must have enough people so that you don't miss things.

But just because the number of interested parties is large doesn't mean that the review itself has to be large. Decide on the proper size of the review based on the effectiveness of the reviewing job, not on the number of interested parties. If the largest effective review is too small to accommodate everyone, then schedule several different reviews, each of which will be of effective size.

Management Participation

Should Management Be Present at Formal Reviews?

This is a difficult question to answer because the word management has different meanings in different places. We are not speaking about excluding a class of people because they have a certain title. Instead of giving the people a title, let's evaluate effects and influences and see the relationships that should be avoided in a review environment.

The main purpose of the review is to assure the quality of the product. Certainly the review has other side benefits, but these side effects must not be allowed to work to the detriment of the original purpose. We must assure that the product is being evaluated on its technical worth.

There are many characteristics that can be involved in technical worth. Correctness is the most important one. Standards, completeness, and understandability are also part of the overall worth of the product.

In order to keep the effort directed to the product, people who evaluate the producer of the product should not be present at the review of the product. If the evaluator of the product also evaluates the producer, two reviews will be occurring at the same time, and they will work against each other. Rather than concentrating on the product, the producer will be concentrating on ways to look good to his or her boss. The individuals who are participating in the review will be aware of the relationship, and peer group pressure might act on them to be "kind" in the review. There is also, of course, the possibility of personal animosity between individuals on the review group and a desire to make another person look silly in front of his or her boss.

In either case, the focus of the review changes from a technical situation to a personal situation.

This is not to imply that management must remain ignorant of the outcome of the review. Part of the standard procedure should be to send a report summarizing the outcome of the review to the relevant personnel. But this report contains only *technical information,* not a blow-by-blow description of the personalities involved. Management should be informed of the information relevant for management: Was the product approved? What was the outcome? Does this outcome affect our schedule or other dependencies? Were any gross oversights found that might affect other parts of the project? Generally, how did the review go?

To generalize on this attitude, we feel that, *people who are in statuses or roles that in any way might cause a conflict in the review situation should not be on the same review committee.*

What About Personality Conflicts?

Personality conflicts do occur, but not very often. It has been our experience that even people who do not like each other personally are quite capable of working together in a review situation. Not all people can work well with everyone, but most can manage to get along. Naturally, if there is a situation of destructive personality conflict, it should be avoided—but in all situations, not just formal reviews.

How Can a Manager Learn About Formal Reviews Without Attending?

As we've seen in other questions, it's important that a manager understand the dynamics of a review, but that's hard to do if you've never attended one. Managers need not be excluded from reviews—only from reviews where their presence might cause a conflict in the review situation. In larger organizations, it would be perfectly permissible for a *qualified* manager to sit in on a review if he or she is not the manager (at any level) of any of the other people in the review.

The important principle is that:

**Nobody should be in a review
who lacks the qualifications
to contribute to the review.**

If nonqualified people are present, they either weigh down the process by their noncontributing presence or disrupt it by their nonrelevant contributions. In some organizations, people having management responsibilities (that is, evaluation responsibilities over other people) retain important technical qualifications. Such managers *should* involve themselves in reviews—provided they can find reviews in which their interests don't conflict.

Quite often, however, technical managers are no longer technically qualified, even though they may once have been. This situation isn't particularly dangerous—*unless those managers don't recognize their obsolescence.* Too many procedures that pass today for "reviews" are merely meetings in which a bunch of underqualified managers make uninformed pronouncements about the value of some product. In such cases, it is best to abandon the "review" procedures altogether, for they have a depressing effect on the people whose work is being "reviewed."

In a real review, where any manager present is not the "boss" and where there are technically qualified people present, the people who are not qualified may find the review a good school. At least they may see their lack of qualification in action, and so will others.

What About Having a Manager as Review Leader?

Quite often, an organization loses a great deal of technical *wisdom* by promoting its top technical people into management positions. Although these people quickly lose— or should quickly lose—their *detailed* technical knowledge, they may have a lot to contribute that their management role inhibits them from giving.

In some such organizations, this wisdom can be fed into the program development and maintenance process by having such managers act as review leaders. As leader, the manager is not expected to contribute the same detailed criticism as other review members, but may have a chance to exercise skills at handling meetings and also get a chance to insert some generalized knowledge—wisdom, if you like—that might slip by in the scrutiny of details.

But just in case you missed the point earlier, let us restate the principle:

> **People who are in positions or roles that in any way might cause a conflict in the review situation should not be on the same review committee.**

Therefore, any manager who acts as review leader must not be responsible for personnel judgments about any of the other people present.

What Happens If a Team or an Individual Producer Keeps Stalling the Scheduling of a Review?

In a well-managed operation, management will notice that a review has not been scheduled on time. What happens next depends on the management. If it's poor management, they will take the initiative and schedule the review even though the producer doesn't feel ready. This review will just be a waste of time, or else it will be a sham that is designed to give management the answer it would like to hear, rather than the true evaluation of the product.

If the management is good at what they do, they will attempt to get to the reasons why the producer feels the product isn't ready. In a few cases this will be because the producer is far too fastidious, but generally the producer will have a pretty good idea that the product isn't ready for review. It may not be very pleasant to find out that part of a project is falling behind schedule, but at least it's better to find out earlier rather than later. It is certainly better not to waste time reviewing something that cannot possibly be correct.

How Can We Tell If Something Really Isn't Ready for Review?

The ultimate test, of course, is to conduct a review and have the product not be accepted. The most common sign, short of that, is the lack of some standard part of the material. Generally, or quite often, this would be the documentation. Probably the easiest way is to ask the producers. It's only in very rare cases that producers will be too pessimistic about their product. Such producers will soon be recognized by the management, who can then make the necessary adjustment for their pessimism. Most producers are optimistic if they can't manage to be realistic.

*Why Not Just Set Up a Regular Schedule of Reviews Every
Two Weeks? Everyone Will Then Have to Report How
Much They've Accomplished in the Two-Week Period, so
Things Can't Get Very Far Out of Control.*

The good thing about this idea is that it may force people
to break down their work into reviewable chunks, none
of which takes more than two weeks to produce. The bad
thing is that these are likely to degenerate into "progress"
reviews, which are old-fashioned management reviews
that never work unless they are accompanied by technical
reviews that ensure that the "progress" is real. Perhaps
the best of both worlds can be obtained in this way: Every
two weeks, schedule each project leader for a short management review in which progress will be reported, backed
up by evidence of progress in the form of review reports.
A computerized or manual data base on reviews can back
up this system in between the biweekly progress reviews.
If a leader "reports" progress that isn't substantiated by
a sheaf of review reports, the managers can spot this and
probe beneath the surface for the causes.

With a system like this in force, people will quickly
come to design their work in reasonable and reviewable
chunks, so that there will be verifiable progress to report.
The leader with evidence in hand will not have to spend
a lot of time making up b.s. charts to cover the lack of
progress, which should be a most productive saving in
itself.

*These Rules Are Rather Reassuring About My Role as
Manager, but I Still Get the Feeling That I'm Giving Up
Responsibility that I, As Manager, Have Been Given by
My Manager. Isn't It True That Under a System of
Reviews, I'm No Longer Responsible?*

You're having a semantic problem that is superimposed
on a sound insight into the manager's role in reviews. You
are *not* giving up responsibility. It's not yours to give. The

reason you direct that reviews be conducted is that you cannot discharge your responsibilities without them. If you lack technical background, how can you render the necessary evaluation of the technical work—an evaluation that must be reliable if the work is to be manageable?

If you *have* the technical background, and if you have the time and confidence to review all technical material and depend completely on your own judgment, then you don't *need* reviews to discharge your responsibilities. If you're like most managers who rose through the technical ranks, however, you are

1. Very short of time to do real technical work in detail;
2. Slowly losing your currency in technology, though retaining overall "wisdom" or "perspective"; and
3. Reluctant to admit to point (2).

Your job as technical manager requires you to retain overall responsibility, but does not allow you time to check everything yourself, any more than it leaves you time to do everything yourself. You must delegate part of the checking function, just as you must delegate part, or all, of the doing of the technical work itself. If you cannot learn to delegate, you will fail in your responsibilities as manager. Reviews are a safe, dependable way to delegate the checking function, which in turn provides an audit on the work you have delegated.

We have not spoken of the other functions of reviews, but just consider one—education—as typical. A good manager is devoted to the development of people. Because you cannot spend sufficient time with your people to directly teach them all you know, you must establish processes that assist you in training them. In establishing reviews, you are carrying out the same sort of management function that you perform when you sign people up for courses—at the same time that you are discharging other responsibilities.

It's our opinion, backed up by years of observation, that the typical manager is always on the verge of going under for the third time. Over these years, we've seen how establishing reviews is the first and most important step for any technical manager to seize true control over the operations for which that manager is responsible. Without reviews, you may succeed for a time, in a limited way, by great personal skill, effort, and dedication, but you ultimately will find yourself at a dead end in what you can achieve as a manager of technical work. This has been true in all other technical fields before programming and analysis. There's no reason to believe it's not true for our business, too. If you want to grow, you have to let go—in a controlled, responsible way such as reviews.

That's a Good Answer, but I Do Have Some Technical Competence, So Why Can't I Have Input to the Evaluation Process?

You can have such input, but it doesn't have to be in the review itself. You have access to the full set of reviewed material. If you have the technical competence, it will be an excellent idea to review it yourself and form a judgment prior to examining the review report. By comparing your evaluation with the review report, you will learn about

1. Your technical competence,
2. The effectiveness of the review, and
3. The product itself.

If you and the reviews are always in disagreement, then you have a serious problem somewhere in your organization. Locate it and correct it—even if it is you!

Allocating Time and Facilities for Reviews

How Much Time Should We Plan on Spending on Formal Reviews?

Obviously, there is no fixed amount or percentage of time to plan on spending in reviews. You should understand how the time will vary with changes in several important factors:

1. Total project size,
2. Complexity of material reviewed,
3. Closeness of material to finished quality, and
4. Competence and experience of the reviewers.

Rather than give a general answer, we'll consider each of these factors in turn.

How Does Project Size Affect Reviewing Time?

The more different parts there are in a project, the more possible interactions there are. Since each interaction is a potential source of mismatch, larger projects will require more reviewing time in proportion to the time spent on other activities. Developers experienced in small systems often fail to take this scaling into account in making estimates for a system larger than any they have yet developed.

A large project can be handled by using more people, by taking more time with the same number of people, or by increasing both people and time. The more people involved in the project, the more people will have to be involved in any particular review—other factors being equal. Eventually, you reach a point where one piece of work cannot be reviewed in a single session because too many people would have to be in the room.

Multiple reviews held simply to accommodate larger numbers of concerned parties quite naturally add to the overhead of reviews. They also create the need for coordinating the results of two or more reviews of the same product.

Other things being equal, a project done with fewer people over a longer period of time will use a smaller percentage of its productive time in reviews. On the other hand, if there is turnover of personnel because of the length of the project, then much of the educational value of reviews will be lost unless material is reviewed more frequently.

How Does Complexity of Material Affect Reviewing Time?

First of all, we have to define *complexity*. It may seem circular, but one of the best ways to define complexity is in terms of the amount of material that can be reviewed in one session.

The first question, of course, is whether the material can be reviewed at all. If *technically competent* people, after preparing in advance, cannot review a meaningful portion of a product in a two-hour review, then that material is probably *too complex* for inclusion in any finished product.

Product complexity is likely to give rise to other problems later on in the system life cycle. The material will be difficult to test, difficult to integrate with other material, difficult to modify, and difficult to use. If, at the conclusion of a well-functioning review session, the committee is unable to state that a complete review has been done, serious consideration should be given to restructuring the reviewed material.

On the other side of the coin, it doesn't pay to review pieces of work so small that only a few minutes work by the committee is required. In that case, review overhead will be too great to tolerate. If the pieces are too small, however, it isn't necessary to restructure the product, but only to schedule reviews for several related pieces at once. In other words, the "review module" should never consist of less than one functional piece of work (or "functional module") but could very well consist of several functional pieces.

What Is Meant by "Closeness of Material to Finished Quality"?

When reviews have been in place for some time, so that the installation has reached some sort of equilibrium level of performance, most reviews will be similar in terms of what issues they raise about the reviewed material. At the outset, however, the quality of the product submitted for review will be so extremely variable that it will be difficult to predict anything about reviewing time. Indeed, one measure of the effectiveness of the entire reviewing system is the predictability of reviews.

As the installation becomes adept at reviewing and producing material that will be reviewed, we will see a stabilization in such measures as:

1. Percentage of products that pass the first review,
2. Percentage of products that must be redone from scratch,

3. Number of issues raised per unit of work,

4. Number of issues missed that are caught later in the cycle, and

5. Time spent per unit of work.

Most of this stabilization comes not so much from better reviewing as from better construction of the material in the first place—as a result of experience with earlier reviews. Once the stabilization takes place, the review process becomes essentially a monitoring of quality to ensure against deterioration of present standards.

Before stabilization, however, the main task of the review process is to expose areas in which gross defects in production are taking place, as well as to educate everyone involved in proper production practices. Consequently, the time taken in early reviews is more a function of the present state of the installation's production ability, rather than any other factor.

Once This Stabilization Takes Place, How Does Review Time Depend on Closeness to Finished Quality?

First of all, there is a paradoxical relationship between quality and time to review. A "perfect" piece of work can be reviewed very quickly, while one with some inadequacies will take more time—if only to write down the issues raised. Eventually, however, the poorer quality leads to a short and sweet review, because participants quickly agree that the material isn't worth reviewing in detail. Thus, the best and the worst pieces of work are reviewed swiftly—only the "good but not perfect" take a lot of time.

What About the Time Taken to Review Rejected Material a Second Time?

Obviously, from an overall project standpoint, material of very poor initial quality will consume large amounts of review time, since all reviews and re-reviews must be counted. On the other hand, passing bad material in an effort to "save review time" will only cause much more time to be spent on other activities, such as testing, integration, modification, and installation. Therefore, there is a danger in monitoring review time too closely—a danger that we may be tempted to pass a poor product just to keep the review statistics looking good.

What About Other Reasons for Multiple Reviews?

We have previously mentioned several other situations in which material must be reviewed more than once. If there are many people concerned with the product, it is best not to violate the standards for the size of the review committee but to schedule multiple reviews instead. Sometimes, many of the interested parties can be satisfied with a *presentation* rather than a review.

In the past, when material was of very poor quality, everyone concerned felt the need to review the material for self-protection. As quality goes up, many of these people will come to see that all they now need from the review is *education*—a purpose that may be better served with a prepared presentation.

A wise project leader will want to ask *why* so many people are concerned about a particular piece of work. Perhaps the overall structure of the work is wrong, with far too many connections between "modules." If that is the case, the extra reviewing time is the least of the worries, and the entire structure ought to be reconsidered.

When multiple reviews are necessary, time may be saved by breaking down the interests according to different criteria. Some parties may be primarily interested in questions of efficiency, while others may be concerned about adherence to standards, operational ease, or potential problems for future modification. By breaking down the reviews according to each particular viewpoint, the efficiency of the review process is increased. More important, however, is the increased quality of the reviews resulting from greater interest (topical focus) and greater involvement (small size.)

We Don't Have Many (Or Any) Places in Which Reviews Can Be Held. Have You Got Any Suggestions?

Look around for conference rooms that can be obtained on a scheduled basis. Don't *assume* they're not available—*ask*. And when you ask, be prepared to argue your case effectively.

If you're having trouble getting a conference room, it may be that you've let your reviews get too large. Larger rooms are usually harder to get than smaller ones, so if you keep your reviews down to the standard size, you'll have less trouble finding an appropriate place.

Longer time periods are usually harder to schedule. Start on time and stick to a two-hour maximum.

If you *really* can't find a conference room, many managers have offices that will serve quite nicely for a review. If no such facility is available, you might question management's commitment to the review process.

If management is truly well intentioned but there still is no time available in conference rooms or offices, you are not yet at the end of your rope. Think about the cafeteria, coffee shop, gymnasium, boiler room, or a nice shady spot under a tree. If people are well prepared, the need for audiovisual aids can be minimized—through naturally a photocopier, blackboard, flipchart, or other material aids don't hurt.

In the final analysis, if the *only* reason you're not having reviews is because you can't find a place—*find a place!*

We Have Lots of Conference Rooms, but We Can't Seem to Get All the Necessary People Free at the Same Time. What Do You Suggest?

We realize that in large organizations, where individuals have distributed responsibilities, it is often difficult to schedule yet another meeting. Part of this problem, however, may be due to the *ineffectiveness* of the existing meetings. Too many people, too diffuse a purpose, too little leadership—all these factors contribute to the bad impression that people have about meetings. Once you get formal reviews *established,* their relevance and effectiveness will encourage people to find time for them—even at the expense of other meetings.

Scheduling difficulties, before you get reviews firmly established, are increased for another reason. While learning new ways, the teams will not be able to predict accurately when their internal product will be ready for review externally. Consequently, they may have difficulty anticipating a regular schedule for formal reviews, but this again should be only temporary. As the team begins to work consistently, it should be able to estimate the project life cycle with adequate accuracy for scheduling purposes.

We Have a Problem with Reviews Involving People from Several Departments. People from Other Departments Don't Want to Come Over to Our Meeting Room for a Review. It Is a Long Way to Walk, So What Can We Do?

First you should realize that their true objection might not be to the walking, as such, but to coming to your "territory." If there is any hint of factionalism, you should take great pains to conduct reviews on "neutral" territory. If no neutral space is available, then it would be a good idea for you to bend over backwards to go to their territory. It will show that you value their contribution enough to be willing to expend some personal effort to be at the review.

If you're pretty sure that there's no real factionalism, then try to alternate rooms—some convenient for one group and some for the other. If the only rooms are *really* in one place, then do other things to make up to the walkers for their trouble: Schedule meetings at *their* convenience. Chip in a little money of your own or of your department's petty cash to come up with free coffee and donuts. Assume some of the secretarial duties on your department's budget. There are many ways to keep the contributions from getting out of balance, which, as you observe, can prove unhealthy for the success of reviews.

The Relevant People for Some of Our Reviews Are Scattered All Over the Country. Is It Possible to Conduct a Review by Telephone?

We haven't tried this, but a number of experiments with phone meetings have indicated that the formal review would be the ideal type of meeting to conduct on the phone. We've obtained permission from T. C. Jones to reprint a report he wrote about some experimental phone meetings IBM conducted. It will give you some excellent guidelines for attempting a telephone review meeting.

Telephone Meetings:
A Tool for Inter-Center Communication

T. CAPERS JONES

*International Business Machines Corporation
San Jose Programming Center
San Jose, California*

Abstract

In 1971 and 1972, a series of six regularly scheduled telephone meetings were held in which as many as 14 writers, managers, and programmers from six different locations were linked into a common telephone circuit via IBM tie lines. The meetings, which did not require conference rooms or special equipment, proved to be surprisingly effective in conveying information and were uniquely inexpensive. The telephone meeting approach appears to offer attractive benefits as a tool to facilitate the coordination of multi-location projects.

Introduction

Early in 1971, *Time Magazine* described a new commercial venture in which up to 20 subscribers were linked into monthly telephone conferences with others who shared their interests in subjects such as European travel, French cooking, etc. The telephone meetings were described as being relaxed, natural and unusually trouble-free.

If such an approach were successful in conveying technical information, it would seem to have numerous applications within IBM, since many projects are spread among multiple locations and this situation often causes communication and coordination problems. It should be pointed out that telephone meetings are neither new nor even uncommon within IBM, but there had never been a conscious attempt to document the findings for wide dissemination. In 1971 and 1972, the Programming Publications Department of the San Jose Programming Center conducted a series of six experimental telephone meetings. These were designed both to assist in solving business and technical problems, and to explore the usefulness of the telephone meeting concept. Following are the results of the study, which in general demonstrated that telephone meetings can convey technical information, and that the approach is practical and offers benefits and advantages.

Preparation Before the Meetings

The preparations for a telephone meeting are quite simple. It is only necessary to call the local telephone supervisor or one of the operators and give the names, locations, and IBM telephone numbers of the participants (assuming that all participants work in cities connected to the tie-line network). On the day and time you select for the meeting, your local operator will dial each of the participants and complete the circuit. No conference rooms, acoustic amplifiers, or special equipment are needed. Each participant may use his own telephone in his own office.

While the above "mechanics" are straightforward when it comes to the actual circuit, following are some observations to help make the meetings smooth and trouble free:

1. We found that it was very helpful to do some advance calling both to firm up an agenda and to establish

meeting times that were satisfactory on both the East Coast and the West Coast. A time of 12:00 San Jose time seemed satisfactory. (Raleigh, for example, quits at 3:45—that is 12:45 San Jose time.)

2. To ensure that all participants have adequate time to review the conference materials and subject matter, it is well to mail agenda, charts, hand-outs, and the like well in advance of the date set for the telephone meeting. Occasionally, this advance notice results in requests for extra participants, bringing additional skills into the conference.

3. We found it desirable to provide an "emergency" number that a participant could call (in San Jose) in case he was accidentally disconnected from the circuit. This happened only twice in the whole series of six meetings, but when it happened the disconnected party didn't know how to get back into the conference hook-up. This proved to be quite a setback since he was the primary participant on one of the major subjects.

4. A number of locations, such as European ones which were not joined directly into the circuit, nonetheless were interested in the results of the meetings. The combination of the agendas and written minutes thus reached an even wider circle than the meetings themselves. As many as 45 people in 17 locations requested copies of the minutes, and many offered follow-up comments for later discussion. The telephone meetings, with the accompanying documentation, became a combination of forum and "newsletter" for topics of common interest.

5. In order to provide increased participation for special groups, some departments attempted to use "squawk boxes" or acoustic amplifiers. In our experience, the results were always unsatisfactory because the devices introduced excessive noise into the circuit.

Startup and Mechanics

With our experimental telephone conferences, a typical meeting would average 14 participants but only 10 different telephone numbers. The additional participation was made possible by the fact that many offices have two phones with the same number. Start-up time for such meetings averaged only seven minutes. This figure is lower than the starting time for most "live" meetings, which typically begin more than 10 minutes after the nominal start time, due to late arrivals, conversations, and so on.

As each person was connected into the circuit by the operator, the speaker would customarily provide identification by name and location. One of the problems which was anticipated, but which did not occur, was confusion over who was speaking. For meetings where the participants knew each other, voice recognition was satisfactory. For meetings where few were acquainted, each speaker would identify himself each time he spoke; then after five or ten minutes of conversation, voice recognition would be possible.

One aspect of the telephone meetings was striking and unusual: there were few, if any, side-track issues, or "private" discussions between people who differed on a given point. In this respect, the telephone meetings seemed a better way of communicating information than most "live" meetings, where it often happens that interruptions or discussions between pairs of individuals slow down the general progress of the subjects under examination.

Another aspect of the telephone meetings that was unusual, since we had anticipated problems, was smooth flow of sequential conversation. There were extremely few (if any) interruptions of a person making a point or describing an issue. This is in marked contrast to many live meetings where statements of "let me finish" are not uncommon. The *Time Magazine* article which described the commercial telephone meeting service commented on this point also. The reasons why telephone meetings should have a smoother flow of conversation than live meetings are not known, but the effect is striking.

The telephone meetings generally lasted between 30 and 45 minutes, including start-up time. The overall impression gained from these meetings is one of a "dense" communications medium compared to live meetings. That is, apparently more information was transmitted and exchanged per unit of time. This can likely be attributed to the unusually low number of interruptions and the smooth flow of conversation typically experienced.

Problems Encountered

The problems encountered can be divided into two groups: problems with the circuit or channel, and problems of a general application or implementation nature. Relative to the telephone circuits, the following four problems were noted:

1. On one occasion an entire meeting had to be deferred when no outgoing calls could be placed from San Jose. This problem came at a period of general tie-line difficulties which lasted for more than a month.

2. On two occasions, one of the participants was (for unknown reasons) accidentally cut off from the circuit. After the first occurrence, each participant was given the number of the San Jose tie-line operator, and could be reconnected in case of difficulty.

3. The use of squawk boxes proved very detrimental. In every case, the noise level of the entire circuit increased so much that shouting was necessary in order to be heard. When the squawk boxes were removed, the sound quality improved.

4. The "normal" limit of 10 telephone numbers is lower than desirable. Conference calls of 20 or more participants can easily be handled from an administrative or procedural standpoint if multiple tie-line circuits were available. An attempt was made to use two "main" circuits and increase the number of telephones in the connection. The attempt eventually worked, but required a 15-minute start-up and reduced the quality of the audibility somewhat.

Listed below are some of the problems encountered because of the way we attempted to carry out the meetings:

1. On one occasion, far too many broad items were placed on the agenda, causing haste and shallow coverage. "In depth" meetings covering and fully exploring the issues turned out to be more satisfactory.

2. On another occasion, the meeting was planned around the participation of a single individual, who had to cancel at the last minute. This left very little of sig-

nificance to cover, and implied a need for either back-up speakers on the primary subject, or for alternate discussion items.

3. On several occasions, problems were placed on the agenda in the expectation of finding solutions during the course of the meetings. It happened from time to time that no one on the circuit knew of any solutions—in part because the problems were complex, but also in part because participation from other locations with experience in the area was not arranged.

Unexpected Benefits

The telephone meeting approach offered several advantages that were not anticipated at the start of the experiment. For one thing, junior and associate writers and programmers, who seldom travel to remote meetings, were able to participate and get immediate answers to technical questions involving other locations. Another advantage was the comparative ease of assembling participants with diverse skills and backgrounds. For example, one meeting had participants representing SDD programming and management, SDD publications and management, DPD publications and management, and Field Engineering Division. Questions involving what kind of information should be placed in maintenance publications were discussed from a number of different vantage points, and fresh insights were brought forth.

A third advantage, although not unexpected, was the way telephone meetings brought all participants "up to the same level" in terms of the items under discussion. A frequent source of trouble on projects spread among several locations is that of varying expectations about which location is responsible for some item, or what the item actually entails. In several of the telephone meetings, it was apparent at the start that participants from various locations had different understandings about some policy or concept. The meetings proved to be remarkably effective in clearing away such misunderstandings. It is this aspect of the telephone meeting approach that would seem to recommend a wider application among multilocation projects.

Costs Involved

All of the experimental meetings mentioned in this report were conducted exclusively via IBM tie lines, and were therefore "free" for practical purposes. There were no department charges or long-distance telephone rates. Administrative time for setting up the meetings ran to perhaps two or three hours per meeting—an hour or so of individual tie-line calls to establish the set of participants and solicit agenda items, and the preparation and mailing of the agenda itself. Such administrative overhead is probably equal to or less than the administrative time for a live meeting; "less than" appears possible because no conference room arrangements are necessary.

The actual meetings themselves are substantially less expensive than live meetings. The participants generally do not have to leave their offices, so there is no travel time or expense. Even to walk to a conference room is not required. The average start-up time of only seven minutes is noticeably shorter than most live meetings, and the average meeting length of between 30 and 45 minutes is also short when compared to live meetings. The effectiveness of the meetings in conveying information is sufficiently high that we considered (but rejected because of embarrassment) the possibility of having telephone meetings *within* a single location.

At the conclusion of the telephone meeting, the minutes were typed and mailed not only to the actual participants, but also to those who had expressed interest in the topics but were unable to attend (either because of the limiting factor of 10 telephones per meeting, or because the location was not on a tie line, such as the European locations). This aspect of the telephone meetings appears about the same as with live meetings.

In summary, the cost of preparing for a telephone meeting, having the meeting, and distributing the minutes appears to net out at substantially less than the cost of a corresponding live meeting. When the effectiveness of the telephone approach is added as a subjective factor, the meetings appear to be uniquely inexpensive—possibly the least expensive way of transmitting information to groups of technical individuals in a timely manner.

Recommendations for Extended Use of Telephone Meetings
Several questions arise concerning the kinds of situations to be profitably used for the telephone meetings. Here are some recommendations for a wider application of the approach:

1. For projects where system design is spread among several locations, weekly or monthly telephone meetings (augmented by specifications sent via mail) would appear to offer a convenient way of keeping all locations abreast of current design matters.

2. IBM has a number of specialized disciplines where interlocation communications would appear useful: standards representatives, compiler experts, cost estimating personnel, and tool development specialists. These groups could profitably form loose "associations" and communicate via telephone meetings.

3. Prior to major conferences (Phase Reviews, Programming Symposia, Technical Information Exchanges, etc.), a series of preliminary telephone meetings might serve to facilitate the establishment of procedural and administrative ground rules.

4. When a new or innovative technical approach is being tested experimentally (HIPO diagrams, "top-down" programming, Design Reviews, Programmer Teams, etc.), other locations interested in the results might find telephone meetings a quick and inexpensive way to broadcast the results in a timely fashion.

5. At key points in the development cycle, certain activities require careful planning at all locations involved in the creation of a system. These activities include writing test plans, processing PTM's, developing performance plans, and creating build plans. Telephone meetings would seem to offer a useful communications means for these important functions, and would facilitate reaching a "standard" level at all locations.

6. From time to time, projects are transferred from one location to another. Telephone meetings of representatives from the sending and receiving locations might help ensure a smooth, successful transfer.

Conclusions

Our initial approach to telephone meetings was one of skepticism. We assumed that lack of visual contact would prove to be a weakness; noise and circuit problems would probably be irritating; confusion and loss of continuity were expected. The excellent results observed in the first meeting, therefore, came as a considerable surprise. None of the expected problems occurred, and the efficiency of the meeting was notable in conveying information without side-track issues or random delays.

As more meetings were held, and were generally successful, a conclusion was reached that telephone meetings work much better than might be anticipated by those who have not taken part in them. They seem to be in that class of awkward subjects which must be directly experienced to be fully comprehended. In other words, positive statements about telephone meetings are perhaps not sufficient in themselves to overcome intuitive doubts as to the success of the approach. In any case, six experimental meetings were carried out with a minimum expenditure of time on the part of those who participated, and with generally beneficial results in solving problems and gaining a common level of understanding. These facts, coupled with the extremely low cost of the meetings, merit consideration for wider use.

Notes on Getting Started SECTION
4

In Our Early Reviews, We Seem to Be Wasting a Lot of Time. Are Experienced, Competent Reviewers Able to Work Faster?

Unless you have a stock of experienced review leaders on hand, you have to count a lot of "wasted" time in early reviews. There is a difference, however, between "wasted wasted" time and "educational wasted" time.

Although it is important to get *everyone* who is developing material involved in reviews at an early stage, it is also important to develop at least a few people with excellent skills as early as possible. Later on, it may be possible to let everyone have a hand at leading reviews, but at an early stage in your experience, it is best to appoint pairs of review leaders who will specialize, for a time, in leading reviews.

In the first reviews, each pair of review leaders can work as one unit in leading reviews, in order to accelerate the process of learning to do reviews. Each member of the pair takes a turn acting as "shadow" to the other—observing the whole review and especially the actions of the leader. After the review, the pair gets together and reviews the review. After a short time—assuming the two were selected properly—each is able to lead reviews independently and provide the proper atmosphere in which others may learn to be effective reviewers.

How, Then, Do We Allocate Time for Reviews When Planning Our Project?

First of all, recognize *explicitly* that reviews will consume time. This time should be scheduled and allocated at the beginning of the project. On the first project, the use of reviews may or may not reduce the *overall* time you must schedule. If you don't schedule adequate review time, however, you will find people shortcutting reviews for other, scheduled, activities. Reviews will not be effective, and the chances of an incorrect or incomplete project will increase. In almost all cases—with the possible exception of a very short project with no people experienced in reviews—the review process will prove extremely cost effective when viewed in the context of the total system costs and effectiveness.

Second, you must establish a *base allocation* founded on your past experience with reviews. If you have no past experience, it's hard to pick a number out of the air, because the experience of others may be quite inapplicable to your situation. As a guideline, however, 2–10 percent of productive labor allocation should go to formal technical reviews. If you are in doubt, *be conservative* with your initial baseline (10 percent). If nothing else, it will demonstrate that project leadership is *serious* about instituting reviews.

Third, raise or lower your base allocation according to the factors discussed above. For example, if the people on this project are more experienced in reviews than the people on the baseline project, you can lower the allocation. On the other hand, if the project is much larger, you must raise the allocation to allow for increased interaction.

We Can See That the Problem of Scheduling Becomes Less Acute with Time. But What About When We're Starting Out?

One effective method is to set aside certain time blocks—projectwide—for reviews. People are requested not to schedule other meetings during this time and to avoid otherwise committing themselves. If people follow this directive, they are usually free to meet at the appointed time. Rarely will it be necessary to postpone a review more than a few days beyond the earliest possible time.

This set time for reviews should be established at the very beginning of the development cycle. Since reviews are needed for all aspects of the product, there should always be *something* to review. Standards, procedures, specifications, designs, code, documentation, test plans, and test results should all be reviewed, so there is little chance of running out of material and letting the scheduled review period go to waste.

What Is the Best Time to Set Aside for Reviews?

With the usual exceptions, most installations seem to find that 10:00 A.M. is an excellent time. Setting an earlier time is likely to involve delays for people who get tied up in traffic or forget to set the alarm. Late in the afternoon is likely to produce rushed and superficial reviews as people look at the clock hoping for an early escape. Right after lunch means that you have to reckon with different peoples' dining habits and also with the drowsiness of the gourmands and epicures.

Starting at 10:00 means that everyone has had a

chance to look at the morning mail (don't let them bring it into the review), have a cup of coffee, and generally get oriented to the business of the day. If everyone brings the remnants of their coffee or other beverage into the review, it adds a warmth and friendliness that is sometimes needed.

If you start at 10:00, furthermore, you should finish before lunch, which tends to prevent the review from dragging on past its appointed hours. Moreover, if review members can lunch together right after the review, wounds can be salved, and rather frequently, an overlooked issue may pop up over the pizza.

If you can't set aside 10:00–12:00 in the morning, that doesn't mean you can't have reviews. The particular time isn't all that critical, as long as everybody knows what that time is for and honors its reservation.

How Much Work Should Be Reviewed Initially?

That depends on how well it is done and how skilled you are at reviewing. It should be no more than can be reviewed in two hours if done badly but correctable or in one hour if done right. This means that the size will change with time as you

1. Learn to review;
2. Learn to write.

In the beginning, this will be a very small piece, but don't be afraid. That only indicates how badly you need the reviews.

Does This Apply to Formal and Informal Reviews?

To any kind of reviewing. It is related to the attention span of adults. If it requires more than this, parts of it will be skimmed over, which is precisely what you don't want.

Our Projects Don't Come in That Size Piece.

Then there may be something wrong with the structure of your projects, because you're building them in pieces whose goodness you can't guarantee. That guarantees disaster. Look at Parts E and F of this handbook for ideas on how to break down the review task into manageable parts, especially when you're starting out.

Our Managers Have the Nasty Habit of Bumping Others out of Conference Rooms to Demonstrate Their Place in the Pecking Order. How Can We Prevent This Practice from Disrupting Our Reviews?

If you are bumped, submit a review report stating that the product was not reviewed because person X preempted the room. Then let the managers solve the problem. If they don't, then they don't sincerely want reviews—at least not more than they want to assert their place in the pecking order. You know what that makes them!

Of All the Things We Might Review, Which Is the Best to Start With?

We're not at all certain which is best, but don't let that stop you from reviewing something. That's the crucial factor—that you get practice, practice, and more practice.
Because you won't be expert reviewers right from the outset, a good strategy is to review something for which the outcome isn't too critical. For instance, you can start by reviewing some production program or a piece

of a production program. Because it's already in production, you aren't feeling scheduling pressure, so finding errors shouldn't be critical, since it presumably "works" satisfactorily. (Don't, therefore, choose that production program that's perpetually crashing—not for the first reviews, though definitely for later ones.)

Beware, though, for many of our clients have found errors in "production" programs, including programs written by their own managers!

Wouldn't It Be Better to Start on Something That Isn't an Actual Program, Like a Document or a Specification?

In some cases that could be better. The advantage of reviewing code is that you can review for errors only and not get into too much unresolvable controversy. Specifications sometimes have that property, but some specifications will engender difficult controversies. Documentation, of course, can always be reviewed for grammar and spelling. As long as you don't have an English teacher in your midst, grammar and spelling should be noncontroversial.

The documentation of an existing program may provide a good subject for an early review because all controversies about what the program actually does should be resolvable by a test, if necessary. In other words, choose something that won't get you entangled in interminable controversies.

How About Reviewing the Guide to Walkthroughs, Inspections, and Technical Reviews?

This is an excellent suggestion and has been tried independently by several of our clients. By reviewing this handbook (a piece at a time, of course), you ensure that the participants clearly understand the philosophies, purposes, and methodologies of the review process. When we conduct review classes, or when our clients conduct them in house, "reviewing the review handbook" is a major exercise, replacing the more traditional examination process with something more relevant and engaging.

In doing reviews of the handbook, we've discovered a number of other useful by-products. Because the outcomes will set the rules for future reviews, it's easier for the reviewers to have a commitment to these first reviews. The list of issues raised will provide a basis for adapting the handbook to the installation's needs, thus making the handbook part of the organization, rather than some foreign body blown in from outside.

Can You Tell Us More About Using the Initial Reviews to Create Guidelines That Will Adapt This Handbook?

From our experience, we can suggest the following general procedure. The first step is to establish the review committee or committees and to assign the various responsibilities. Obviously, this document is too large to review at one sitting. Moreover, some sections will not be relevant to the installation or perhaps not relevant to the earliest reviews. Segmenting this material into workable, relevant sections will give the leaders experience in determining reviewable pieces of work.

The material can be reviewed for technical correctness and for applicability to the installation, either in a single review or in two functional reviews.

Remember the rules. The review process itself is to raise issues, not resolve them. Using the issues lists generated, a group of interested individuals can then form a working group or groups to address the specific problems. Once their work is complete, the review groups can review the proposed solutions. In this way, the transition from reviewing "their" material to reviewing "our" material is achieved with minimum strain. The review committee gains immediate feedback on the rules they are criticizing, while the work groups must experience the effects of the modifications they make.

After a while, the reviewers will probably get bored with reviewing the handbook and will eagerly welcome the chance to review something with more technical meat. If and when that happens, don't drag out the handbook reviewing, but switch to code, specifications, or some other readily available material. The final adjustments to the review handbook will iron themselves out once the people gain actual experience reviewing their own work. The important thing is that they review well, not that the handbook is perfect.

I'd Really Like to Get Started with Reviews, but I'm the Only Technical Person in My Shop, so What Can I Do?

First of all, consider whether there are, in fact, other technical people in other departments who could share reviewing with you. If there truly are no other technical people in your organization, then the issue is certainly complicated.

One thing you can certainly do is institute formal reviews of such things as specifications and user documentation, for there is a large component of these in which many nontechnical people in your organization would be interested.

We know of several of our clients with one-person or one-team shops who exchange reviews with other organizations in similar circumstances. User groups or professional societies are often good places to find such people.

In one case, three programmers—all working singly at remote sites on similar systems—met at a course and decided to cooperate on reviews. They mail the material to each other, allowing sufficient time for both postal delays and adequate study. Then they arrange a conference call, late at night when the phone rates are low, and hold the review over the telephone. Although this is certainly not the ideal situation in which to hold reviews, they all felt it was well worth the expense and effort and certainly better than no review at all.

Even if you cannot find *anyone,* inside or outside your organization, prepare for a review anyway. For example, for a code review, you can walk through or inspect the code just as if other people were present. The preparation itself will give you a changed perspective on the material and help locate errors. If you actually make the presentation of a walk-through—to your spouse, your dog, or your mirror—you'll do even better—if you can get over the feeling of being silly.

You can extend this approach by finding *someone* in your installation who, though not technically qualified, is interested in what is going on in the data-processing function. This person might be a user, machine operator, data entry clerk, or summer help college student. All you need is a willing ear, and you'll be surprised what they and you will hear.

We Are About To Become Involved in Structured Systems Development. Should We Give Our People a Chance to Become Familiar with These New Methodologies Before Starting Reviews in Addition?

NO. START NOW. Formal reviews should be an integral part of ANY system methodology, whether you are wiring program boards or using a "front-end word-processing macro-generating prelinkage-compiler." Products are not products unless they are reviewed. There is little danger of reviews working to the detriment of any worthwhile idea.

But Won't That Be Too Many New Things Going On at One Time?

Perhaps—in which case, you should delay the introduction of "structured systems development," whatever it means to you, until your reviews are working reasonably well. If you start reviews later, how will you *know* what's happening with your "structured systems development"? In our experience, we've seen clients institute one "new" technology after another, with much hoopla, much money, and sometimes much resentment. But with little or no effect, when you get down in the pits and see what they're actually doing. If we showed you some of the "top-down designs" and "structured programs" that we've turned up when reviews were instituted *after* the "new" technologies, you would lose your lunch.

On the other hand, you may be right to delay reviews if they are just going to be an excuse for not doing anything because "we've got too many new things to do at once."

So You Really Think We Should Start Reviews First?

Why not consider the benefits; then decide for yourself? First of all, the review process will spread the word about the new technology—at little or no additional expense. Second, reviewing will teach you valuable lessons about the new technology, such as which new ideas are being tried first, which are gaining easy acceptance, which are being resisted, which are misunderstood, and which aren't being tried at all. Third, the participants themselves will point out flaws or minor inconsistencies in the new methods. Fourth, reviews will uncover conflicts between the proposed methodology and existing practices or conditions in your shop.

Fifth, as time passes, the reviews will provide a historical perspective on the new technology. Many practices will become part of the daily routine. Others will disappear. Fortunately, this evolutionary process will be monitored, and installation practices and standards will remain consistent rather than "speciating."

But the most important reason is the first—dissemination of the new technology. If it's worth doing, it's worth spreading, and there's no more effective or efficient way to get results for your training dollar. People who haven't been formally introduced to the new technology will get exposure and motivation. They will know who knows—who can teach them and answer those questions that one never asks of the instructor.

In short, if you think you can truly introduce a new technology *without* reviews, you're on shaky ground. At least you'll never be able to *prove* your point.

We're Still Not Satisfied with the Answers on Where to Start. There Are So Many Areas to Cover, Where Can We Start?

Because organizations differ so much, you will appreciate that there is no single answer. Obviously, in the end you will wind up reviewing from the very beginning to the very end, but most people in the past started with code reviews because that was the most obvious place. You know that code has errors, but you don't know what the errors are. So you start code reviews and eventually get code pretty well under control. Then you realize that there were errors in the designs, hidden by the coding errors. So you start design reviews and get design under control. Then you discover the hidden errors in specifications.

The specifications end is in many ways the hardest to start with, but when possible, it may be best to start close to the user right at the beginning. There's no sense doing a good job on the wrong problem, so there are far greater savings to be gained by starting to review at the specification end. Still, it's harder to show management what these great benefits are, because the effect of the review is not as dramatic or as quantifiable and doesn't show up until much later, when everyone has forgotten what trouble you might have had if you hadn't reviewed the specifications.

Would You Suggest Starting on One Completely New
Project and Working with That, Rather Than Starting on
a Particular Type of Review and Working on a Number of
Projects at One Time?

If you are project oriented, with many small projects, the
answer could be yes. But consider starting on *two* projects,
roughly at the same time. Two projects side by side introduce a spirit of friendly competition, plus much learning that can be transferred back and forth. The people
from one project can serve as a body of experienced reviewers for the other.

We've learned from several of our clients that this
sort of double pilot project, assuming each is quite small,
is very successful. It provides incentives and avoids certain
accidental features of one project or another that may not
be a good model for all the others.

We've also had a situation where a successful single
pilot was not accorded much attention, so that reviews
were dropped. Other people said, "Well, this project is
really unique (or why would you have done reviews).
Therefore, what they've done is not really applicable to
what we do, so we can ignore it." If there are two projects,
it's much more difficult to make this argument sound
convincing.

I Suppose That Leads to the Next Question. Do You Need
to Train People Formally in Doing Reviews, or Can You
Simply Build Upon the Experience of Actually Doing
Reviews?

Our current feeling is that if we can spend a small amount
of time training the review leaders for an organization,
then the review leaders will train the others, so it's not
really necessary to send all the people to a special review
course. It may be helpful, though, to kick off a large
review effort with at least a day of conceptual training for

the mass of reviewers, so that they understand what the trained leaders are trying to accomplish in the reviews.

Actual behavior in the review, however, is best trained in actual reviews or simulated reviews, not in large training classes. We find that we can train the leaders in a workshop, guide them through a few reviews on the job, and perhaps come back and check up on them after a month or so of experience. With this much training, ten to sixteen review leaders can then start the process of training an organization of two hundred people in a year's time. You can't go much faster than that by any method.

How Long Do You Generally Find That It Takes for Your Clients to Get a Formal Review System Functioning at Full Capacity?

Let's first answer a different question: How long does it take before the formal review system starts to pay more than it costs? Management should be more concerned about this question, because it tells them what their risks are going to be, and we often find that people are more worried about the risk of something new than seduced by the potential benefits.

One of the beauties of the formal technical review is that it may be introduced with minimal risk, yet begins to return benefits from the first day of the first review. Thus, any time you decide that a system of formal reviews is not for you, you can quit and still be ahead. We don't know of many quitters, but there are some people who don't do it right at first. If you're *not* getting benefits right from the start, then it's probably a strong indication that you're doing something wrong.

The answer, then, is that to get started you need enough time to read this book a few times, find some material, schedule a review, and get going. A few days, or perhaps two weeks at the outset.

That's a Useful Answer, Particularly Where Management
May Not Be Committed to the Idea in Advance, But I'd
Still Like to Know, How Long Would It Take for the
Practice to Permeate the Entire Organization

Your distinction between committed and uncommitted management is an important one. Let's talk about fully committed first, in which case it depends mostly on the size of the organization.

The fastest we've experienced with fully committed management is in organizations with twenty technical people or less. We have a number of clients of that size, and if they're willing to pay the price, we can bring in courses, workshops, and consulting and have them doing very effective reviews of all phases in a matter of a month. Of course, for a long time after that they keep improving as they develop leader skills, individualized checklists, and variant review practices. The whole organization is changed in a month, but the soil was prepared. Management was ready and the organization was usually doing similar things, informally, so they were not afraid to look at each other's work or to have their own work looked at.

At the other end of the scale, we have a client with about 600 technical people, fully committed management, but no real experience in working openly. There it took about three years to turn the organization 180 degrees, from a failing software producer to a highly successful one. One rule of thumb you might use is about one month for each twenty people in the organization, but that's with a management that's fully committed in advance and a lot of help in the beginning.

What About a Management That's not Committed One
Way or the Other?

If you start out with no commitment by management, then there's really no reliable way to say how long it's going to take. First you must get things going in small parts in order to produce some striking results. If the results are striking, you can begin to get the attention and commitment of management, after which things can progress fairly rapidly.

But it's hard to get striking results when people don't have any measurements to gauge how well or poorly they were previously doing. Management can discount the results, and because striking results may appear critical of prior management behavior, there is a tendency to do just this. For instance, if you document a reduction of errors by a factor of five, you may hear, "Oh, that's typical. We never really had that much trouble with errors except on a few really poor projects."

In such a situation, you could go on forever without persuading anybody. This is why we encourage people, whatever stage they're at, to start writing things down and to be quantitative, explicit, and nonjudgmental. Even before you start actually doing any reviews, you will be speeding up the process of acceptance of reviews if you start keeping better records of what you're doing now. Management will usually be won over by facts. If not, then it will take forever to do anything worthwhile, so go somewhere else.

Your Handbook Clearly Distinguishes Three Types of Review—The Informal Review That a Team Might Carry Out on Its Own Work, the Formal Technical Review, and the Project Control Review Conducted by Management. If You've Got an Organization That Is Carrying Out Fairly Successful Informal Team Reviews and Project Management Reviews, How Do You Initially Justify to Management the Expense of Formal Technical Reviews?

If the informal reviews actually are working that well, it may not indeed be cost justified to introduce formal reviews. But we've never seen an organization where infor-

mal reviews were that consistent. And even if they were
that consistent, management has no way to know it, so the
formal reviews would be "ulcer justified," even if not cost
justified.

In very small organizations, the distinction between
formal and informal procedures of all kinds becomes
blurred. If there are informal reviews, management is
likely to know what the results are, even without formal
reporting. But as an organization grows above the face-
to-face level, things begin to slip out of everybody's sight
and not be noticed.

As we've had to remind people so many times, the
cost of one mistake can be so huge that it shouldn't be
hard to justify another level of review with a little more
formality to put management at ease. But in a way, the
very magnitude of the exposure to error makes it harder
to convince management. We've had the experience of
coming out of a most productive review and saying to
management, We found one error in your specification
in there that, if it had slipped through, would have cost
you a million dollars five years from now.

A million dollars pays for a lot of reviewing, but
it's awfully hard to convince someone that you've saved
them a million dollars in the future. Unfortunately, a
large percentage of the shops we visit have management
that has been motivated *after* the million has already been
spent. When we come in and demonstrate that the million
could have been saved by a system of formal reviews,
people are not always delighted.

The best we've been able to tell people is that other
people have had these experiences, with such and such
results. Then we tell them that if they are always within
schedule, within cost, and don't get surprises that aggra-
vate their customers, then the system they have is OK and
should probably be left alone. But we don't get many data-
processing managers who are willing to say that their present system is that good, no matter how proud they are
of what they've accomplished. It's a hard business we're
in, and it's no disgrace to admit that you could do better.

*Are You Suggesting, Hidden in That Answer, That Smaller
Organizations Might Not Have the Full Spectrum of
Formal Technical Reviews or That Smaller Organizations
May Delete the Formal Review Altogether?*

We have noticed the tendency of smaller organizations
to deformalize technical review procedures as time goes
by. They become comfortable and develop their own informal way of handling things that produces the same
result. They evolve what you might call a semiformal review process.

In larger organizations, because of the nature of
large organizations, this tendency is much less pro-
nounced. Even so, we live in an informal society, and
people, being human, even large organizations inevitably
develop their own informalities and unspoken rules.
There's nothing whatsoever wrong with this. It's both
natural and nice. The only question is whether the process
continues to do the job.

*In This Answer and in Other Parts of the Handbook,
There Seems To Be an Implication That Formal Reviews
Are Preferred to Informal Reviews. Doesn't the Formal
Review Create a Negative Learning Environment for the
Producer, Who Could Be Forced Into a Defensive Position
During the Review?*

Let's be as clear as possible about this, because it seems
to keep coming up. First, the only absolutely essential
difference between the formal and the informal review
is the report to management. Without this reporting, the
reviews must be called "informal"—even though some
"informal" reviews have much more structure and real
formality than some "formal" reviews.

Second, *we prefer less formality to more formality.* We
always recommend as much informality as you can get
away with. But no more! It all goes back to whether the

system works—and that means whether it reliably produces the information desired by the people who inaugurated the system of reviews.

For instance, if "informal" reviews have been inaugurated by the chief programmer within a team, but are not working well because nobody prepares seriously or people behave irresponsibly during the meeting, then the chief programmer might want to consider introducing some formality into the proceedings. Or, if "formal" reviews have been producing reports to management that fill in all the blanks but merely go through the motions of raising real issues, management might want to consider ways of loosening up the procedures a bit so that people are more comfortable with them.

Then Why Do You Emphasize Rules So Much?

The "formality"—in the sense of rules—is primarily an aid through the difficulties of getting started, just like the formalities of getting married. Every bride and groom in the world must have thought of running out on the whole process on their wedding day, but the gown and the tuxedo and all the rest help carry them through an unfamiliar and emotionally charged experience. However, it would be a pitiful marriage if the bride wore a gown and the groom wore a tux for fifty years! Indeed, if your organization *doesn't* loosen up a bit in its review practices after a short time, then *that's* something to see a consultant about.

The formality does strike people as curious before they start, just as a wedding ceremony might seem curious to someone from another culture. But we've seen a lot of reviews now, and we know there are some universal feelings in the first reviews. People are concerned. People are nervous that they're going to be criticized or that they're going to have to say bad things about their friends and colleagues. In these cases, it helps people to know that this process is something that is done routinely in other organizations and that nobody has ever died from it.

The "rituals" may seem silly and arbitrary, but they do show people that they are not the first people ever to do this. They also are arranged to protect people—and to let people know they are protected—from the most common abuses of inexperienced reviews. The rituals get people over this very difficult first review period, after which they can become less formal. They get better at reviewing and being reviewed, they are less nervous, they learn more in each review, and the results are more reliable.

As a result of watching established reviews, you might get the impression that getting started is easy, just as you might forget, after twenty-five years of marriage, just how frightening your own wedding can be. If you forget, then formality seems stupid. Try to remember.

Technical Reviews And Project Management

Are Technical Reviews a Form of Project Management?

No, technical reviews are a *tool* that can be used with any form of project management, in much the same way, say, as a Source Program Library (SPL) is a tool of project management. Like a SPL, formal technical reviews serve an essential *control* function. Without the source library, management has no assurance that the software is secure against accidental or deliberate change. Without the formal review, management has no assurance that the software was any good to begin with, even before it went into the source library.

We Paid a Lot of Money for the X System of Project Management. Just How Does This System Fit with Technical Reviews?

We are often asked this question, with various names substituted for X. In order to understand how technical reviews can fit into *any* form of project management, we need a general picture that encompasses all such systems. In particular, we are concerned with how *technical facts* are linked into the project management system, as the technical review's concern is with technical facts, rather than the many other facts a manager needs to manage a project.

Figure B.5.1 shows a general picture of the role of management in a development project. Plans are made, resources are allocated, and activities are begun to accomplish the task. If the outside world (environment) did not intervene, and if people and resources were perfectly predictable, there would be no need for management once a project was launched. But there is an outside world, and nothing is perfect. Thus the need for management.

Management during a project operates by comparing partial output with the planned output. As discrepancies arise, management acts. More resources are allocated; resources are moved from one place to another; activities are speeded up or slowed down; new activities

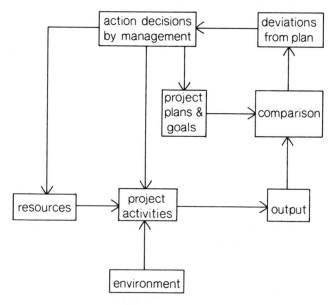

FIGURE B.5.1.   *A General Picture of Project Management*

are initiated and old ones closed down; some activities may have to be repaired or redone. Ideally, the plans and goals can stay constant, but if deviations are too great, the initial hopes for the project have to be adjusted to meet the reality of what can be accomplished within a given schedule and budget.

This model is only one way to look at the project management task and naturally falls far short of telling all about its complexities. Nevertheless, it is a true and useful picture for understanding why *technical* projects are more difficult to manage than nontechnical projects.

What characterizes a technical project, in this model, is the problem of *comparing output with plans.* In a nontechnical project, the project management staff can simply *look* at the output and *know* whether or not it matches the plans. In a technical project, "looking" is a job that requires very special—that is technical—abilities.

Let's make this point explicit in the programming context. Suppose the project plans call for module A, consisting of 300 lines of code, to be completed on 17 January. On 16 January, a programming secretary hands management a report that a module named A, consisting of 303 lines of code, has been placed in the development library in object form. Has this activity been completed according to plan?

If the project were nontechnical, the answer would be quite easy. Suppose the "module" consisted of 300 barrels of aviation fuel delivered to a certain point. The delivery report would show 303 barrels delivered and passing inspection, presumably by qualified inspectors, so the work of that activity is completed. If the report shows only 212 barrels delivered, then the activity is not completed, and perhaps only about two-thirds completed.

The difference between these two cases is instructive. If the only way to test aviation fuel were to fly a plane, then the two cases would be the same. But although flying is the *ultimate* test of fuel quality, it is too dangerous a test to use for management purposes. In order to make the use of aviation fuel *manageable,* we have evolved over the years *a series of reliable intermediate tests of quality.*

In programming, when this series of reliable intermediate tests does not exist, good project management is not possible except by circumstances of good luck.

In Our Organization, Our Chief Programmer Teams Usually Produce Reliable Evaluations of the Quality of the Software They Are Producing. Why Do We Need Technical Reviews?

If you have full confidence in the evaluation of these producing units, then you don't need technical reviews. But what does the term "usually" mean in your question? Is "usually reliable" an adequate basis on which to risk perhaps millions of dollars of development money?

The question of *risk* is uppermost. Most programming teams can produce reliable output a good percentage of the time, but once in a while they slip up, and one slip can delay an entire system for months. The formal review is designed as a check and balance system to protect against such slips. Like any checking system, it cannot *correct* a seriously disturbed situation. Instead, it can only provide information that management can use to begin corrective measures.

Information normally comes to project management by two routes, as shown in Figure B.5.2. *Cost and schedule information* comes in channels relatively independent of the producing unit and thus can be relied upon to detect when a unit runs over cost and schedule. But what if the technical work isn't done right? It's easy to be on schedule if the work doesn't have to be right! But because management is not usually in a position to evaluate the technical output directly, it receives the unit's own evaluation—a dangerous game if the unit is malfunctioning.

In this system, the producing unit is both defendant and judge—a good system for controlling the work in the short run, but utterly inadequate for overall control. If

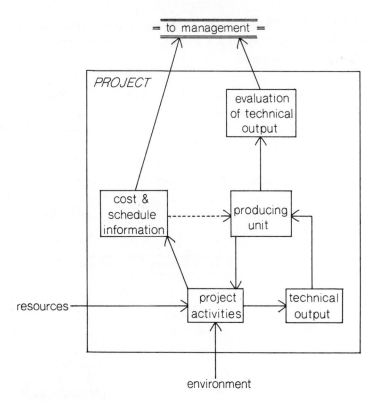

FIGURE B.5.2.   *Management's View of the Output of a Programming Effort*

the unit is technically weak in a certain area, the unit's judgment will be weak in the same area. Just where the work is the poorest, the evaluation sent to management will be least likely to show the weakness.

With perfect people on perfect teams, the problem still exists, because of information overload. As the unit becomes overloaded, the work quality may suffer because there is inadequate time for supervision. Not only may the work quality suffer, but for the same lack of time, the evaluation suffers. The unit *wants* to be done on schedule and *wants* the work to be correct. Under pressure, any human being will see what is wanted instead of what exists. This is simply no way to control the expenditure of millions of dollars nor to risk many millions more when the programs are run.

*And You Say That Formal Technical Reviews Can Solve
the Problem of Creating a Reliable Link to the Project
Management System?*

Yes, as we can see in Figure B.5.3., which shows how the formal technical review fits into any system of project management. As before, the unit controls its own development work, perhaps conducting informal reviews internally. Nothing need be changed at this level, which makes the introduction of reviews much simpler.

As the diagram shows, the formal review is conducted by people who are *not part of that producing unit.*

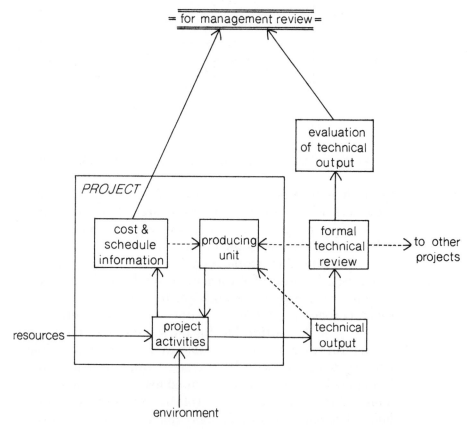

FIGURE B.5.3. *The Place of the Formal Technical Review*

Hopefully, these are people who have no conscious or unconscious reason for favoring or disfavoring the project's work. Moreover, their report—the technical review summary report—goes to management, regardless of whether it is favorable or unfavorable, thus providing *reliable information* to be used in *management reviews* of the project.

The diagram also illustrates the difference between a *technical* review and a *management* review, sometimes called a "project review" or some other name. The technical review committee is staffed by technical people and studies only technical issues. Its job is to put the evaluation of technical output on the same reliable basis as, say, cost and schedule information and then to deliver this information to management. Using both sorts of information, management can now make informed judgments of what is to be done in controlling the project.

There are (or may be) other outputs from the formal technical review concerning technical issues raised by this work either for this project or other projects. We shall discuss these later in Part D. For now, we wish to stick to the single dominant reason for instituting a system of formal technical reviews—reliable evaluation of technical progress for management purposes. Even if there were no other benefits of the formal technical review—and there are considerable ones—this single purpose would justify many times over the effect needed to install such a system.

It should be noted that most "project control" systems do not concern themselves with the accurate and reliable evaluation of the *quality of technical output*. Instead, they concern themselves with measuring what can be measured *without* technical review, assuming, more or less, that one module of 300 lines of code is more or less like any other module of 300 lines of code. If that assumption of quality is correct, then these systems can provide excellent management information for project control.

If that assumption is incorrect, then only the "cost" side of the "cost effectiveness" ledger has any meaning.

Under such conditions, the best project control system can provide only an illusion of control. The consequences are familiar enough—surprised customers when schedules are missed, cost overruns, specifications not met, performance not up to expectation, errors plaguing production systems, and maintenance huge and never ending.

You Seem To Be Saying That the Review Is a Device for Tracking Progress. How Often Should We Hold Reviews, and How Does This Relate to Our System of Project Management?

There are two related questions here. The answer to both of them is implied by something one of our clients told us: "They have to design their work so that they don't go longer than two weeks without having some reviews of the product to do." In short, you must *design* to be reviewable.

Many installations get into trouble because they don't do this. Instead, they plan an enormous chunk of work—like 10,000 lines of code—with nothing in the middle that they can review. After working for several months, they present it for review and find out it isn't done—or is half done, but coded so poorly it is unacceptable. Their problem is designing, not reviewing, but it's the review that shows up the problem.

So you must choose the time between reviews according to the longest time you can afford to be in the dark about how the work is going. This probably will turn out to be from two to four weeks in most cases. It may be shorter than the time prescribed between "phases" by your project management system, but it should not be longer. Using this frequency, management can know something is behind if it has gone for several weeks without being ready for review or if it has failed to pass its review. Either case is a signal for management action to get the project back on course before the deviation is too great.

You've Emphasized that We Should Review Early and
Review Often. But Is It Possible to Do Too Much
Reviewing?

It certainly is. Anything done to excess is bad, even moderation. So although it's possible to do excessive reviewing, don't worry about making a mistake every once in a while by doing too much. It's OK not to be perfect all the time, for that would be excessive, too. You're going to make mistakes, no matter what you do, so perhaps it's a good strategy to err on the safest side—and that would be the side of too much versus too little reviewing.

If you are reviewing too much, there will be self-correcting factors. People will find themselves having little or nothing to contribute to reviews and will begin to opt out of reviewing. Most commonly, though, when this happens, the problem is too many reviewers not too many reviews.

For instance, if you typically have seven people in a code review, but the leader perceives that the same result could have been achieved with any three or four of those people, then you are probably inviting too many reviewers. Perhaps people are asking to be invited, which enlarges the review. In those cases, we find that the excess reviewers soon stop asking. In other cases, just try cutting down the review size one member at a time until you find a size that has the right energy level to conduct an effective review.

That Answer Addresses the Workload on the Individuals,
but What About the Total Number of Reviews Themselves?
Even with Small Reviews, You Can Spend All Your Time
Reviewing If Too Many Reviews Are Scheduled.

The number of reviews to be scheduled depends on the project management system. If management is controlling at a certain level of detail, then that is the level that needs reviewing. For instance, if the completion of fifty lines of coding is a "milestone" for your project management system, then there had better be a review of each fifty-line hunk of code.

Managers sometimes worry when they see that their system of reviews no longer turns up the large numbers of errors it did when first installed. They are tempted to save money by cutting out these "unnecessary" reviews. This temptation is based on a short-sighted and incorrect view of what the review system does—that the purpose of the review is to find errors.

Actually, the ultimate purpose of a system of reviews is to *prevent* errors. If the knowledge that the work is going to be regularly reviewed prevents errors, then the review system is paying for itself and shouldn't be abandoned.

It's possible to experiment with slightly less frequent reviewing, but we prefer that the review leaders simply learn to terminate reviews quickly when there is little or nothing to discuss. Learning to terminate reviews at the proper time is one of the hardest things that review leaders have to learn. If there are complaints about too much reviewing, examine the leaders' technique for bringing the meetings to a close.

Could We Reduce the Number of Reviews By Sampling— That Is, By Reviewing Only Randomly Selected Pieces of Work?

It's true that random sampling will retain the feeling that any piece of work *might* be reviewed, so motivation to prevent errors can be kept at a high level if the sampling process is well designed. But can you afford even that one rare error that slips through the sampling? It may depend on your applications. In Australia, a single error costing an estimated $235,000,000 was traced back to a piece of a system that was missed by the sampling procedure. They did review the specifications, but only on a sampled basis. Bad luck? Yes, but can you afford to depend on good fortune in drawing the sample? If you can, sampling may be well worth considering.

PART C

Conducting the Review

The Review Leader

What Are the Responsibilities of the Review Leader?

Leading a review can come to carry much prestige, but the job also carries real work responsibilities, not all of them glamorous. The review leader's responsibilities can be summarized easily:

> **The job of the review leader is to obtain a good review—or to report the reasons why a good review wasn't obtained.**

What Do You Mean, Report the Reasons a Good Review Wasn't Obtained?

A few examples should make this principle clear. Suppose one or more members of the review come unprepared, after having been given the appropriate material sufficiently far in advance. If this lack of preparation means that a good review cannot be conducted, then the review

89

should be terminated and a report created for management explaining the reasons in detail.

Or suppose the committee arrives at the meeting room only to find that the plasterers are tearing down the walls, making the review impossible. If too much time is lost finding another room, the review should not be conducted, but a report should be sent to management in place of the review report. Management has a right to expect that each scheduled review will produce *either* a good review report or a report on the reasons the review wasn't good.

But What If the Product Being Reviewed Just Isn't Very Good?

This question hinges on a misunderstanding of what is meant by a "good review." A good review means a review that produces an *accurate assessment of the product* as it now stands. The goodness of the *review* has no necessary connection with the goodness of the *product being reviewed.*

Suppose a piece of code containing serious errors is reviewed and reported to management as being error free. The review that produces such an inaccurate report must be judged a bad review. Conversely, if the product is actually well done, but the review labels it as full of errors and problems, the review must again be judged as bad—even though the product itself is very good.

The review leader *cannot and must not* be held responsible for the goodness or badness of the product as it arrives for review, but only for the goodness or the badness of the review itself. Of course, once the review has declared a product to be good, the review leader has acquired a portion of the responsibility for the product— because the review for which the leader was responsible declared it to be a good product. Without such responsibility on each member of the review committee, there can be no long-term guarantee of the accuracy of reviews—and without accuracy, reviews become useless as management tools.

How Do We Choose a Review Leader?

The review leader should be chosen for a combination of technical and personal qualities. Without adequate technical skill, the leader wouldn't be able to understand the comments and criticisms raised in the review. It is essential, for instance, that the leader be able to detect when the meeting is drifting into an interesting technical discussion that has no clear application to the material being reviewed, in order to steer the review back on course.

On the other hand, the review leader is not necessarily honed to a sharp edge on the particular application being reviewed. The intricate technical details should be assured by experts—the review leader's job is to assure that these experts do their jobs.

Whatever the review leader knows or doesn't know about the details of the material being reviewed, certain technical knowledge will be essential. The review leader should definitely be well versed in the development process, the development tools being used, modern software methodologies, and in particular, the relationship of reviews to the entire development process.

The prerequisites on personal qualities are harder to define, for there are a number of styles of leadership that can produce an effective review meeting. A good rule to follow is that

Results are more important than mannerisms.

If a leader gets a good review by shouting at everybody, then why worry about shouting? On the other hand, there are leaders who can cool a boiling meeting by raising an eyebrow or coughing, and who could quarrel with that approach?

But Aren't Certain Mannerisms Always Fatal to a Review
Leader's Success?

"Always" is a pretty strong word, but there are some mannerisms that could be viewed as dangerous signs. Anyone who thinks that "leader" means "boss" is a rather poor candidate for leading a review of technical peers. Also, anyone who is afraid to contradict someone else on the review team may have serious trouble keeping the process in order. Perhaps the worst personal trait for a review leader is the inability to step back from a technical discussion that happens to be of great personal or intellectual interest. Once the review leader gets caught in some technical whirlpool, who will rescue the review?

Shouldn't the Review Leader Be Someone Who Can Follow
Through on Administrative Details Responsibly?

The review leader certainly must take responsibility for a variety of administrative steps vital to a successful review—steps we shall discuss elsewhere in this section. On the other hand, none of these steps requires extraordinary administrative powers. We would be highly suspicious of someone who claims to be a professional programmer or analyst who tries to be excused from review leadership on the grounds of lack of administrative ability. If someone is lacking in experience in administrative follow-through, perhaps the role of review leader would provide an excellent training ground for skills that would prove invaluable in day-to-day technical work.

We Use Chief Programmer Teams. Shouldn't the Review
Leader Job Be Given to the Various Chiefs?

The team leader—chief or otherwise—is often delegated the responsibility for reviews. Certainly the qualities that make a good team leader should prove to be assets in the review leader role. On the other hand, don't overlook other people who may have the technical and emotional maturity to lead reviews.

For example, more than one installation routinely assigns the backup programmer most of the review leader duties. The chief is already heavily burdened with both administrative and technical duties within the team, while the backup is often left with idle hands. By leading reviews, the backup programmer gets an opportunity to gather both breadth and depth of experience that will one day be needed to step up to the chief programmer role.

There may be numerous people other than designated team leaders who would do an excellent job as review leaders while gaining immeasurably from the experience. Indeed, one of the major roles of the review in the development cycle is as training ground for future technical leaders.

But Can the Team Leader Really Be Objective When Leading a Review of His or Her Team's Work?

Although team leaders may lead reviews, they should *never* lead reviews of their own team's work. As we discussed in the case of management,

Nobody should be present at a review whose role might create a conflict of interest.

Obviously, leading a review of one's own team's work would create a great conflict and must therefore be avoided.

How Does the Review Leader Prepare for Each Review?

After the review leader has been informed by the producing team that a work unit is ready for review, the first step is to collect the relevant materials needed for the review. Once assured that all relevant materials are actually ready and available, the review leader schedules the actual review at a time and place agreeable to all who are to attend. In some installations, the review leader must have consultative power concerning attendees in order to be able to take responsibility for the quality of the review.

After the materials have been gathered, the review leader is responsible for getting them reproduced and distributed sufficiently far in advance of the meeting to permit everyone to prepare. The distribution can be done by any convenient method, but the leader should follow through in some way to confirm that the materials have been received, are complete, and are not just sitting unnoticed in the in basket.

Some review leaders set the meeting time and place when confirming the arrival of the materials. If there has been a specified period of time allocated for reviews, there should be no great difficulty in getting the meeting together.

On the day of the review, the leader should verify that the facility is available and ready for use. We have provided a checklist for this task that is essential to assuring that the meeting doesn't fail for mechanical reasons.

Finally, if for some reason the review must be cancelled or delayed, the review leader is responsible for notifying all participants.

What Materials Are Needed in the Review Packet That the Leader Must Assemble?

The principle here is that *anything* relevant to making a correct technical judgment of the product must be in the packet. If participants have to go hunting around for relevant information, they probably won't prepare at all.

What is relevant material? Naturally, the answer depends on the particular sort of material being reviewed.

Code reviews would involve the code, test data, test results, specifications, documentation, and other such materials. Design reviews would involve specifications, design constraints, standards, implementation scheme, and one or more alternative designs. The requirements for each type of review will be discussed in detail elsewhere. The important question for the review leader is, Can we make the proper technical judgment without resorting to additional material? If the answer is no, then that additional material should be added to the review packet.

Doesn't That Involve a Great Deal of Copying Cost?

If the copying cost is that big an issue, one of two situations is at fault:

1. The project is *seriously* underbudgeted.
2. The design is so poor that great masses of material are needed to assure each little piece—in which case, no review is needed to tell you what to do!

Don't try to save on copying costs by *circulating* one set of materials. *It doesn't work.*

What Does the Review Leader Do During the Review Itself?

The job of the review leader is to obtain a good review. Once the advance preparations have been made, the best way to assure a good review is to conduct an orderly, well-paced meeting. Very few people are born with the ability to read and guide the mood and pace of a meeting, but most people can learn. As the leaders acquire practice, they acquire skill. During the transition, they may need some guidelines and/or some help from a backup leader acting as a "buddy" or as a "shadow."

The first and foremost requirement for an adequate review is advance preparation by everyone involved. At least 80 percent of all review failures can be traced to lack of advance preparation. Therefore, the leader should be monitoring constantly to ascertain how well the advance preparation was carried out.

As the review progresses, the leader should make certain that each member of the review committee has an opportunity to comment on the product. Anyone who has prepared for a review and finds no opportunity to contribute what has been prepared is unlikely to prepare for the next review. Equally important, significant points about the product are likely to be lost. Better to have a few points raised twice than to miss even one point entirely.

In pacing the review, the leader must be certain that sufficient time is spent covering the material. If the meeting is being rushed because there is too much material to be reviewed carefully, the leader should simply announce that there will be another review to cover the remaining material. Or if the meeting is being rushed because there are too many problems with the material, the leader should ask the committee to concentrate on obtaining a list of the most important points. If there are that many points concerning the product, another review must be scheduled *after the major points have been corrected.*

If the course of the meeting starts to deviate from its mission, the review leader's job is to bring the members back on track. Usually, a simple reminder will do the job, but there are techniques to use in case a reminder doesn't work.

At the conclusion of the meeting, the review leader has the responsibility of polling the committee to reach the consensus opinion. The review leader is then responsible for the preparation of the review report and the transmission of the report to the participants, to management, to the producers, to the project library, and to other interested parties.

How Can the Review Leader Bring the Meeting Back to Order When It Drifts Into Irrelevant Subjects?

The first step is to observe the drift with an eye to discovering if it's merely a way of concealing lack of preparation by one or more members. If it's not, a reminder of the purpose of the meeting is usually adequate, but if this fails, there are several effective courses of action.

The leader can usually stop overly detailed technical discussions by interrupting with, Yes, that's a good point, and asking the recorder to write it down. Writing down the point tends to focus the discussion on the most important issue and also acts as a natural terminator to that topic.

If some member ignores this hint to stop, the next step is to remind the group that the purpose of the meeting is to *raise* issues, not to resolve them. Usually, the problem comes from someone who has a great deal to say on the issue. The leader should acknowledge the potential contribution of that member by asking the recorder to add a note to the issue requesting that the producing group consult this member before attempting a resolution. Once the member feels assured of eventually being heard out, the discussion should cease. It will behoove the review leader to follow through on such notes after the review, for if people come to feel that they are just being shut up by a ruse, they will cease to respond to the technique.

The leader should *never* accelerate the meeting by *putting down* some member. If the leader assumes that each member is *trying* to make a contribution, the members will usually respond by acting in a mature manner. Some people are not as articulate as others. It may take some time, effort, and patient listening to extract the truly important point the person is trying to make. Most people, after they have been put down once or twice for trying to make a sincere effort to communicate something they deemed important, will stop trying.

Another common source of meeting slowdown is a long explanation of something in the product to a member who doesn't understand it. This kind of slowdown is particularly common in the "walk-through" type of review, where a member of the producing team is making a presentation. Here, there is a tendency to "explain away" problems, in order to get a favorable review report on the team's product. The leader must monitor these explanations and decide when to cut them off.

A good principle to follow is that each reviewed product is *supposed* to be self-documenting. If someone is having a hard time understanding the product based on the review material, then either:

1. That person hasn't prepared, or

2. the product is not quite "self-documenting."

It's up to the leader to determine which is the case. In the first instance, the review should be handled as in any other instance where a member is unprepared, as mentioned elsewhere. In the second, the leader should terminate the discussion by asking the recorder to write down, as an issue, that such-and-such is not adequately clear from the documentation.

But What About Someone Who's Really Just Being Obstructive and Noncooperative in the Review?

If the above tactics are adopted, and particularly if you, as leader, have assured that everyone has prepared and everyone gets to contribute, you will rarely experience such a situation. Still, when you start out with reviews, you may find people who are determined to sabotage the whole process by making a mockery of the early reviews. This isn't a pleasant situation, but there's no need for the review leader to be intimidated by it.

Once you have convinced yourself that someone is really *trying* to be destructive, you should simply announce that you feel that this review is no longer being productive and is therefore terminated. The leader *always* has the prerogative to terminate the meeting, so there can be no argument with this approach. Having terminated the meeting, however, you will be obliged to report to management the *reason* why a good review wasn't obtained. Therefore, you will have to be prepared to defend your conclusion that a member was acting obstructively. This acts as a check on arbitrary judgment by you, the leader.

If this obligation of the leader is carried out fairly and conscientiously in the earliest reviews, your installation is unlikely to experience this kind of difficulty in later reviews. The obstructors will either learn how to be constructive participants or else stop being invited to reviews—or perhaps stop being invited to work at all. On the other hand, if a particular review leader habitually accuses other people of obstructing reviews that are actually being badly led, management cannot fail to notice before long. There is nothing to keep any review member from making a personal report to management on the poor conduct of a review.

We must emphasize that such obstructive tactics are *very* rare in a reasonably healthy organization and almost entirely confined to early reviews, when leaders are inexperienced and a few recalcitrants may still be left over from the "good ol' days." In fact, an experienced leader, faced with apparent obstruction, will first assume that the person is actually acting out some situation *outside* the review situation itself. Perhaps a child is critically ill at home or a spouse has just taken a lover. Perhaps the person has a terrible stomach ache or just came from an argument with the boss, or both. The remedy is to *try* reasonable steps to bring the meeting on track. Then, if reasonable efforts fail, to suggest that the meeting be terminated if it continues in the same vein. If that mild threat doesn't work, then it really isn't a problem for the review leader, but a problem for management, and the meeting should be terminated.

What About the Really Quiet Person Who Just Hasn't the Nerve to Speak Up?

If the leader notices someone who isn't saying anything, the first step is to examine the behavior of everyone else to look for intimidating factors. It may be, for instance, that people are just jumping in with comments without waiting for explicit recognition from the leader. There's nothing wrong with a spontaneous meeting as long as *everyone* is being spontaneous. If someone is being cut off or shut off, then the leader must take explicit steps.

One way is to ask that the meeting take one point from each person in *rotation*. If someone has more points to raise than others, the extra points can be brought up after everyone else is finished. The rotation is easily recognized as a "fair" way to allocate time, so it is easy to bring the meeting back to the rotation if it deviates. It is usually *unwise* to have everyone take a turn to give *all* points on a particular matter, for someone with a long list will discourage everyone else from contributing.

Even when explicitly asked, some people have difficulty in speaking in a meeting. If the leader is aware of this situation in advance, a meeting with the shy person can be arranged to help prepare a list of points. Many people can read from a prepared list more readily than they can speak extemporaneously. During the meeting, the leader can assist the shy person by asking direct questions, such as, What did you find difficult to understand in these instructions? Very few people are so shy as to be unable to respond to direct questions, especially if the leader prevents anyone else from jumping in while the person is stoking up the courage to respond.

How Can the Leader Be Sure All Important Points Are Covered?

If everyone speaks, most points will be covered, so anything that ensures a fair share of speaking time to each member should help ensure adequate coverage. If there are many points, it may help for the leader to provide an *organizing principle*. For instance, the leader may ask that each person, in rotation, give their *one most important point.* Each successive rotation will take the next most important point, so that if there are too many points to cover, at least the most important ones will be sent back with the rejected product.

Sometimes, the first round will reveal such serious shortcomings in the product that it will be best to terminate the meeting early, rather than waste any more time. There's absolutely no need to fill up the time allocated to the meeting, once some fatal point has been raised and agreed upon.

There is a tendency to go through the product from "beginning" to "end." For instance, when reviewing a document, the first page might be reviewed in detail before any other pages are considered. Generally, this "sequential" review is a poor review, unless there has first been time for *overall* comments to be made. It has been said that "an expert is someone who catches everyone else's trivial errors on the way to his own grand fallacy." The leader would be wise to assure that the review group isn't this kind of "expert."

We've Seen a Tendency for Some Impatient Persons to Rush Through the Review and Produce Superficial Comments. What Can the Leader Do About This?

If the review procedures require *consensus,* nobody can be rushed into approving a superficial review. All anyone needs to do is to vote for rejection of the product on the grounds of inadequate review. The need for consensus then forces the product to be reviewed again.

Actually, it is the *threat* of such a "veto" that generally protects against a rushed, superficial review. Once people understand that trying to rush things will actually mean it takes longer, they will slow down. Of course, if a product is to be re-reviewed because of inadequate review, the *same* people must be chosen for the review. Otherwise, people will use rush tactics as a technique for getting out of review responsibilities.

Some People Find It Hard to Say Bad Things About Someone Else's Work. How Can the Review Leader Encourage Them to Contribute?

Not only do some people find it hard to say something *bad,* others find it hard to say something *good.* For a long time we've, encouraged review leaders to insist that each participant have *at least one positive and one negative remark.* Having made a positive remark, the "nice" person tends to feel less trepidation about saying something negative. Conversely, forcing the "cynic" to say *something* positive may provide an opportunity for a new way of thinking about the product.

The positive-negative ritual may seem silly, but it actually serves a number of useful functions. By *insisting* that each participant make a negative comment, the leader *ritualizes* criticism, in much the same way the Catholic church ritualizes criticism of candidates for sainthood by appointing a Devil's Advocate. Without this ritual authorization to criticize, who could say something bad about a saint?

Once the ritual nature of criticism has been established, no person need feel that making negative comments is impolite. The ritualization of positive comments, on the other hand, has at least two other important functions. First, it tends to encourage the producers, who might otherwise be discouraged by a long list of negative comments. Second, it helps ensure that the producers will not destroy something positive while trying to remedy something negative.

For example, a code review might produce the criticism that the specified memory allocation has been exceeded. If the review group also compliments the producers on their use of meaningful error messages, the messages will not be destroyed in an effort to meet the memory criterion. Without the positive remark, the producers might seize upon the first memory saving that came to mind—and then be shot down in the next review for not having meaningful error messages.

We Have One Person Who's Always Late for the Review. Should We Wait for This Person or Start the Meeting Anyway?

Neither. We assume the person was put on the review for a purpose. Therefore, you cannot start without this person without making the review appear more thorough than it actually is. But if you wait, then soon everyone will be coming late, and a bad practice will have been established. You should wait a reasonable time, depending on the "culture" of your office (perhaps five minutes), then convene the meeting for the purpose of declaring the review INCOMPLETE. An explanation is written to management that the review was not complete because this person did not attend. The problem will soon cure itself.

But Sometimes There's a Good Reason for a Person to Be, Say, Fifteen Minutes Late. Isn't This a Rather Severe Procedure?

Now you're asking a different question. The previous question was about a *habitual* latecomer. Certainly if someone calls the review leader at or around the appointed time and informs the review leader of an upcoming short lateness, the review leader has several other reasonable options. Everyone can be informed to come back in fifteen minutes or just to wait. In some cases, there will be *parts* of the review that don't really involve the late person. If so, perhaps the review can be structured to do those parts first. But *don't* restructure like this for the habitual late-comer, or you'll only be rewarding the very behavior you find objectionable.

Our Problem Is Just the Opposite. What Can We Do About a Person Who Always Leaves Early?

The problem seems opposite, but is actually pretty much the same as habitual lateness. Each person is trying to say, by actions, that the meeting is not sufficiently important for such an important person. The first attack on the early leaving problem is to be sure that your meetings do not run over schedule, which would give people a valid excuse for leaving early. If meeting times are clear in advance and enforced, there are few real excuses for leaving early. Therefore, if the habitual early departer rises to leave, declare the meeting adjourned with a report of NOT COMPLETE, with accompanying reasons. This brings the problem to the attention of management, whose job it is to handle such problems.

When the early leaving is not habitual, but really necessary (as in an emergency), do not be afraid to adjourn the meeting with a NOT COMPLETE report explaining exactly why. Unlike a late start, for which you can compensate, there is no substitute for a relaxed discussion at the end of the meeting—by *all* participants—of what the final decision should be. Management will certainly understand that life's many contingencies sometimes upset the best planned and best run review meetings, so there should be no problem if the occurrence is rare and actually justified. What management *doesn't* want is a review report that falsely claims that the review was completed.

Do You Have Any Good Ideas How to Handle the Person Who Tends to Want to Redesign, Rather Than Raise Issues?

One approach we've heard sounds worth trying. When the offender tries to redesign the product to "make it better," you stop him or her and require that instead they come up with some way to "make it worse." This adds a little humor, forces them to see that the product can't be all bad, and shows that they, too, are capable of generating less than perfect ideas. It soon stops the "here's how to make it better" syndrome.

Is There Any Special Way the Leader Should Start the Review?

Each installation soon develops its own style of kicking off a review. A typical protocol might look like this:

1. The leader announces, We're here to review product X, for the purpose of Y.
2. The leader then introduces each person, saying something like, Charlie Smyth is here representing auditing. He's particularly interested in the control aspects of this product and also in the user manuals.
3. The leader then introduces the recorder and describes the method of recording to be used, if it has any new aspects or is unfamiliar to any of the members.
4. The leader then reviews the list of materials, checking that each person has received the full set, all of the same versions. (Ideally, this checking should be done by the leader when or soon after the material is distributed.)
5. The leader then begins the particular form of review that is being carried out by introducing the form (walk-through, inspection, etc.) and explaining it to any who have not used it previously.

Shouldn't the Leader Ask If Everyone Is Prepared?

The leader should certainly *find out* if everyone is prepared, but *asking* may or may not do the job. In many
installations, nobody would reply, No, to the question,
Are you prepared?

Then How Can the Leader Discover If People Are Not
Prepared for the Review?

Let's begin to answer that question by putting it in perspective. Once reviews have become firmly established,
unprepared participants will seldom be a problem. But
when you first start reviews, people don't believe that
reviews will be different from other meetings, for which
they traditionally didn't have to prepare. Thus, it's extremely important to establish once and for all that reviews
will be aborted if even one participant is unprepared—
and that the reason for the abrupt termination will be in
the review report.

How, then, can the leader know if someone hasn't
prepared? There's no 100 percent method, but here's a
checklist of methods various clients of ours have found
useful:

1. Visit each person the day before the review to check
    whether the entire packet has been received. If they
    haven't even counted the documents, you know they
    haven't prepared yet and aren't likely to prepare be-
    fore tomorrow.
2. Leave one (inconsequential) page out of the packet
    or have the pages numbered with a gap in one place.
    People who don't call the leader to find out about the
    missing page obviously haven't prepared.
3. Ask everyone to mark their copy in red for typos and
    other points too minor to bring up in the review itself.

Have these given to the recorder ten minutes before the review starts, so the recorder can post them to a master copy while the others are having coffee. The recorder should be able to tell from the level of marking who hasn't looked at the documents. Be careful, though, for some people just don't spot typos. Use this information as an indication to question someone further about preparation.

4. Start the review by having everyone make a general comment, perhaps one good and one bad, about the product. Look for vague generalities and ask for clarification as a way of spotting bluffers.

5. Keep a little checklist of comments made by each person as the review progresses. Have several columns, labeled

   NONSPECIFIC   SOMEWHAT SPECIFIC   SPECIFIC

and check for each person as each comment is made. After a while, you'll begin to see a pattern emerging. If someone is never making specific comments, it may mean they are not prepared—or it may mean that they just don't know how to be specific. In either case, the review leader ought to intervene, though differently in each case. This list will also help the review leader keep involvement at a high level for *all* participants.

Here is an example of a leader's checklist from an actual review:

Name	Nonspecific Comments	Somewhat Specific Comments	Specific Comments
Oswald	/ /	/	┼┼┼ /
Dorothy	/	/ / /	┼┼┼ ┼┼┼ / /
Lynn	/ / /	/ / /	┼┼┼
Arthur	┼┼┼ ┼┼┼ /	┼┼┼ /	/
Robbie	/		/ /

The leader should be able to form some hypotheses by the time this much data has been collected. Arthur is very likely not prepared and bluffing, but he may just be a poor reviewer. Robbie could be just a very quiet person, in which case the review leader should draw him out. In doing so, we'll soon find out if he's prepared or not. Dorothy may be monopolizing the review and shutting out quiet ones like Robbie. The leader might watch for times when Robbie and Dorothy are competing for the floor and push the balance in favor of Robbie a few times. Arthur might be tested with some direct questions or perhaps stopped short when making nonspecific or irrelevant comments by telling him that the particular comment isn't contributing.

6. The review leader can keep a checklist of little dodges or habits that people may get into when they are not prepared. On the list might be such things as:

   a. *READING:* Much reading of documents rather than listening to the other participants.

   b. *DITTOING:* Making comments such as, Yes, I feel exactly the same way, or, I noticed that, too. This may be a way of encouraging others, but it may also be a way of *appearing* to know what's going on.

   c. *TWISTING:* Making comments that seem specific but are actually grammatical tricks on what someone else said previously. One person remarks, I think Section 7 is too detailed in relation to Section 6. Then the bluffer says, Yes, but it could be that Section 6 is not detailed enough with respect to Section 7. This could be a good observation, or it could be a coverup.

   d. *NIT-PICKING:* Making an unending stream of nit-picking points.

   e. *PHILOSOPHIZING:* Trying to get the meeting involved in grand philosophical issues.

   f. *ANNOTATING:* Making marks in the document as the meeting progresses, perhaps just a little ahead of where the meeting is currently.

    g. *DRONING:* Dragging out one argument, or bring-
ing it up over and over, rather than merely recording the issue and getting on with the next
item.

Other items may be added to this checklist as your
experience grows. Be conservative, though! Each of
these habits is *also* a natural habit of some people,
which is exactly why they make good disguises. Of
course, most of them are not very good habits from
the point of view of the successful review, so the review leader could rightly object to them on those
grounds.

7. Sometimes it pays to ask directly if people are prepared—or a little less directly by such a question as:
How much time did you have to spend preparing on
this product? Which section gave you the most trouble? Why? You may actually get a straight answer, or
you may be able to tell something from the hesitation
upon answering.

8. Ask the entire review group to watch for you as you
lead the review. After all, *everyone* is responsible for
a good review. We've prepared a consolidated checklist for review leaders or review watchers, including
the two ideas above and a classical list from social
psychology called the Bates Category System. We use
one or all parts of this form in review classes to assist
participants and observers in rating each others'
performance.

*Well, That's an Interesting Checklist, But Why Is It So
Important If One Person Out of Five or Six Isn't
Prepared? Won't the Review Be Pretty Good Anyway? And
Besides, We Can't Afford to Delay the Whole Process If
Just One Person Isn't Ready.*

If you can't delay the process, it's better if you excuse the
person or persons who aren't prepared and conduct the
review with a smaller group. What we're trying to avoid

is a review that *looks* like it's the work of six people when it's only the work of three or four or five. This gives management a distorted view of the amount of authentication that went into the review report, which will ultimately lead to poor decisions.

Why Not, Then, Invite a Few Extra People, Knowing That It's Just Human Nature for a Few of Them Not to Be Prepared?

You could, of course, ask seven or eight people to prepare for the review, hoping that five or six will actually prepare. But think how you would feel preparing for a review if you knew that was the policy. Would you really do it if you thought that management thought your opinion was so dispensible?

No, in order to make reviews work in the long run, they must be based on full preparation and participation by all the people who are invited, with very few exceptions. Naturally, if someone has a heart attack, you may want to conduct the review with a somewhat smaller group, but in any case, you don't want to pretend that the victim actually participated in rendering a sound technical judgment of the product, do you?

How Do You Use This Consolidated Checklist?

There are several methods, depending on what you're trying to accomplish. In our classes, one of the ways we use it is by assigning an observer for each person in the review. The observer has the responsibility of checking off each behavior seen in the assigned subject. At the end of the review, the observers present their findings, which are discussed. This method can be used in actual reviews to help people improve their review performance, but it is best supervised by someone experienced in the method.

We can also use the checksheet for "scoring" videotaped practice reviews. With the videotape, each person can check his or her own behavior and compare this perception with the perception of other observers.

There are a number of other variations, including the use suggested earlier as a help for the review leader, perhaps with a "buddy" leader doing the checksheet. The most important thing about the checksheet is to realize that it is a tool for making people *aware* of their behavior in reviews, so that they may improve and run *better* reviews.

The checksheet is *not* a method of ranking people, and all checksheets should be destroyed after they have been discussed. One good idea is to code the names of the participants on top of the sheet, so that nobody who finds the checksheet in the wastebasket could make any use of it.

Checksheet Contents

Part I: Tabulate each participant's comments in one of the three categories when substantive matters are being discussed.
Specific: e.g., The comma in line 53 should be a semicolon.
Somewhat Specific: This part of the program isn't too clear to me. It seems backwards, somehow.
Nonspecific: I don't like this page. This design is clumsy. This is better than some programs.

Part 2:   Tabulate behaviors that may be habits or may be ways of covering up for lack of preparation:
Reading: Reading the document instead of listening.
Dittoing: Simply echoing what someone else just said.
Twisting: Echoing what someone else said, but with a different grammatical twist.
Nit-picking: Everyone knows what *this* is.

Philosophizing: Trying to involve the review in grand philosophical issues.

Annotating: Writing in document rather than listening.

Droning: Dragging out an argument or coming back to the same point over and over after it has been recorded.

Part 3: Classify each behavioral act, verbal or nonverbal, in one of these categories:

Shows Solidarity, raises others' status, gives help, rewards.

Shows Tension Release, jokes, laughs, shows satisfaction.

Agrees, shows passive acceptance, understands, concurs, complies.

Gives Suggestion, direction, implying autonomy for others.

Gives Opinion, evaluation, analysis, expresses feeling, wish.

Gives Orientation, information, repeats, clarifies, confirms.

Asks for Orientation, information, repetition, confirmation.

Asks for Opinion, evaluation, analysis, expression of feeling.

Asks for Suggestion, direction, possible ways of action.

Disagrees, shows passive rejection, formality, withholds help.

Shows Tension, asks for help, withdraws out of field.

Shows Antagonism, deflates others' status, defends or asserts self.

No single mark or small number of marks means anything in particular. It is the overall pattern of behaviors in a period of time that may indicate something worth noting about the person or the meeting. Don't worry about being absolutely precise. Just capture most things as best you can, as you see them.

CHECKSHEET FOR REVIEW LEADER AND/OR PARTICIPANTS TO
MONITOR PRODUCTIVE AND NON-PRODUCTIVE PARTICIPATION

PERSON

BEHAVIOR						
Specific comments						
Somewhat specific comments						
Non-specific comments						
READING						
DITTOING						
TWISTING						
NIT-PICKING						
PHILOSOPHIZING						
ANNOTATING						
DRONING						
POSITIVE EMOTION						
Shows solidarity						
Shows tension release						
Agrees						
ANSWERS						
Gives suggestion						
Gives opinion						
Gives orientation						
QUESTIONS						
Asks for orientation						
Asks for opinion						
Asks for suggestion						
NEGATIVE EMOTION						
Disagrees						
Shows tension						
Shows antagonism						

Checklist for Review Leaders

Your Qualifications

Do you understand the purpose of reviews in general?

Do you understand why this particular review is being held?

Can you be objective on the subject of the review?

Have you ever participated in a review as reviewer and reviewee?

Do you have any personal difficulties with any of the reviewers that might interfere with your ability to lead the review?

Prereview

Is the product ready for review?

Are all relevant materials in your possession?

Have all relevant materials been distributed on time?

Have all the reviewers received the materials?

Have the reviewers confirmed their acceptance of the schedule?

Has the conference room been scheduled?

Have arrangements been made for the necessary physical equipment?

During the Review

Are all participants well prepared?

Is there agreement on the objectives of the review?

Are all the participants contributing?

Is the review well paced?

Is interest waning?

Has everyone been heard?

Has anyone tuned out?

Has someone (such as the producer) swayed people by emotional arguments or smooth presentation?

Is there agreement on the outcome of the review?

Is that agreement truly understood by all participants?

Postreview

Was the review successful?

Did it reach a workable conclusion?

Was anybody responsible, if the review was not successful?
Is the report prompt and accurate?
Are all participants satisfied with the outcome?
Did the product get a fair and adequate treatment?
Does the producing group have a reasonable basis for clearing up the issues?
Have all relevant people received the appropriate information?
Have the producers and participants profited from the review?
What can you do to make the next review better?

When I'm Leading a Review, I Frequently Get the Feeling That One of the Participants Is "Somewhere Else" or Trying to Accomplish Something That Isn't the Function of the Meeting. What Can I Do to Ensure Full and Relevant Participation?

What you're talking about is called a "hidden agenda." Here are some notes we wrote for one of our workshops on how a leader can handle just the type of situation you describe.

Agendas

We are all familiar with the idea of an *agenda* for a meeting. Sometimes the agenda is published before the meeting, sometimes it is decided or amended during the meeting, and sometimes it is understood through standards or long practice. The agenda can be a trivial matter to decide, or it can be the longest, most political issue of the meeting. One of the reasons formal technical reviews work so well is that they establish an agenda:

1. That is set prior to the meeting,

2. That is known to be productive in practice,
3. That is standard for a particular type of review, and
4. That is understood and accepted by everyone in the review.

Private Agendas

No matter what public agenda has been accepted, each participant in any meeting will have a variety of *private* agendas, such as:

1. Needing to use a toilet,
2. Wishing to make a phone call,
3. Hoping that the meeting ends early,
4. Trying to make another participant look foolish,
5. Desiring a favorable opinion of the product under review, or
6. Dreaming of a forthcoming vacation or retirement.

Private agendas may run contrary to the public agenda of the meeting, as when someone desires to obtain a favorable review of a poor product. Private agendas may also *reinforce* the public agenda, as when someone desires to end the meeting early and thus contributes to keeping the meeting orderly and on track with the public agenda.

A good review leader will guide the meeting so that private agendas do not interfere with the public purpose of the meeting—to obtain an accurate review of the product. An outstanding review leader will turn many of the private agendas to the advantage of the public agenda.

For instance, if someone wishes to obtain an unfavorable review of a product, the review leader will guide that person toward well-reasoned, factual criticism of the product as the best way to obtain the private goal. If the product withstands such criticism, then the private goal will not be reached, but the public good will be served.

Hidden Agendas

Unlike public agendas, private agendas are not always known to the review leader and other members of the review committee—or even to their possessors. When an agenda is *hidden,* it can distort the purpose of the review without anyone noticing what is happening.

For instance, if some member has a desperate need to use the toilet, but keeps this fact hidden through sheer force of will and mental concentration, the review is, in effect, losing the participation of one member. In this case, it would serve the review better if the member would ask for a "time out" for "personal privilege." The meeting would stop for a few minutes, but when it resumed it would have full participation.

Sensible participants in a proper review environment will feel safe in asking for such times out, but not all people are always sensible and not all environments feel safe. Everyone has experienced times (such as when receiving a lecture from the boss) when it didn't feel safe to ask to be excused for a minute. The review leader and all participants must work hard to keep the environment "safe" and to observe when some member seems to feel "unsafe."

Other hidden agendas are not so sensibly handled. For instance, if Harry wishes to make Jackson look foolish, he's not likely to admit this hidden purpose, even to himself. One way to avoid problems in such a situation is by choosing the review committee in a way that avoids as many such personal clashes as possible. That's why we recommend keeping bosses and subordinates out of the same review.

But not all such personal clashes can be anticipated. Perhaps Harry wants to make Jackson look foolish because Cynthia is in the meeting and he's trying to woo her away from Jackson. Cynthia may not be aware of Harry's interest, nor may Jackson or even Harry himself. Certainly the review leader is unlikely to know, so such clashes have to be handled *on the basis of behavior in the meeting.*

Handling Hidden Agendas

Harry's feelings for Cynthia are no business of the rest of the review committee—unless they interfere with the public agenda of the meeting. If and when they do interfere, the review leader and other review members must observe the interference and take action to stop the interference. Otherwise the review will be less productive than it might have been.

To a great extent, sticking with the formal rules of the technical review will minimize this kind of interference from hidden agendas. But it's not always easy, when starting reviews, to stick to the rules. Moreover, there will always be situations in which the rules don't seem to apply, so human judgment is always needed. It takes a while to learn to handle these situations, though some review leaders are instinctively better than others in certain situations.

Once an organization has practiced technical reviews for a while, most review leaders and committees have developed an instinct for handling hidden agendas. Unfortunately, when you start doing technical reviews, you have many things on your mind besides the personal agendas of each and every participant. Many organizations have failed to establish a system of technical reviews because they were unable to handle hidden agendas successfully in their earliest reviews. It's not that it's so difficult to handle these situations, but only that we lack experience when we're getting started.

Practice with Simulated Agendas

For this reason, our Implementing Technical Reviews Workshop emphasizes practice with hidden agendas. In every simulated review, each participant is given a "Hidden Agenda Sheet" containing zero or more hidden agendas to pretend to carry to the simulated review. The first thing these sheets do is remind all participants that it's always safest to assume that everyone in the meeting has *some* hidden agenda.

Second, they accelerate the process of learning to handle situations that can arise in reviews, but might not arise naturally for a long time. Third, they do give each participant a chance to feel what it's like on *both* sides of the hidden agenda, because learning what it feels like to *have* an agenda is the fastest way to learn how to spot agendas and deal effectively with them.

Handling Real Agendas

You can use the concept of the hidden agenda sheet next time you're in a review meeting or any meeting. Just imagine that you're in a workshop and that each person in the meeting has been handed a confidential hidden agenda assignment just prior to the meeting. As the meeting progresses, try to determine what each person's hidden agenda might be. If one of the agendas seems to be harmful to the purposes of the meeting, test your hypothesis directly, but not accusingly.

For instance, you might say, "Jack, I have the impression that you would like this meeting to end early. Am I correct, or is there something I'm missing? If you do have something else that's more important, we can stop the meeting early and resume at another time."

Notice that you're not accusing Jack, but only suggesting that if he does have something more important, you'd be glad to cooperate with him by postponing this meeting. And if there's some other reason for his peculiar behavior, he has a chance to share it with the rest of you.

When I demonstrated this technique at a recent review we observed, Jack told us that he was concerned about his four-year-old son getting home from the day-care center. His wife was out of town, and a neighbor had promised to pick the boy up. The review committee happily agreed to a ten-minute break for Jack to phone the neighbor. After the break, Jack was relaxed and participated fully. Later, he thanked us for giving him the chance to call, but wondered how we knew his mind was elsewhere.

"It's easy to see," we replied, "once you assume that everyone has other important things on their mind. Next time, though, try just asking the group if you can be excused for a few minutes. We don't think anyone will argue that ten minutes in a review meeting is more important than the safety of your son." It's a positive step when everyone is watching for other peoples' hidden agendas, but it's much more positive when everyone is watching for their own.

If You Asked People, at the Outset, What They Felt Was Missing from the Material Reviewed, Wouldn't That Give You a Good Idea If Someone Wasn't Prepared?

That's an excellent idea, raised by one of our clients. It's very hard to be definitive about what's missing if you haven't read the entire set of material. You're likely to be embarrassed by someone pointing out that the "missing" material is actually conspicuously present.

It's All Very Nice to Talk About the Importance of Preparation, but We Just Don't Seem to Be Able to Handle It in Our Organization. People Aren't in the Habit of Preparing, and Review Leaders Find It Too Hard to Actually Stop the Review Because One Person Isn't Prepared. What Should We Do?

Yes, it is hard—the first time—to do what's necessary, but if you do it, you won't have to do it often, because people will prepare. Over and over again, we've found there is no better way than this: If the people are not prepared, the leader simply terminates the review and writes a report that says, "Review not finished. John and Mary were not prepared, so we could not perform the review as planned. The review will reconvene at . . . ."

Now perhaps this is not a serious delay, so that management is not concerned. In that case, John and Mary won't suffer; it's not too important. But if management is concerned, they will give the matter their attention, and it will be rectified quite quickly. We find that where people are, as you put it, "in the habit" of going to meetings unprepared, they tend to assume that reviews will be the same. But once the problem has been brought to the attention of a management that cares, it doesn't happen a second time without good reason. It really works, and it's a lot easier on everyone in the long run.

But Suppose John and Mary Have a Legitimate Excuse for Not Being Prepared. Do You Want the Review Committee to Act as Ratfinks?

No, but that's not what you're doing. You're simply reporting a fact to management—you couldn't do your work for this reason. It's a *management* job to decide if there's good reason and what action to take if there is or isn't. If your management can't handle that one, you're not going to solve the problems of your organization by technical reviews. Besides, you don't like it when managers try to do *your* job, do you?

What About When the Unprepared Person Comes from a Different Department and Reports Not to Your Management but to Someone Else? Do You Have Any Experience with That?

If you've chosen your review committee properly, there is a reason for each person to be there, regardless of which department they come from. You'll generally find that their management will take it quite seriously when they receive the review report they've been waiting for and discover that the review was not completed because their own people were not prepared.

If they don't take it seriously, and the same people keep coming unprepared, then perhaps that management doesn't care about this review. In that case, discuss the problem with your management and suggest that the next time it happens, you do the following with the approval of your own management. Simply get the committee to agree to reduce itself by one member and continue with the review. Say to the unprepared person, "Your part in the review is finished. Please leave now." Then in the report, state what happened: Milton was not prepared, so with the prior approval of Harold, the committee voted to remove Milton from the review committee. Milton then left the review, and the process went on without him, conducted by the people whose names appear on this report.

Then you let management, using these facts, fight it out. In no case allow yourself to proceed with unprepared people in the room.

Yes, but How Can the Review Leader Bring the Meeting to a Close?

The best way for a review leader to bring the review to a close is to announce to the committee his or her intention to end the review and the reasons for these intentions.

The decision to end the review is strictly the responsibility of the review leader. Many of these reasons are obvious and should receive little opposition. For instance, if a portion of the material was not included in the review packet and was discovered missing during the review, clearly, the review should be terminated. If a member of the review committee is not present or is not prepared, the review should be terminated. Fire, plague, earthquakes, volcanic eruptions, and other natural catastrophes are also good reasons to end the review.

Unfortunately, the review leader may not have such

concrete reasons for wishing to end the review. The review leader may feel that personalities are getting involved, or one of the other participants has a "hidden agenda" that is getting in the way of conducting the review. The review leader might feel something as intangible as not being in control.

The review leader will have an easier time by remembering a simple rule: I, as review leader, am responsible for getting an effective review. If I believe that isn't happening, it's my responsibility to terminate the review. With this thought in mind, the review leader merely has to announce, I'm no longer able to conduct this review in an effective manner, so I'm terminating it. Of course, the review leader may have to justify this termination to management, but that's the way it should be. Let's consider some examples:

1. There's a personality clash that's reducing the meeting to a two-person argument. The leader tries to control it, but fails. Whether it's the leader's fault or the fault of party A or party B, the review isn't being productive and should be terminated.

2. In situation (1), when the leader announces the intention to terminate, A and/or B might be brought to their senses. In this case the leader has unleashed the ultimate weapon for bringing the meeting under control. Most of the times we've observed A or B or both acting in an infantile manner, this act by the leader clears up the matter immediately. In the other cases, where the behavior continues, management *should* be given this information and act on the situation.

3. The leader may simply feel out of control, for no identifiable reason. By announcing, I can't control this meeting, so I'm terminating, the leader gives the others a chance to change their behavior, if that's the problem, but without placing blame. This should not be a threat, but only a simple statement about the leader's inability to control. Threatening will only make matters worse.

The Recorder

What Are the Responsibilities of the Recorder?

The primary responsibility of the recorder is to provide information for a report that accurately reflects the review. The variations in content and format of this report will be discussed in another section, but the need for accuracy is always paramount, regardless of the form of the report or the method by which it was obtained.

There are many variant ways in which the recorder function is accomplished. Whatever variations you explore, never forget that

The primary function of the recorder is to provide information for an accurate report of the review.

What Is the Most Common Way of Carrying Out the Recorder's Responsibilities?

Most commonly, a single person (other than the leader) is chosen by the leader to keep the records that will be needed to prepare a report on the review. The recorder writes short notes on a flip chart in full view of the participants—notes that capture the essence of each issue and serve to identify it uniquely if further elaboration is needed. If an issue requires some very careful wording, the recorder may transcribe that wording in full, for checking by the participants.

Minor issues may be recorded in other ways. For instance, if part of the reviewed material is a textual document, typographical errors can be noted with a minimum of fuss on a copy kept by the recorder for this purpose. In such a case, no further record is needed, except for a single point on the main list stating, Please see the marked copy for corrections.

At the conclusion of the meeting, the leader will call upon the recorder for a brief review of all the notes to ensure that they correctly represent the conclusions of the review group. The recorder, therefore, has the responsibility of ensuring that the group has *reached a definite conclusion*. The recorder should state the committee's point and poll for agreement.

Once the recorder is certain of the contents and accuracy of the notes, a final copy must be produced. This report is the responsibility, ultimately, of the review leader, though the recorder certainly will assist in the preparation.

Our Company Doesn't Like Flip Charts. Do We Really Need to Use Flip Charts?

Those who use flip charts favor them over private recorder's notes because they save a lot of time at the end of the review. With private notes, only the recorder knows exactly what is written down, which often leads to arguments and mistakes. Indeed, with private notes, nobody else knows for sure whether the recorder is writing down *anything*. In videotaped practice reviews, we've found that a recorder who writes private notes is likely to miss several points that are made in too rapid succession during the review, so the *public* character of flip charts is essential.

Some people prefer blackboards to flip charts. They are public, but they have the problem of running out of space. When the blackboard fills up, the meeting must stop while its contents are recorded permanently. With flip charts, the filled page may be ripped off and attached to the wall with masking tape. This role is traditionally given, in one installation, to anyone named Jack who happens to be on the review—and who becomes known as "Jack the Ripper." Having a ripper serves two important functions. First, it speeds up the meeting, for the recorder can continue without pause while Jack is ripping or at least taping. Second, knowing that the recorder won't be disturbed by the filling of the sheet, people aren't so hesitant to raise new issues as the sheet fills up. With blackboards, we've noticed a strong restriction of the flow of new ideas as the amount of free space diminishes. Nobody wants to force the recorder to stop and copy everything.

Several organizations get the same effect, more or less, of flip charts by using foils with an overhead projector. One advantage of this method is that the foils may be copied on an ordinary copier—something that you can't do with flip charts. On the other hand, the flip chart pages contain *notes,* not the finished report, so the advantage isn't that great. Disadvantages of the overhead projector method include noise, heat, and possibly darkness. Most crucial, however, is the inability to post all previous sheets for public scrutiny as the review progresses.

Are There Any Other Recording Methods in Common Use?

Sometimes an instant camera is used to capture notes from a blackboard. If a unique document is presented in support of some point, someone might leave the room to copy it—but this is generally better left until the end of

the review unless there is a copier in the room. An audio
tape recorder has been used, especially to capture the
exact wording of a long issue. Tape recording the entire
review will simply produce a pain in the neck for the
person who has to prepare the report, though on delicate
political matters it can be useful to keep a recording as
a backup. Still, if there is so much tension and hostility
in the review that a recording is needed to nail down
agreements, there will probably be more serious problems
with the report. Why not just keep the delicate political
matters out of the technical review in the first place?

What About Videotaping the Meeting, so No Recorder Is Needed?

We often videotape reviews in the course of our training,
but we don't advocate the practice for actual reviews. First
of all, a video (or audio) recording doesn't provide a visible
record of progress for the participants to survey as the
meeting advances. Therefore, a recorder is needed in
addition to whatever effort is needed to keep the video
going. Except for educational purposes, the video camera
captures *too much,* while at the same time it misses things
outside its peripheral vision. We don't need to know who
had an itchy chin at each point in the meeting.

A video (or audio) recording can be just one more
disturbing element in a sensitive meeting. Some people
behave quite differently when on camera than when off,
and we also must reckon with the technical difficulties in
getting and keeping the equipment working.

All things considered, we cannot recommend the
use of recordings. Even if they are used, they are *not* a
substitute for the recorder function. And as far as the
educational function is concerned, please think several
times before you try to use the video approach. It's not
as easy as it looks and can precipitate a disaster.

Who Should We Select as Recorder?

Almost any person competent to serve on a review can act as recorder. The recorder can greatly influence the pace of the meeting, for better or for worse. In order not to be a bottleneck, the recorder ought to be able to record the meeting in "real time." Once the concept of the recording as *notes* is understood, most people can write fast enough to keep the meeting from pausing for irritating amounts of time.

Some detailed points, however, may require a volume of writing, on the spot. In that case, the meeting must be slowed down so everyone can pitch in and help the recorder get it down on paper.

Ideally, the recorder is technically competent to the degree of being able to understand the vocabulary, acronyms, and "numbernames" such as 370, 3275, 1108, 470/7, 11/45, 6027, hike! This knowledge will help prevent undecipherable notes. Obviously, the more the recorder understands about what is going on, the higher the degree of accuracy attainable without severely disrupting the flow of the meeting.

Why Not Have the Leader Act as Recorder?

There are some definite positive points in favor of allowing the leader to act as recorder. Most positive of all is that the leader can control the pace of the meeting so that all points are recorded. With recording and leading responsibilities cast into one person, there is no chance of slippage in communication between the two functions. By centralizing the responsibility for managing, recording, and preparing the report, we make the review process appear to run most efficiently.

On the other hand, this veneer of efficiency may conceal serious difficulties. In practice, the leader trying to act as recorder tends to lose control of the meeting, for it is difficult to follow the meeting's dynamics while you're writing on the wall.

By separating the two jobs, we allow ourselves to choose the best person for each function. A good leader and a good recorder will work smoothly, especially if the recording is done in public, as it should be. Rather than *creating* communication problems, the leader-recorder pair is likely to clear up problems that would have gone undetected by one of them alone.

Finally, we have observed that the centralization of these two functions in one person can seriously bias the review—consciously or unconsciously. Studies by political scientists have shown that the recording position is one of great power. The recorder can conveniently forget to record things or can record things that were never said or actually agreed upon. By recording in public, and by separating the powers of the recorder and the review leader, we are only applying the time-tested method of "separation of powers" to the problem of obtaining a good review—one that is accurate and free of bias.

We Use a Program Librarian, Whose Functions Are More or Less Those Described by Harlan Mills of IBM. Is It a Good Idea to Use the Librarian as Recorder?

In some situations, the librarian can be a most effective recorder. The librarian should have the technical skills for recording meetings quickly and accurately and probably possesses technical knowledge at least to the level of nomenclature. Also, the librarian is intimately involved with the project and has a commitment to its successful outcome. Therefore, to the librarian the review would be more of an ongoing responsibility than an occasional chore.

Because the librarian may be assigned to the team or project from beginning to end, a continuity is established and maintained. The review reports and documentation become part of the historic records of the project, which are a major responsibility of the librarian. Moreover, since the librarian is often aware of the *real* progress of the project, he or she can anticipate when reviews will be necessary and can inform the review leader about planning for upcoming reviews.

The major drawback in using the librarian for recording reviews is that this activity takes time away from other tasks. Before using the librarian as review recorder, be sure that the time is available. It would be most unfortunate if review recorder duties placed on the librarian caused a degradation in turnaround time, for example. Don't overwork the librarian, but do consider using the recorder role to educate and occupy an underworked librarian, if you have one.

But What if We Don't Have a Librarian?

We aren't particularly recommending the librarian as recorder, but only asserting that a librarian can be used in that way. Our own preference is toward keeping the number of people in the room at a minimum, so that using one of the participants as recorder is the better way, if it can be managed. In our experience, any competent person can act as recorder. Moreover, it will help achieve more productive reviews if each participant has had some personal experience with the recorder role.

People can take turns based on project, time period, rotation of the job, or a roll of the dice. In some places, each participant (other than the leader) takes a fifteen-minute turn as recorder during each review meeting. This certainly spreads the work and smooths out any gross differences in recorder skill. It also gives everyone a chance to stand up once in a while, both for exercise and for the feeling of power that comes with having the stylus in hand.

The major differences between recorders will be in the pace of the meeting. "Amateur" recorders may require a slower pace than a "professional," but that slower pace may prove advantageous in getting clear communication of technical points.

Can More Than One Person Be Recorder in the Same Review?

Yes, and it may be an excellent idea to rotate the recording job. One of our clients taught us the following scheme:

1. At the start of the review, the leader polls the participants to find out if anyone has little or nothing to say about a particular phase of the review. The person with the least predicted participation assumes recorder duties for that phase.

Another client uses a different scheme:

2. A small pocket alarm is used to time fifteen-minute intervals during the review. Each participant other than the leader takes a fifteen-minute term as recorder, in sequence.

There are many possible schemes. Just be sure that the scheme you use fairly distributes the task among the participants. Also remember that each recorder will have to work on the reports, so, for example, it wouldn't be wise to choose someone who will be out of town immediately after the review.

Are There Any Other New Ideas About the Recorder Task You've Learned About Since the First Edition of the Handbook?

We've seen a lot of variations, each of which makes the particular people feel more comfortable with their local situation. Most of them are so small and special that it wouldn't be worth explaining them, but one was really exciting and may represent a breakthrough on a whole host of recorder problems.

One client is experimenting with a large screen video projection system tied to their time-sharing text editor. The recorder sits at a terminal in the review room and types the issues directly into the text processor. Some of the anticipated advantages are:

1. Typing is faster and clearer than writing;
2. Everyone can see exactly what is being written on the large screen;
3. Changes can be made instantly and easily because of the text processing;
4. The review report can be constructed easily by editing and rearranging the issues that are stored;
5. Particularly difficult points requiring much precision can be worked out in detail and captured exactly while everyone watches; and
6. If the reviewed material is in the text-processing system, material can be copied directly into the review reports.

It remains to be seen whether or not the mechanics of the process prove too cumbersome, but since this client already has all the supporting hardware and software, the experiment is easy to perform. Early indications are in favor of success, but with a few anticipated problems:

1. There is only one room in which reviews can be held using this method, so a scheduling problem arises.
2. During the World Series, the Employees' Club had first priority on the large screen projector.
3. Very occasionally the time-sharing system was down for part of the review.

One unanticipated positive result is that people who never before used the text-processing system learned about its availability and the mechanics of using it.

We Have Started Using an Audio Tape in Our Reviews to Record the Points Raised and Agreed Upon, Rather Than the Entire Proceedings of the Meeting. We Have Found This Practice to Have Several Advantages and No Disadvantages. How Do You Feel About It?

We've begun using this procedure ourselves and now feel we can recommend its use under many circumstances. Here are some things we've learned:

1. The equipment must be reliable; otherwise it will prove disruptive. However, since it is merely being used as a quick substitute for writing, no great harm need be done if the equipment fails, as long as you are prepared to switch to writing on an easel pad instead.

2. It is still a good idea to have a method of writing in public, for several reasons, such as,

    a. breakdown, as in (1);

    b. drawing diagrams, which are very hard to record in audio; and

    c. writing an index to the audio tape.

3. It is good to keep a visible index to the points on the audio tape, in case there is need to refer back to some earlier point. Sometimes the index entry alone is sufficient, but at other times you will have to backspace and search for the point, which can be very time consuming and annoying. An index helps, and so does a fast rewind and fast forward. Best of all is a tape counter, so that the position on the tape can be recorded in the index. The index will also help whoever has to transcribe the tape.

4. Since the tape will have to be transcribed, transcription equipment for the tape system used should be readily available. *Do not* make someone transcribe from a tape recorder without transcription equipment. *Do* provide the transcriber with the index. *Do* provide the transcriber with a list of acronyms and technical terms.

5. Do not merely accept the transcription without editing and the usual approval process by all review members.

6. The process of shaping the exact wording of the point for recording is very helpful in keeping everyone's attention. When points are written, everyone can be looking elsewhere, but when someone is talking for the recorder, everyone has to listen or at least not be talking.

7. It's a good idea to save the tape until after the final report has been signed by everyone. Then erase it immediately.

How Should the Recorder Be Placed Physically with Respect to the Other Members of the Review Group?

Every member of the review group should be able to see the recorder without turning. Curiously, we've noticed that the most frequent violation to this rule in practice is by the one person who most needs to see the recorder— the review leader. That's because the table is often set up so that the recorder and review leader are side by side, so when the recorder stands up to record, he or she is actually over the leader's shoulder. If you are recorder, be sure the leader can see you at all times, because the nonverbal signaling between you two is essential to the proper conduct and flow of the meeting.

Speaking of Flow of the Meeting, We Often Find That the Recording Is Slowing Things Down and Draining the "Energy" of the Review. What Can We Do About This?

You're right about the importance of keeping up the energy level. Try one or more of the following ideas:

1. Get a recorder who writes faster;

2. Get everyone more involved in the recording, so they won't simply be waiting impatiently for the recorder;

3. Let people take turns recording;
4. Have two recorders, each one taking every other point;
5. Help the recorder with such jobs as ripping and numbering sheets;
6. Teach and encourage the recorder to abbreviate;
7. Record key words on paper and use a tape recorder for more exact wording.

At the very least, speak up about this situation when it arises in your review. Don't just sit there and sulk or make trouble. You are smart people and should be able to solve this problem once you recognize it.

When I've Acted as Recorder, I've Had Trouble Making My Own Points, so I Feel It's Been a Waste to Prepare. Any Suggestions?

Why not pass the pen to a second string recorder to record the points you're bringing up. When you're done, take the pen back. If you're having trouble getting attention, be sure everyone can see you. If they can and you still have trouble, learn to be more assertive. Simply say, I have a point to make, or, I have something to add to that. If you're still ignored, or if you have trouble saying things to a group, write them on the flip chart, in BIG letters, and refuse to write anything else until someone reads what you've written.

Don't, however, simply write your own points on the issues list without bringing them up to the entire group.

Have There Been Any Attempts to Automate the Review Recording Process?

There have been some small attempts to using existing text-editing and word-processing facilities to record the review process. Some of our clients are attempting to build software tools to aid them in their review processes.

For the most part these tools are designed specifically for a particular installation with a particular way of doing things. None that we have examined so far seems to have a general enough character to be considered a product.

A warning about automated review packages. Like any tool, they should be helpful to the process. As soon as the tool becomes more important than the process itself, pitch the tool. It's very easy for software people to become enamored with developing a "review-recording tool" and then to delay introduction of reviews because "the tool isn't quite ready." Postpone any ambitious recording tool projects until you have installed reviews. Lack of a tool will never be the cause of failing to implement reviews, but presence of a tool could well be.

Checklist for Recorders

Your Qualifications

Do you understand the purpose of reviews in general?

Do you understand why this particular review is being held?

Do you understand the jargon used and the formats used in this material?

Are you able to communicate with the type of people who will be in the review?

Can you be objective on the subject of the review?

Have you ever participated in a review as a reviewer and as a reviewee?

Prereview

Can you identify, by name, the review leader and other participants?

Have you arranged your schedule to allow time for the review?

Have you allowed time for the work you will have to do after the review?

Do you have the materials necessary for keeping an accurate record in the proper formats?

Do you have the resources available to carry out your job, during and after the review?

During the Review

Do you understand what an issue is?

Are you recording all issues?

Are you recording things that aren't really issues?

Are your notes accurate reflections of the comments?

Are you making a flip chart or other visible record of the issues?

Do your detailed notes actually correspond to the flip chart abbreviations?

Do you have copies of any supplementary material introduced as a part of any issue?

How much of your report consists of editorial commentary?

Is the outcome stated explicitly and unambiguously?

Are the issues recorded in neutral language?

Postreview

Was the report promptly prepared?

Was it accurate?

Was the report properly reviewed and signed?

Was it distributed to all relevant people, including participants?

Was a complete copy of the reviewed material and the report placed in the historical record?

If there were related issues raised, was a related issues report prepared?

When you are given the job as recorder for a review, survey your own qualifications before accepting the job. If you don't feel you fit the checklist or don't understand something, discuss the matter with the review leader.

If you've accepted the recorder job, complete the prereview part of the checklist long before the meeting is scheduled to start. Be sure you understand the other parts of the checklist before the meeting starts, so you can carry out your responsibilities.

Helpful Rules and Customs for Reviewers

*How Can I, as a Participant with No Special Role, Make
Certain That the Review Runs Correctly?*

You are right in assuming that the job of making the
review run well is not the sole responsibility of the leader
or the leader and recorder. No leader in the world is good
enough to create a good review out of uncooperative, ill-
prepared participants. Therefore, each member of the
review group has personal responsibility for the outcome
of the review and thus for helping the review process.

There are a number of universal rules that help
smooth out the interpersonal relationships of a review
situation. We've abstracted these rules from our own and
others' experiences with reviews. It will help if you learn
and practice them.

RULE I
BE PREPARED

If you are unprepared for the review, tell the leader at
the outset so the review can be rescheduled. If you try

141

to fake it, the worst that can happen is that you will succeed, in which case the review will be less good than it could have been. If you are caught, as you eventually will be, your associates will come to bitterly resent your wasting their time.

While trying to fake preparedness, you may have a tendency to defend your opinion with unjustified vigor in order to cover up. Or you may try to divert the session to trivial points or to points that are so general they could apply to any material, without even having to study it. At best, you could sit quietly and let those who did prepare conduct the review with minimal interference from you. In any case, being unprepared creates unpleasant situations—so, as the Scout Motto says, BE PREPARED.

RULE II
BE WILLING TO ASSOCIATE

Whatever else you do in a review, be nice to your fellow person. The product you are reviewing is the creation of a group of people who, theoretically at least, worked hard at it. They have an ego involvement and are in a real sense exposing their creation to potential ridicule—always a sensitive situation.

Be reasonable. Remember that you are evaluating the product, not the people. Anyone can make a mistake— if you don't believe this, wait until your first product is reviewed! The other reviewers and the producers are your *peers*, not your enemies. Don't think you can conceal your own sense of inadequacy by railing rudely at your peers. They know you, or soon will, for the review process opens everybody's aptitudes to public knowledge.

If it does turn out that the producers are incompetent or malicious, these facts will soon become evident to management through the outcomes of a series of reviews, so don't take it upon yourself to decide if this is a mistake or a habit. Assume it's a mistake, and act accordingly.

Rule III
Watch Your Language

Even when we mean well, we often create a most negative impression with a careless choice of words. For example, a sentence starting with the words "Why *didn't* you. . ." immediately establishes in the listener's mind that you think you are smarter, which may or may not be true, but certainly isn't relevant or helpful.

"Why did you. . ." is not much better, and it might be helpful to avoid the use of personal pronouns that imply fault. Instead of asking, Why did you do it this way?, you could ask, Why is the product this way?

But any question starting with why could be taken in a negative sense. An excellent starting phrase, which has stood the test of hundreds of emotion-charged reviews, is "I don't understand. . . ." Uttered in a sincere tone of voice, this phrase begins with the humble (and quite likely true) assumption that the difficulty rests in your own head, rather than in the product. And if you represent a typical person who is *supposed* to understand this product, it is an important criticism of it that you don't understand something, so you need not be apologetic about using the phrase.

Watching for irritating phraseology may not seem important, but over the long and short run, it does tend to reduce difficulties.

Rule IV
One Positive—One Negative Comment

Each participant should have *at least* one positive and one negative input. First of all, this rule guarantees that each participant will *have* an input. Second, it protects against certain extreme personality tendencies.

To some people, this rule seems silly—perhaps juvenile—and unnecessary for mature individuals. Our own experience says otherwise. In the worst case, some of the positive or negative comments may be more humorous than content oriented, like "Gee, I really like the color ink they used for their report." Or "I believe it would be better to have the report less clear, so it would impress management more."

There's nothing wrong with such humor, which at the very least helps give the participants a feeling of unity or relieves some of the tension in a charged situation. As our products improve over time, we certainly hope that serious negative remarks will become more and more rare, so we'll have to invent funny things to say.

Rule V
Raise Issues, Don't Resolve Them

Issues should be raised, not resolved. Technical people love nothing better than talking about technical issues and how they would approach them. If the review starts to discuss the remedies to each problem, it will never end successfully.

Even when there seems to be time to work out a resolution, the "patch" is not likely to be well worked out. If the producing group has been working conscientiously on the product and yet still has the problem, perhaps it's not so simple after all. Or, if it *is* that simple, they'll be able to work it out on their own.

Time should be taken in making changes. Some organizations have reported that most of the errors appearing in a system were introduced during the last two weeks of development. Others have measured that "patches" have ten times the likelihood of error than does "original" code. Therefore, it's best to avoid the quick "fix"—which may not be a fix at all.

Since programming is what they like to do, programmers will tend to be frustrated by this rule. But notice that we're not saying that programmers can't discuss interesting technical issues and ideas for solving them. We're merely saying that they cannot carry on these discussions during the review. After the review adjourns, perhaps over lunch, those parties interested in some idea can continue to meet. By all means offer your ideas to the producers—but as a separate and private matter that won't tie up the whole review and won't become a contest of "I have a better idea than you do!"

RULE VI
AVOID DISCUSSIONS OF STYLE

It is wise to outlaw discussions of style. The primary concern of the review committee is the accuracy and quality of the product. If something is *wrong*, it's *not* a question of style. If something will make the product *difficult to maintain*, it's *not* a question of style.

On the other hand, a question of efficiency when efficiency is not a relevant specification *is* a style question. Unless the specifications explicitly address a particular issue, most discussions of the issue turn out to be questions of style. Of course, if someone believes the specification to be incomplete, this is a serious matter—which should have been caught in an earlier review of the specification. In such a case, the issue to be raised is, There is some question as to why the specification omitted mention of efficiency (or called for such a low efficiency figure), not, This product isn't efficient enough, even though it meets the specification.

RULE VII
STICK TO STANDARD—OR STICK THE STANDARD

Style shouldn't be confused with standards. If code, for example, doesn't adhere to programming standards of the installation, an issue should be raised for each deviation.

It is not unusual for the first products to be reviewed to be rejected on matters of standards. If this situation occurs, it would be well to review some of your current production systems to see if *they* meet standards. If a majority of these systems aren't meeting standards, you might consider revising the standards (which aren't, in fact, "standard") rather than criticizing the reviewed products.

Above all, don't let violations of standards pass without *any* comment—about either the product or the standard. Habitual violation of *some* law inevitably produces contempt for *all* laws, so if you want *any* standards to be followed, you'd better stick to them or stick them in the trash.

RULE VIII
ONLY TECHNICALLY COMPETENT PEOPLE
ATTEND REVIEWS

You must establish at the outset that reviews are restricted to technically competent people. If someone does not have the ability or interest to be a useful member of the review committee, that person should not be on the committee at all.

This rule is not intended to exclude trainees, who hopefully are *in the process* of becoming technically competent. Part of that process—an essential part—is participation in reviews. And aside from the educational value to the trainees, the review itself usually benefits from the fresh opinions and questions of the less experienced—and even more from their high degree of interest and enthusiasm.

What this rule *does* mean is that people should be prevented from attending reviews for politics, prestige, nosiness, or noisiness.

RULE IX
RECORD ALL ISSUES IN PUBLIC

A review will be far healthier if the participants insist that the issues be recorded in some form that they can watch, both while the issues are recorded and afterwards. Only in this way can they be sure their statements are adequately represented and correctly presented. Nothing is more destructive to *full* participation than to have each contributor wondering whether or not his or her personal contribution has, indeed, been recognized. Nothing is more creative of dull, repetitious meetings than to have no public version of past issues to refer to when someone starts tracking over ground already traversed.

RULE X
STICK TO TECHNICAL ISSUES

Matters of schedule, budget, staffing, and the like should not occupy review time. There will, no doubt, be other meetings on these matters, but they are not the job of the review. Schedule, budget, and staffing are *already visible* to management and do not need the technical review to make their status clear. While it may be fun to play at being the project manager, the technical review isn't the place to do it.

Even when the review is able to avoid these serious management problems, it may fall the other way—into a strictly social situation. We must expect a certain necessary minimum of time to be spent on social situations—particularly on the exchange of pleasantries that reduce the friction of interpersonal differences. Each reviewer has a share of the responsibility for preventing social situations from becoming the sole activity of the review.

RULE XI
REMEMBER EDUCATION

Since every review serves an educational function, make certain that *all* participants understand *all* the issues that were raised. Clear up any confusion as to the technical content of the final report, for each participant is taking responsibility for the product, if approved. If this responsibility is to have any meaning, each participant must be in a position to make an intelligent judgment. Therefore, each issue must be explained to a sufficient level for this judgment to be made.

Some people consider education to be a side effect of the review, but as with many medicines, the "side effect" may turn out to be the main effect, at least in the long run. Review participants communicate an incredible amount of information among themselves, far overshadowing the amount of information that appears in the final report. Some of this information is project directed, in which case it contributes directly to the improvement of the project. Even more important, however, is the information of a general technical nature, for that information raises the quality of the technical staff—a no cost method of improving all *future* projects.

RULE XII
DO NOT EVALUATE THE PRODUCERS

If reviews become a management tool for evaluating *programmers,* rather than *programs,* it will defeat the major purpose of the review—error detection and reliability assurance. Producers are exposing their product—which they may feel is an extension of themselves—to public scrutiny. If they are being punished for the number of errors detected, how can we expect them to work in ways that make errors easy to detect?

We cannot emphasize this point strongly enough. If management wishes to evaluate the review, then evaluate in a way that will encourage the *desired* behavior. Evaluate the review leader on how well the review was conducted. Evaluate the participants on their preparation and contribution. Evaluate the recorder on the quality and promptness of the report. But don't destroy the channel that brings bad news; otherwise you'll get no news at all.

The principle is to evaluate the individuals based on the display of desired behavior. Since everyone makes mistakes, we cannot evaluate people on whether or not they make mistakes. But we can evaluate them on how helpful they are to others who are commissioned to find those mistakes.

By evaluating on the proper bases, we make the evaluation procedure reinforce the things we wish to encourage, rather than work at odds with our objectives. Through time, the review process itself can be evaluated on the quality of the systems developed. If the reviews are not leading to a better product, the review process should be reviewed.

RULE XIII
DISTRIBUTE THE REPORT AS SOON AS POSSIBLE

The formal review process is the "rite of passage" of a system in the programming environment—the process that marks the change from one status to a more advanced one. In human societies, birth, marriage, and death seem to be universal rites of passage. In our culture, we have other such rites, including graduation, confirmation, and promotion. For a programming project, the rite is the formal technical review.

With reviews, there is no way a part of a project can slip unnoticed from, say, the design stage to the coding stage, as was so often done in the past. Each module will be incorporated into the system based on a rite of passage (a review), and each document will enter in the same way. Nothing becomes part of the system until it has passed review.

Rites of passage supply a public pronouncement that the change of status has occurred. The wedding, for example, is a public statement of the existence of a marriage. A couple cannot be married without the knowledge of the authorities, religious or civil; neither can they pretend not to be married once they have had a public wedding.

The same reasoning applies to reviews. Not everyone attends the review, but the fact of its happening is public. So is its result. The review thus becomes a public indication of the progress of a project—an indication that cannot be used to fool anyone about how things are progressing. Without the review, management cannot manage effectively nor can other producers plan related work. Therefore, long delays in reporting the outcome of a review have the same effect as not conducting the review at all. Report the results promptly, or else report that the review was not, in fact, completed.

RULE XIV

LET THE PRODUCERS DETERMINE WHEN THE PRODUCT IS
READY FOR REVIEW

If the producers feel their product is not ready for review, the review will usually be a waste of time. Management may *wish* that the product were ready—indeed, the whole project schedule may depend upon it—but wishing won't make it so. If management *forces* the producers to put their product through a review, they will be forcing the reviewers toward acceptance in spite of their best technical judgment.

If the producers say they are finished, you can't really bank on it—hence the review process. But if they say they *aren't* finished, chances are ninety-nine to one they're right. Sure, there are some programmers who seem to be enamored of perfection beyond any reasonable bound, but that's hardly what makes so many projects go down the drain. The fatal mistake occurs when management pushes people to deliver *something,* regardless of quality, in the vague and vain hope that somehow things will work out all right in the end.

If the producers don't produce on time, by all means give 'em hell, if that's the kind of motivation they need. But don't waste more time preparing for a review, and don't force other people to participate in a charade of a review. At best, they'll reject the product, which we already knew would happen. At worst, they'll yield to the implied management pressure and pass something that really shouldn't pass. Then you'll pay the price later—and the later price is *always* higher. In either case, reviewing shoddy or unfinished work will have a depressing effect on the review group and the development team. It will also sour everybody to the very idea of reviews.

Summary of Helpful Rules and Customs

Be Prepared

Be Willing to Associate

Watch Your Language

One Positive—One Negative

Raise Issues, Don't Resolve Them

Avoid Discussions of Style

Stick to Standard—Or Stick the Standard

Only Technically Competent People Attend Reviews

Record All Issues in Public

Stick to Technical Issues

Remember Education

Do Not Evaluate the Producers

Distribute the Report as Soon as Possible

Let the Producers Determine When the Product Is Ready for Review

Helpful Rules for Management

SECTION

4

*Since They Can't (Usually) Attend Reviews, How Can
Managers Participate in the Review Process?*

We've been able to distill a number of rules for helping
managers participate to the fullest in the establishment
of effective reviews in their organization. Most of these
rules are stated or implied elsewhere in this handbook,
but for convenience of reference, here's a condensed list:

RULE I
SHOW A COMMITMENT TO THE REVIEW PROCESS

Unless all levels of management show through action, not
words, a real belief in the review process, reviews will
become as meaningless as most other meetings. Other
rules in this series are largely a working out of ways to
show this commitment.

Rule II
Budget Time for the Review Process

Reviews do take time, though that time is saved in other places. You can show your commitment from the very first by explicitly budgeting time for reviews. You can continue to show your commitment by not preempting reviews for more "critical" tasks.

Rule III
Be Prepared to Assign Real People to the Review Task

A generalized budgeting of time is important, but the real test of your commitment comes when you're willing to assign someone full or part time to some review responsibilities. This might involve an assignment of a pair of review leaders to act as "buddies" for the early reviews, providing a full-time recorder, or perhaps establishing an entire team of review specialists for quality assurance.

Rule IV
Encourage the Participants to Prepare

For many managers, this rule merely means that they shouldn't question someone spending time reading someone else's work, rather than "doing their own." If you're the least bit suspicious of the real value of reviewing, you may unconsciously communicate this in very subtle ways when interacting with your people.

Rule V
Help Out with the Physical Arrangements

Nonmanagement participants in the reviews won't have the political clout to schedule proper facilities in the face of competition from management. By obtaining the facilities yourself, you can relieve the review leader of this responsibility—but don't do it if the review leader will resent it. If no other adequate facilities are available, you might consider relinquishing your office for a couple of hours. Spend the time out of your office reviewing the troops in the field. This will certainly be an effective way of showing your commitment. And, if *you* don't have an office, get money in the budget to rent conference space. In other words, do whatever is necessary, especially what's in your power as manager and not in the power of the technical staff.

Rule VI
Don't Be Penny Wise and Pound Foolish

It is tragic to see otherwise well-conceived and well-executed reviews fail because of insufficient copying budget, secretarial help, or audiovisual supplies. If the review isn't important enough to justify fresh marker pens, who's going to believe it's important at all?

Rule VII
Reward Good Reviews of Bad Products

Don't confuse a disappointing product with a disappointing review.

Rule VIII
Punish Poor Reviews of Any Product

When something turns out bad, after being reviewed as good, make sure you don't focus all your wrath on the producers. Be certain that each reviewer is held in some measure accountable for having failed to give an accurate appraisal. On the other hand, come down hard on review groups that unfairly condemn a truly good product— though this situation is naturally harder for you to detect.

Rule IX
Punish Poor Review Behavior

Treat any report of noncooperation or maliciousness in
a review with great care and seriousness. If it becomes
known that you will tolerate childish behavior of some of
your favorites in reviews, there will be no way to convince
people you really do believe in the process.

Rule X
Override a Review Judgment Only at Your Peril

You must be willing to *believe* the decision of the review
group, no matter how unhappy you are with the outcome.
If management overrides the decision of the technical
review committee for political considerations, the whole
procedure can become a farce. If you think you *must* act
in a manner that seems to contradict the review judgment,
first reconsider your thinking in view of the long-term
damage done by undermining reviews. Then, if you still
feel you have to act, call a short meeting with the review
committee to:

1. Explain that you do *believe* them, but that you must
    take the risk of acting in what seems like a dangerous
    way; and
2. show your reasoning, based on factors other than the
    technical quality of the product, for making your
    decision.

Usually, this overriding decision will be to proceed with
a product not meeting quality standards. We understand
the kinds of considerations involved, but we implore you
to reflect a hundred times about what happens to your
organization when you sacrifice quality, "just this once."

Summary of Helpful Rules for Management

Show a Commitment to the Review Process

Budget Time for the Review Process

Be Prepared to Assign Real People to the Review Task

Encourage the Participants to Prepare

Help Out with the Physical Arrangements

Don't Be Penny Wise and Pound Foolish

Reward Good Reviews of Bad Products

Punish Poor Reviews of Any Product

Punish Poor Review Behavior

Override a Review Judgment Only at Your Peril

The User and the Review

*As a User, What Do I Do if I Don't Understand What I
Am Reviewing?*

The best thing that anyone can do if they find themselves
reviewing something they don't understand is to say so.
It defeats the entire purpose of the review if you just "go
along with it." In the best case, the system might turn out
to be what you wanted, but probably it won't. If you don't
understand the material, be prepared to explain what you
don't understand.

It may be that you're the wrong person to be attending the review. For instance, if you are reviewing
messages that will appear to prompt a clerk at a display,
and you personally never use the system, you may not be
in a position to say much of value about the messages. It
would probably be best to have someone experienced with
the actual procedure attend the review. As a user, this
person will be in a better position to evaluate the product.

It could also be the case that the material is im-
properly prepared. Pieces might be missing, or the document might be full of jargon. In the first case, if when

159

preparing for the review you feel that some essential information is missing, call the review leader and find out about the missing information. If indeed the information is missing, the review should be cancelled. If the document is riddled with jargon, this should be brought out at the review meeting. A rewrite might be in order.

We Find That the Programmer Wants Us as Users to Review the Code. We Don't Understand Code.

It's surprising that the programmers expect you to read code. There are certain technical issues that you as a user should be aware of, but rarely on the code level. It's possible that the reason the programmers want you to read the code is that they have failed to prepare some sort of intermediate document or design that would present the system logic accurately. If this is the case, the entire programming procedure should be examined. But it might also be that they think you *want* to see the code. Try talking to them. Again, the principle of competence applies. *No one should be at a review who lacks the technical capability to contribute to that review.*

Does That Mean That If Anything Is Presented That I Don't Understand, Then I Shouldn't Be There?

Not at all. When you don't understand something, it could be you, but it could be the product. Just say you don't understand, without blaming the product or yourself. If someone in your category is *supposed* to understand, then you are a test case. Most of the time, the producers will try to bully you into feeling inferior for not understanding their wonderful product. Stand your ground. Make them put a statement in the Issues List stating that the user representative didn't understand thus and so, without a value judgment as to whose *fault* it is. A tough stand on your part may save hundreds or thousands of users from the same problem. Perhaps it is *neither* party's fault. Perhaps you should understand but don't—indicating a need for some form of education of the users. Your job is to be open, honest, and nonjudgmental. Can anyone argue with you when you say, simply, I don't understand? What can they say—Yes, you *do* understand?

PART D

Reporting the Results of the Review

Functions of Reporting

What Is the Major Reporting Function of the Review?

Although many people in a project may have an interest in the information generated by a review, the major purpose of any review is to provide *management* with a *reliable* answer to the fundamental question:

> **Does this product do the job it's supposed to do?**

Why Is This Function So Fundamental?

Once any piece of work has been reviewed and accepted, it becomes part of the system. Subject to a very small risk factor, it is:

1. Complete,
2. Correct,

3. Dependable as a base for related work, and

4. Measurable for purposes of tracking progress.

Without reviews, there are no reliable methods for measuring the progress of a project. *Sometimes* we get dependable reports from the producers themselves, but no matter how good their *intentions,* they are simply not in a position to give consistently reliable reports on their own products. Historically, without reliable progress measures, several classic syndromes for project failure have developed. The most familiar of these syndromes is

> **The project is on time—until the due date is reached.**

When neither management nor programmers have an accurate means of measuring progress, how can anyone know that the project is on schedule? How can they detect slippage early enough to take constructive action? The "crisis" at the project's deadline is merely the end of an illusion that has been built up, module by module, since the beginning.

How Does the Review Report Solve These Crisis Problems?

With formal reviews, the review report serves as a formal commitment by technically competent and unbiased people that a piece of work is complete, correct, and dependable. The review report states as accurately as possible the completeness and acceptability of a piece of programming work, be it specifications, design, code, documentation, or whatever.

By themselves, these review reports do not guarantee that a project won't end in crisis or failure. It is up to the management of the project to use the information in the review reports to make the management decisions needed to keep the project on track. Good review reports are not sufficient to make a project succeed, though bad reviews or no reviews are sure to get a project in trouble — no matter how skilled the management may be.

Are Review Reports Always That Accurate?

There is always the danger of the review process not fulfilling its function, which is why we have to educate ourselves in what makes good reviews and good reviewers. When we first start doing reviews, there will be many mistakes—review reports that do not accurately represent the status of a piece of work. Fortunately, management will be wary, in the beginning, of placing too much reliance on the outcomes of the reviews, so the trouble caused by an inaccuracy can be kept to a minimum.

Much more dangerous are inaccurate reviews once we have come to depend on review accuracy. Consequently, an essential secondary function of review reports is to furnish *historical* information — information by which the review process itself can be evaluated.

How Does the Historical Record Help Evaluate the Review Process?

After a substantial number of review reports has been accumulated, information on a number of important questions can be extracted and correlated with other project control information. For instance, how many work units that passed the review procedures had to be altered subsequently? Were these alterations user-initiated changes or were they corrections to problems missed in the review?

It is often difficult to determine a clear demarcation line between a user change and a correction. Many "user changes" come about because of an oversight in an earlier phase of the project. Analysis might have missed a crucial factor that later turned up as a change. The design might have ignored flexibility, so what should have been a minor correction escalated into a major revision. Therefore, even though the demarcation is difficult, try to determine the true origin of difficulties—whether the problem was in the analysis, in the design, or perhaps in the review of the analysis or the design.

Does Historical Analysis Provide Specific Information to Show How the Review Process Can Be Improved?

Some of the information can be extremely specific. For instance, many installations classify the types of problems turned up in each type of review and tabulate the frequency of the various types. A similar tabulation is made of the types of errors that slip through the review only to be caught at a later stage. (Nobody knows how to tabulate the types of errors that slip through but are *never* caught.)

Comparison of these tabulations—in total, by review group, and by producer—provides clear guidance for future educational and reviewing practices. As always, it is essential that this information be used for improvement, not punishment, lest the whole scheme backfire and produce better methods of concealing errors and deficiencies.

To illustrate the use of such tabulations, let's say that most of the flaws detected during code reviews centered around the module interfaces. If this deficiency was installationwide, the training department could set up special training for everyone, guided by the specific types of interfacing errors recorded in the review reports. If the tabulations showed that only certain individuals, as reviewers or as producers, tended to make these errors, the training could be focused where it was most needed.

Or perhaps the interfacing errors, upon analysis, reveal a weakness in the installation's standards concerning interfaces. Whatever the source, the historical records should first make the problem evident and then help narrow it down to its true source.

Our Problem Has Always Been the Inability to Know When
Some Phase of a Project Is Actually Complete. We Don't
Even Have a Clear Definition of the Beginning and End of
a Phase, So How Can Reviews Help Us Understand What
Happened, Even with a Good History?

An accurate, complete review report history can be compared with the schedule projected at the beginning of the
development cycle. In which phases did the estimated time
match the actual time? Where did the deviations occur?
Were the deviations problems in production? Were there
mistakes made in the original estimate?

As the question indicates, however, this information
will be meaningless if the "phases" of the project plan
don't correspond to units of work marked at both the
beginning and the end by reviews. In other words, your
problem is that there is some supposed "phase" of your
project development cycle that doesn't produce a defined
measurable unit. No wonder you have a problem!

You might think about eliminating such unmeasurable phases from your system life cycle—or else figure
out some meaningful reviewable document that would be
representative of the end of each phase and the beginning
of the next. If there is nothing that can be reviewed, then
nothing has been produced, and if nothing is produced,
why do you call it a phase?

What Are Some of the Other Benefits of the Historical
Record of Reviews?

We've already seen how the report history, as an assessment of the skill level of the technical staff, can serve the
education function. The education function is always
fighting an inevitable lag between the need and the training in a particular area. The longer the delay between
need and fulfillment, the less effective the education program. By continuously tracking the problems actually experienced by developers, the education function can re-

spond more quickly and more precisely—or as the old evangelists used to say, "preach to their condition."

Another important piece of information in the history of review reports is the list of names of all people who were in any way associated with the product or review. If there are subsequent maintenance or enhancement needs, or merely questions arising about some aspect of the system, there is an accurate record of people from whom information might be obtained. Of course, one of the side benefits of the whole review process is that more people are involved in each piece of work, so the chances of finding a knowledgeable person still around are greatly increased.

We are constantly surprised by new uses of information from the review history. One client was able to gain a better understanding of the pattern of machine utilization, thereby improving computer operations. In another, management was able to locate a long-standing bottleneck in the development cycle and institute improvements. And many clients have used a careful tabulation of error conditions to establish more meaningful standards—based on actual experience, rather than theory or opinion.

You've Emphasized the Value of the Reports to Management, but What Do the Producers Get for Submitting to This Procedure?

Of course, the first thing the producers get is relief from the impossible responsibility of giving an unbiased report on the quality of their own product. If, at some later time, it turns out that the product wasn't as good as the review said it was, the producers can rightfully claim that the responsibility falls at least as heavily on the reviewers. Therefore, once having passed a review, they can relieve their minds of that piece of work.

If the work doesn't pass review, the producers get

an explicit and meaningful list of issues to work on. These issues were raised and thought important by a "jury of their peers"—not by someone whose opinion they don't value. If they settle those issues and then fail to pass the next review, they have a right to place some responsibility on the first reviewers.

Placing responsibility on the reviewers is not for purposes of assigning *blame,* but to ensure that reviewers act responsibly and that producers are not asked to produce unmeasurable work to some hidden measure. The end result will not be finger pointing, but successful projects—though the road to that end result may contain a few rocks that some people will be tempted to throw.

Do Other Technical People Benefit from the Review Reports?

Because the reports are part of the visible project record, anyone can study them and learn whatever they can find in them. The value of this kind of general perusal of the efforts of others cannot be overestimated, but there is a more specific benefit that also radiates from the review reports—a list of *related issues.*

During the course of a review, an issue may be raised that turns out not to be an issue with the product at hand. For example, someone may question the adequacy of the specification, even though the product itself meets the specification as given. The producers may use a library function in a way that is technically correct but that is outside the limits of testing of that function. A reviewer may suddenly realize that a common table is being used incorrectly in some *other* routine, by seeing its correct usage in the routine under review.

Since the people who need to be informed of these related issues are unlikely to be in the review, some form of related issues list is created and distributed by the review leader to management and, as far as is known, to all interested parties. In more than one case, a single related issue has been worth the cost of a month of reviews, including coffee and donuts.

What Are the Various Reports Issued by the Review?

The one report that is always generated by a review is the TECHNICAL REVIEW SUMMARY REPORT, which contains the conclusions of the review. If any issues are raised that must be brought to the attention of the producers, a TECHNICAL REVIEW ISSUES LIST is produced. If issues are raised about something other than the work itself, a TECHNICAL REVIEW RELATED ISSUES REPORT is created for each issue.

The details of these three reports will be discussed in the following sections. On occasion, an installation will institute some other report for research purposes, such as a detailed breakdown of standards used and broken, but each such report will be unique to the installation.

In those cases where the review leader has to give a report of a failed review (not a failed product), there will undoubtedly have to be other material generated, but the form and content will again be unique to the installation and may, in fact, be verbal. The same observation would apply to any personal report a participant would want to give to management—as, for instance, objecting to the behavior of the review leader.

The Technical Review Summary Report

What Information Goes on the Summary Report?

Although different installations will vary the format of the report to meet their own standards, the basic contents are the same for all technical reviews. The report format given at the end of this section is illustrative of the contents, which, in any case, should fit on a single sheet of paper. The summary report must identify three items:

1. What was reviewed?
2. Who did the reviewing?
3. What was their conclusion?

Under *What was reviewed?* comes the work unit identifier, expressed according to the product development standards at the installation. This might consist of a code and a line or two of descriptive information. In some cases, there will be references to related documents, such as specifications. We recommend the practice of listing *all* materials that were used in the review, as illustrated in the sample report. Finally, the producers should be uniquely identified—either as a team or as individuals.

Under *Who did the reviewing?* comes the name of each person present, along with a signature. One date should suffice, since all are expected to sign at the end of the review, and no review should take more than one day. Some installations specifically identify the recorder as well as the review leader.

Under *What was their conclusion?* comes, as a minimum, a checkoff of one of the possible conclusions. If other reports have been produced to support or supplement this decision, they should be referenced here.

Why Is It Necessary to Have the Individual Reviewers' Signatures?

The signature in our society is the symbol of *commitment.* Everything is based on signatures—alimony, bills of lading, contracts, deeds, eviction notices, foreign exchange, grades, hospital releases, invoices, job tickets, knighthood, leases, marriage licenses, notarizations, overdrafts, purchases, quitclaims, releases, stays of execution, treaties, usurpations, voter lists, waybills, x-ray authorizations, yearbooks, and zoning variances. Everything from a parking ticket to the Yalta Agreement must be signed, and millions of dollars are spent educating the gullible public to *read the fine print* before signing anything.

In the review situation, we want to encourage people to read the fine print before signing and then to take the responsibility denoted by their signatures. If your name is signed on the report, you cannot later claim that although you were there, you didn't agree. Many times, a review meeting seems to have concluded its business, only to be thrown open again when someone realizes the gravity of signing one's name while holding back some serious reservations. Therefore, to those who don't want to sign their names, we always ask, Why *don't* you want to sign your name?

Why Single Out the Review Leader and Possibly the Recorder for Special Notice and Mention?

The review leader is responsible for the report, so if there are any questions concerning the *report,* they should be addressed to the review leader. In those installations where the report is considered a joint leader-recorder responsibility, then both should be identified. Anonymous reports serve little purpose.

Can You Explain What It Means for the Review Group to Accept the Work Unit?

Acceptance means that the review group feels that the work is—with high probability—what it purports to be. It is complete, accurate, and in conformity with all specifications and standards. If other work depends on the completion of this work unit, then that work can proceed with confidence.

In order to come to a decision to *accept as is,* the review group must be *unanimous.* To be otherwise would mean that someone still has reservations about the work unit—in which case it could hardly be certified with high probability to be complete, accurate, and in conformity to all specifications and standards.

What About a Decision to Rebuild?

This represents the other extreme of the decision spectrum. It says that in the opinion of at least one member of the review group, the work unit has zero or negative residual value and should be thrown away and that, perhaps, a new effort should be initiated. The work is so full of errors or is so error prone that it is not worth retaining or modifying.

Hopefully, this decision is rare, and very little work

will actually have to be discarded. Nevertheless, it is important for the success of reviews that the *rebuild* decision always represent a viable alternative. If the review group were not allowed to recommend rebuilding a truly inferior piece of work, then a severe bound is placed on work quality in the installation.

Managers sometimes dread this possibility and try to outlaw it. Actually, the meaning of the *rebuild* decision makes perfectly good business sense, which any manager should be able to appreciate. When the committee says rebuild, they are saying that in their most conservative technical opinion, it would cost more in time and money to try to fix the unit than to build it over. If that is actually the case, what the manager should fear is a decision *not* to rebuild, for that will be costlier and slower.

How Is the Decision to Rebuild Made?

The actual decision to rebuild is made by management, based on the recommendation of the review committee. If the work involved is expensive, management may be loathe to accept such a rash step and could conceivably convene a second review to consider the matter again. The job of the review committee is to make sure that the work doesn't just slip by management's notice when there is a good chance that something very costly is about to happen.

The decision to *recommend* rebuilding is made by the committee if *any one member,* after full consideration of the matter, still feels that rebuilding is justified.

But How Can We Let One Person Dictate a Rebuild Decision? Won't That Subject Us to Irresponsible Behavior?

Quite the contrary. Knowing that a single recommendation for rebuilding will carry the entire committee's weight, each individual is forced to consider such a strong recommendation with utmost seriousness. At the same time, the other members of the committee will not be able to walk over or outvote a member with serious reservations. All will be forced into careful consideration of the dissenter's views, if they are to convince the holdout to vote for a less serious conclusion. You can be sure that if a decision to rebuild is made, the issues supporting that decision will be carefully scrutinized, both within and without the review committee.

What Is the Difference Between Major and Minor Revisions?

Quite simply, a revision is "minor" if the review committee feels confident that it can be made correctly *without the necessity to reconvene to check it.* For instance, code might be correct but a little difficult to understand in certain aspects, such as lack of documentation, poor choice of variable name, or lack of pagination in the listing. In such a case, the committee can recommend *accept with minor revisions*—sending the code back with the list of issues to be resolved without further review, within a specified period of time.

If, however, there is *any* change that any member of the committee feels should be reviewed after completion, the decision must be *major revision,* and a new review must be scheduled.

Are There Any Other Decision Possibilities for the Review?

We find a number of variations and finer distinctions made, formally and informally, in diverse organizations. Some places recognize a category of revision that requires a new review, but where the changes are simple enough that the review can be scheduled on the spot not longer than three days hence. The new review doesn't require the full formality of prior organization, for it is more or less a continuation of the first review. Naturally, this means that no major new pieces of documentation are needed.

A good example of this level of decision occurs when code has been reviewed and nothing has been found wrong except some overlooked test cases. The committee asks the producers to add these cases to the test set and run them. The committee then reconvenes to review the results of these cases. If they check out, the decision of the second review becomes *accept.* In some instances, running these extra cases gives the committee members a few more days to reflect on the product package—which could result in a more serious fault being uncovered. To keep matters under control, no *second* decision can be of this "informal re-review" type, lest the whole process degenerate into an endless regression.

Yet another slight variation is to accept with minor revisions and to delegate one committee member the task of checking that the changes have actually been made within the allotted time. A good choice for this delegation is the person who is most concerned about the most serious change. Otherwise, the review leader usually gets the job. Alternatively, the producers could be required to make up a report demonstrating that the changes have been made, or the change could be checked informally. It is not so much a matter of distrust as a method of ensuring that the procedures are followed without the changes falling through the cracks.

Are There Any More Decision Possibilities?

We could concoct other outcomes that would be useful for specific cases, but one general caution is in order: Do not establish so many outcomes that the review committee will have difficulty determining if it is an A− or a B+ product. The committee should expend its efforts on reviewing the product, not on ranking it. Keep the choices simple so people can readily come to consensus.

Can You Explain the Consensus Idea a Bit More?

Because the major job of the review is to assure quality, its decisions must lean to the conservative side whenever there is doubt. Therefore, all must understand that the decisionmaking process is based upon the principle of *shared responsibility*. We want to set up the decisionmaking process so that no member, after the product has been proved to be of poor quality, can claim, "I told you so, but I was outvoted by the rest of the committee."

The easiest way to assure shared responsibility is to require that the decision of the entire committee must be *equal to the most severe decision of any member*. If three say *accept* and one says *rebuild,* the decision must be rebuild, if there is any decision at all. The committee can continue discussing the decision in hopes of swaying somebody, but it cannot "outvote" the minority member calling for a rebuild decision.

The *consensus* we speak about is a consensus to be conservative and to *accept the doubts of the most doubting member*. In effect, if you feel the decision should be *accept* but someone else feels it should be *major revision,* you agree to acknowledge the possibility that the major revision position *could* be right. If it *could* be right, then you would be taking a great risk in simply accepting the work, so you agree to let the committee decision become *major revision*.

Once the producers get to work on the major revision, they may be able to persuade the doubting member that the matter is not so serious after all. For instance, instead of needing a change in the code, all that may be required is clearer documentation of the existing code. Consequently, major revision doesn't *necessarily* mean that a major revision will have to be made. What it may mean is that a minor revision will have to be made and then reviewed by the committee to convince them that no major revision is necessary.

But What Happens If, in the End, the Committee Cannot Even Agree to Accept the Doubts of the Most Doubting Member?

At some point, the leader will decide that no progress toward consensus is being made—either persuading the doubter or getting the accepters to accept the doubts. The leader then closes the review with a decision of *no decision,* which is marked on the Summary Report and sent to management with an explanation. In such a case, it is best not to attach any names to the various opinions—unless, of course, the leader believes and documents that someone is acting in bad faith.

In this case, the Issues List is given to the producers, who may wish to do something about the issues while waiting for a new review, with a new committee, to be convened.

Just so we don't give the wrong impression, the no decision is a *very* rare occurrence, once the committee members understand both how and why the decision-making process works.

We Occasionally Have Trouble Getting Agreement If the Product Needs Major Revision—or Rework. What Should We Do?

As long as the review committee can come to agreement about whether the product needs re-review or not, major mistakes will be avoided. The greatest mistake a review committee can make is to assume that a questionable product is correct. This mistake can result in an expensive error. As long as the review committee can agree about the general outcome, the detail may not be that important.

The recommendation about major rework or rebuild is just a recommendation. It is the best judgment of the group given the review process. It should be the "considered technical judgment of prepared technical people." The decision about reworking the product is ultimately that of the management not of the creating team—or of the review team. Although the review team may feel that a product should be "rebuilt," the creating group may feel that "rework" is sufficient.

Management has to weigh these technical opinions and also consider various business aspects of the decision. Because the creating team almost always tends to be optimistic and management can easily suffer from the same outlook, it behooves the review team to be as conservative as possible in their decision. You will *never* see management deciding to do *more* work than the review team recommends.

In Our Reviews, We've Had the Problem of Being Unable to Decide If, Say, a Design Was Bad or Simply the Document Describing the Design Was Bad. What Is Our Decision in a Case Like This?

We've found that the best thing to do in a case like this— which is quite frequent in some organizations—is to decide *review not complete*. The letter explaining this decision would then say something like this:

> The review committee was unable to decide whether the design was fuzzy or merely the description of the design was fuzzy. We will be unable to complete this review until we get a design document that we can understand. Here are some of the points we didn't understand: (Then attach a list of points that will help the designers know where they must work if they want their work to be reviewed).

In a sense, the decision is "work not reviewable." It's the same thing that you would do if you were missing parts of the design document. You can't review what you don't have, and you can't review what you don't understand. It could be that all the reviewers are stupid, but perhaps they are typical of the people who will have to read the design document later on. In that case, it should be written so that stupid people can understand it—or else it shouldn't pass review.

TECHNICAL REVIEW SUMMARY REPORT

REVIEW NUMBER _____   STARTING TIME _____

DATE   _____   ENDING TIME   _____

WORK UNIT IDENTIFICATION _____

PRODUCED BY _____

BRIEF DESCRIPTION _____

_____

MATERIALS USED IN THE REVIEW: *(check here ____ if supplementary list)*
    IDENTIFICATION   DESCRIPTION

_____   _____

_____   _____

_____   _____

_____   _____

_____   _____

_____   _____

PARTICIPANTS:
    NAME   SIGNATURE   I.D.

LEADER_____   _____   _____

RECORDER_____   _____   _____

3._____   _____   _____

4._____   _____   _____

5._____   _____   _____

6._____   _____   _____

7._____   _____   _____

APPRAISAL OF THE WORK UNIT:

ACCEPTED *(no further review)*   NOT ACCEPTED *(new review required)*

_____ as is   _____ major revisions

_____ with minor revisions   _____ rebuild

                                     _____ review not completed

SUPPLEMENTARY MATERIALS PRODUCED: DESCRIPTION AND/OR IDENTIFICATION

_____ ISSUES LIST   _____

_____ RELATED ISSUES LISTS   _____

_____ OTHER   _____

                                     _____

TECHNICAL REVIEW SUMMARY REPORT

REVIEW NUMBER ___3.2.2.1___   STARTING TIME __10⁰⁰__
DATE ___MAY 5, 1976___   ENDING TIME __10³⁰__

WORK UNIT IDENTIFICATION EDIT-FILE-IB7 TRANSACTION EDITOR
PRODUCED BY PAOLILLO, NOWACKI, AND GARFIELD
BRIEF DESCRIPTION EDITS AND FORMATS INPUT TRANSACTIONS FOR
                   UPDATING SX-PARTS CATALOG

MATERIALS USED IN THE REVIEW: (check here ____ if supplementary list)
       IDENTIFICATION   DESCRIPTION
COMPILED CODE LISTING   ALL SYNTAX ERRORS CORRECTED
TEST FILE LISTING   INCLUDING ERROR CASES
TEST RESULTS LISTING   SIMULATED BY DEVELOPER, NOT USER
CRITICAL ASSUMPTION LIST   ANY OF THESE WOULD REQUIRE MAJOR
                                  REVISION OF THE SYSTEM IF CHANGED,
                                  IN THE OPINION OF THE DEVELOPER.

PARTICIPANTS:
        NAME   SIGNATURE   I.D.
LEADER J. TAO   Junior Tao   ------
RECORDER A. MARIETTA   A. Marietta   ------
3. P. SCHWARTZ   P. Schwartz   ------
4. L. BARMAN   L. Barman   ------
5. L. NOWACKI   L. Nowacki   ------
6. P. THOMPSON   P. Thompson   ------
7._____   _____   _____

APPRAISAL OF THE WORK UNIT:
ACCEPTED (no further review)   NOT ACCEPTED (new review required)
_____ as is   ✓ major revisions
_____ with minor revisions   _____ rebuild
                                 _____ review not completed

SUPPLEMENTARY MATERIALS PRODUCED: DESCRIPTION AND/OR IDENTIFICATION
✓ ISSUES LIST   3.2.2.1 – Wrong spec used for price
_____ RELATED ISSUES LISTS   field edit.
_____ OTHER

SAMPLE

TECHNICAL REVIEW SUMMARY REPORT

REVIEW NUMBER 3.2.2.2   STARTING TIME   10:00 am
DATE   5/25/76   ENDING TIME   11:00 am

WORK UNIT IDENTIFICATION   EDIT-FILE-1B7 TRANSACTION EDITOR
PRODUCED BY PAOLILLO, NOWACKI, AND GARFIELD
BRIEF DESCRIPTION SEE REVIEW REPORT 3.2.2.1

MATERIALS USED IN THE REVIEW: *(check here ____ if supplementary list)*
    IDENTIFICATION   DESCRIPTION

  CODE LISTING (COMPILED)
  TEST FILE LISTING   TEST RESULTS, NEW CASE INCLUDED
  REVISED SPECIFICATION   REVISED & CLARIFIED FOR FIELD EDIT
  CRITICAL ASSUMPTION LIST

PARTICIPANTS:
    NAME   SIGNATURE   I.D.
LEADER   J. TAO   *Junior Tao*
RECORDER A. MARIETTA   *A. Marietta*
3. P. SCHWARTZ   *P. Schwartz*
4. L. BURMAN   *L. Burman*
5. L. NOWACKI   *L. Nowacki*
6. P. THOMPSON   *P. Thompson*
7.

APPRAISAL OF THE WORK UNIT:

ACCEPTED *(no further review)*   NOT ACCEPTED *(new review required)*
   _____ as is   _____ major revisions
   _____ with minor revisions   _____ rebuild
                        _____ review not completed

SUPPLEMENTARY MATERIALS PRODUCED: DESCRIPTION AND/OR IDENTIFICATION
  X ISSUES LIST
  _____ RELATED ISSUES LISTS
  _____ OTHER

TECHNICAL REVIEW SUMMARY REPORT

SAMPLE

REVIEW NUMBER _SP-1098_____   STARTING TIME _3:00 P.M._____

DATE _____6/6/76_____   ENDING TIME __4:45 P.M._____

WORK UNIT IDENTIFICATION Specification of input forma statement R-399A

PRODUCED BY __Accounting Department--Haven Gladstone_____

BRIEF DESCRIPTION _Describes the desired input format for on-line_

_____data entry for the interactive year-end system._

MATERIALS USED IN THE REVIEW: *(check here ____ if supplementary list)*
      IDENTIFICATION   DESCRIPTION

Original description____   5/25/76_____

Model formats_____   3 new screen layouts_____

Current formats_____   5 old formats copied from Run Book

_____   _____

_____   _____

_____   _____

PARTICIPANTS:

NAME	SIGNATURE	I.D.
LEADER_T. Sinatra____	*t. sinatra*	149280
RECORDER_Bill B. Smith__	*Bill Bob Smith*	883726
3. J. Smith_____	*J. Smith*	185544
4. ~~P. Fried~~ *A.Franklin*	*A. Franklin*	~~190218~~ 66 2015
5. M. Fierro_____	*M. Fierro*	093189
6._____	_____	_____
7._____	_____	_____

APPRAISAL OF THE WORK UNIT:

ACCEPTED *(no further review)*   NOT ACCEPTED *(new review required)*

____ as is   _____ major revisions

_X__ with minor revisions   _____ rebuild

                                        _____ review not completed

SUPPLEMENTARY MATERIALS PRODUCED: DESCRIPTION AND/OR IDENTIFICATION

_X__ ISSUES LIST   _____

____ RELATED ISSUES LISTS   _____

_X__ OTHER   _suggestions to standards for_

                                    presentation of format layouts.

TECHNICAL REVIEW SUMMARY REPORT

REVIEW NUMBER ___1217___   STARTING TIME ___2:35 p.m.___

DATE ___4/4/78___   ENDING TIME ___3:55 pm.___

WORK UNIT IDENTIFICATION ___QK-001___

PRODUCED BY _HAROLD FULKERSON_

BRIEF DESCRIPTION _IN-CORE QUICKSHOT SUBROUTINE FOR FORTRAN LIBRARY_

MATERIALS USED IN THE REVIEW: (check here ____ if supplementary list)
     IDENTIFICATION   DESCRIPTION

IDENTIFICATION	DESCRIPTION
QK-001-1	MODULE LISTING WITH DRIVER
QK-001-2,3,4	3 TEST OUTPUTS
QKS-001	SPECIFICATION FOR MODULE

PARTICIPANTS:

NAME	SIGNATURE	I.D.
LEADER PAT LITTLEWOOD	Pat Littlewood	
RECORDER BUD SLYVER	Bud S. Yver	
3. MARJOE WEST	Marjoe West	
4. ART BONDER	Art Bonder	
5.		
6.		
7.		

APPRAISAL OF THE WORK UNIT:

ACCEPTED (no further review)   NOT ACCEPTED (new review required)

_____ as is   _____ major revisions

_____ with minor revisions   ✓ rebuild

                                   _____ review not completed

SUPPLEMENTARY MATERIALS PRODUCED: DESCRIPTION AND/OR IDENTIFICATION

✓ ISSUES LIST

_____ RELATED ISSUES LISTS

_____ OTHER

SAMPLE

SAMPLE

TECHNICAL REVIEW SUMMARY REPORT

REVIEW NUMBER ___ED -319_____   STARTING TIME ___*1:30 pm*___
DATE _____14 Oct. 1977___   ENDING TIME ___*3:45 pm*___

WORK UNIT IDENTIFICATION __3rd Assignment--Structured Prog. Class__
PRODUCED BY _____H. Kaminski_____
BRIEF DESCRIPTION __Self-study assignment for control structures.__
_____

MATERIALS USED IN THE REVIEW: *(check here ____ if supplementary list)*
    IDENTIFICATION   DESCRIPTION

Video Tape #227_____   20 minute tape--17 minutes used_
Self-help exercise_____   Tutorial & problem set_____
Self-assessment material   Evaluation instrument & results
_____   _____
_____   _____
_____   _____

PARTICIPANTS:
    NAME   SIGNATURE   I.D.
LEADER_B. Lincoln_____   *B. Lincoln*   495500
RECORDER C. Cavello____   *C. Cavello*   637920
3._Marcia Rodrich_____   *Marcia Rodrich*   486692
4._C. Brown_____   *C. Brown*   311021
5._N. Alvarez_____   *Nadia Alvarez*   443885
6._P. Schneider_____   *P. Schneider*   696981
7._D. P. Freedman_____   *D. P. Freedman*   Visitor

APPRAISAL OF THE WORK UNIT:

ACCEPTED *(no further review)*   NOT ACCEPTED *(new review required)*
____ as is   ____ major revisions
____ with minor revisions   ____ rebuild   *(mechanical problems)*
        ✔ review not completed *(too much material)*

SUPPLEMENTARY MATERIALS PRODUCED: DESCRIPTION AND/OR IDENTIFICATION
✔ ISSUES LIST   *ED-319*
✔ RELATED ISSUES LISTS   *question on DO WHILE/UNTIL syntax*
____ OTHER   *sent to compiler group.*

The Technical Review Issues List

What Is the Purpose of the Issues List?

Whereas the Summary Report is primarily a report to management, the Issues List is primarily a report to the producers. The Issues List tells the producers *why* their work was not fully accepted as is, hopefully in sufficient detail to enable them to remedy the situation.

Does Management Get a Copy of the Issues List?

Practices vary, but our recommendation is that management *not* routinely get the Issues List. In instances we have seen of managers getting this report, there has been a tendency to *count* issues as a means of evaluating producers and/or reviewers. Because the issues can be highly technical, the manager generally has no other way of making sense out of the report than to count the number of issues, rather than weigh their seriousness. Besides, the Summary Report already contains, in its assessment of the work, a weighted opinion of the seriousness of the issues, so why burden management with extra paper and technical details.

What Form Should the Issues List Take?

Unless the issues are to be classified for feedback purposes, there is no need for some specialized form for listing the issues. Of course, whatever is sent to the producers should be clearly identified, but other than that, the watchword is *communication*.

The Issues List is a communication from one technical group to another. It is not intended for nontechnical readers and therefore need not be "translated" for their eyes. Moreover, it is a *transient* communication, in that once the issues are resolved, the list might as well disappear. (We exclude, for the moment, research use of the lists.) Therefore, it need not be fancy, as long as it is clear.

Don't be restricted by the word "list." Some issues are best communicated by red pencil markings on a listing or other document. Sketches or diagrams can be extremely helpful in getting a difficult point across from one technical mind to another, and since there is no need to be fancy, the effort required is reasonable. If you *do* send miscellaneous items, however, it's a good idea to make up a master list referencing each item sent, just to keep track of things. The master list also serves as a convenient checklist for reviewing the issues after they have been resolved.

What Form Should We Use If We Intend to Classify the Issues for Research Purposes, to Feed Back Information About the Nature of Issues Raised Over a Period of Time?

In our experience, a review can be seriously disrupted by forcing the participants to classify issues as they are raised.

Rather than demand the use of a special form of Issues List, one of two other approaches should be tried. First, the researcher can simply work with a copy of the "natural" issues list, after the review. If necessary, the researcher can recode the information onto any form convenient for the research, perhaps with the assistance of somebody who was in the review.

The other approach is to have the researcher sit as a *silent observer* in the review, taking notes on the issues in whatever form suits the research. All participants, of course, must be informed in advance of the role of the researcher and should be entitled—even encouraged—to look over the researcher's notes after the meeting.

Even when the researcher's notes are open for inspection, the presence of a nonparticipant in the review can arouse suspicion or create a "performance" atmosphere—either of which might be disruptive to the main purpose of the review. We strongly recommend *against* this approach for the first few rounds of reviews, in any case. There will be enough problems to work out concerning review behavior, without having to handle the problem of being "spied on." Once everyone is comfortable with and skilled in reviews, trials can be conducted to see if the "researcher in the room" technique will actually prove viable.

In Our First Few Reviews, We Felt That We Wanted to Make Positive Comments and Have Them Recorded Along with the Negative Comments, but You Seem to Prohibit This Practice. Is It Ever Permitted to Record Positive Comments?

First of all, we definitely don't want to prohibit positive comments *in the review itself,* for reasons noted elsewhere.

Second, there is one case in which positive comments *must* be recorded along with issues on the Issues List. Whenever it is feared that changing the product to eliminate an issue might at the same time destroy some important positive feature, the positive feature should be noted along with a statement of the potential conflict. The example Issues List from Review 5.6.2.1 (page 198) shows how this might be done in the case of a users manual that was hard to use for finding answers to specific questions.

Third, it isn't a good idea to have other types of positive comments part of the *official* output of the review because *absence of positive comments* will eventually be seen as a negative comment in itself. Then the review procedure can easily degenerate into an exercise in mutual admiration aimed at impressing management and stimulating raises — a fine idea, but one that will destroy the error-finding quality of reviews.

Could We Have an Extra Report, Unofficially Giving Positive Points?

You could, but we're wary of what happens to such pieces of paper once they get into circulation. It's better to have the things communicated orally to the producers, either during the review or immediately after.

How About Conducting a "Positive Comments" Review, in Addition to the Review Oriented to Error Finding?

That could prove an excellent idea, provided it's done only *after* the product has been accepted. Be careful, though! Positive comments are much more subjective than a list of errors or issues and could lead to endless arguments or the development of political factions or buddy groups. Whenever possible, try to find *measures* of the positive qualities of the product, measures that can eliminate some of the subjectivity.

*There Are Times When We Don't Get Agreement About an
Issue on the Issues List. Does Everyone Have to Agree
About an Issue Before It Goes on the Issues List?*

> Certainly not. The Issues List is the opinion of the members of the review committee. It does not mean that everyone agrees with the issue, but that someone thought it was important enough to put on the list. Our experience has been that when reviews first begin there are a lot of issues that may appear minor in nature. As the review process matures and the reviewers become more familiar with reviewing techniques and develop a better sense of the material itself, minor issues come into perspective.

*When the Issue Is Not Agreed Upon Unanimously, Should
That Fact Be Noted?*

> Sometimes it is helpful to record an issue in this form:
>
> > Several members of the review committee were unable to understand the description of the data elements.
>
> These reviewers who didn't understand may be considered a *sample* of the other people who will have to look at this material later on. It may not always be necessary for everyone to understand, so it may help to qualify the issue further by a description such as:
>
> > The people without experience in COBOL were unable to understand the description of the data elements.
>
> Another informative description of the issue might be:
>
> > People without COBOL experience were unable to understand the description of data elements, but were satisfied with an explanation that it wasn't necessary to understand them in detail to follow the rest of the report.

The point here is to put the information in the producers' hands that they will need to resolve the issue intelligently.

Should the Review Leader Decide What Should Appear on the Issues List?

Censorship in any form is dangerous. If the leader or any member of the review team wishes to change the wording of an issue, it should be with the agreement of the person raising the issue. This probably need not apply to grammatical corrections, but grammar and meaning sometimes interact.

When a Product Is Rejected Because of Major Issues, What Should Be Done with the Minor Issues That Were Raised?

The sample Issues List from Review 3.2.2.1 (page 196) gives one possible situation. Here, the wrong spec was used for one field, so the code could not be accepted even though most of it was correct. The committee felt, however, that the remaining issues were in parts of the code unaffected by this issue and could be useful to the producers.

The purpose of the Issues List is to be useful to the producers, so keep this criterion in mind when deciding what to pass on and what to ignore. If, for example, the wrong spec had been used for the entire code, there would be little sense in criticizing the heading comment or the name of a variable, since the code is to be thrown away.

But Couldn't the Producers Learn Good Techniques from Some of the Minor Issues, Even If the Code Is Discarded?

Yes, if they pay attention to them. Consider the psychology carefully here, before you crash down on someone who has just heard the difficult message that their hard work has gone to waste. They may not be eager to learn new coding techniques just now, so it might be best to hold your tongue.

There is also another psychological matter. Suppose your teenager came home and was told three things:

1. Don't leave your chewing gum in the ashtray.
2. Don't drive the car down the wrong side of the highway.
3. Tie your shoelace.

How effectively would the crucial message about highway safety be communicated? If you surround an important message with relatively trivial ones, you dilute the impact of the important message. Better to leave a few shoelaces untied than have a dead child.

Are You Implying That the Committee Need Not Report All Issues in All Cases?

Absolutely.

But Won't the Reviewers Feel Frustrated and Angry If All Their Points Are Not Captured?

Perhaps, but only if they've prepared in an unintelligent way. Once you start finding major flaws in a product, you should leave nit-picking aside and simply look for other flaws of the same magnitude.

And in the review itself, the review leader should take care to ensure that *major* points are brought up early, because minor points may waste everyone's time if the product fails for reasons of the first magnitude.

Besides, if someone really feels that they have something they *must* tell the producers about their use of commas, they would be well advised to communicate this privately outside the official channels. That way, they're far more likely to elicit a changed behavior, rather than a defensive public posture. Of course, if the purpose of the issue is not to help the producer, but merely to show off the reviewer's prowess, then it's better done privately in any case.

The ability to apply judgment in such cases is one of the principal advantages a good review committee has over a collection of anonymous reviews collected by company mail.

SAMPLE

ISSUES LIST FROM REVIEW 3.2.2.1   May 5, 1976

The following issue was deemed serious enough to cause termination of the review.

1. <u>Wrong spec used for price field edit</u>. After a smooth review of about half of the code, we reached the section that edited the price field. After much disagreement, we realized that the specification for the price field was not the one currently in use.

Between the time of release of the program spec and this review, the data administrator had released a new spec for the price field, to take account of possible higher prices. Somehow, that change doesn't seem to have been reflected in the spec of the program under review.

We were unable even to resolve the controversy over what is the correct spec, so the review committee decided to recommend that coding be brought to a halt until this specification issue is resolved.

The review committee felt that it was likely that only a few parts of the routine would have to be changed in response to point #1. Therefore, we have listed below the minor points to be cleared up--in case those parts of the routine are retained.

2. <u>Wrong name for loop variable</u>. It was noted that J, the name of a loop variable, was not in conformity with installation standards.

3. <u>Heading comment not completely clear</u>. The comment at the head of the program doesn't seem to make completely clear the distinction between this routine and other edit routines on other transactions.

4. <u>Additional test cases</u>. Two test cases to cover open areas of the spec were suggested for the test set. They were noted on the master test data listing and given to Louise Nowacki for incorporation in future tests.

5. <u>Typographical errors</u>. A number of typographical errors were noted in the prose of the code, and marked on the master copy for correction.

_____   Junior Tao, Review Leader

_____   A. Marietta, Recorder

SAMPLE

ISSUES LIST FROM REVIEW 1217

4 April 1978

Although the review committee was satisfied that the Quicksort
module apparently sorted all test cases correctly, and that the
tests were fairly comprehensive as to types of sequencing, it
was (eventually) the unanimous view of the committee that the
module was not up to the standards now required of our FORTRAN
library.

In the specifications for this project, the explicit reason for
building this module was to provide a <u>faster</u> in-core sort for
FORTRAN arrays of moderate size. The tests for this module have
all been functional tests, with no particular orientation to the
question of speed, apparently under the assumption that any
Quicksort would just naturally be faster than other sorts in the
library.   However, the times given for the sorts actually done
do not compare favorably with the experienced times listed for
the two fast sorts now in the library, SRTF007 and SRTF008.
SRTF007 is faster by 20% or more on arrays of less than 100 elements
in the Quicksort tests, while SRTF008 is at least 40% faster on
the one array of 200 elements used. It may be that the Quicksort
would be faster on much larger arrays, but none were tested.

Even if the Quicksort module proved faster on larger arrays, it
was the consensus opinion of the reviewers that the coding style
was so esoteric that none of us would have confidence in using
this sort in an important job. We would rather take the penalty
of somewhat longer machine time than risk our job in the hands
of a module which we could not convince ourselves was correct or
incorrect.

Perhaps 10 years ago this module would have been acceptable for
the Library here, but not today. Certainly none of us would want
the responsibility for maintaining this module, once it was accepted.
In addition to the unfathomable design, the documentation is
completely mysterious, and actually makes the program harder to
understand than it would be without the documentation.

There was not unanimous opinion concerning whether such a module
is actually needed in the Library, even if it were up to present
standards. In the end, we concluded that we may have been negatively
influenced by the poor quality of this work. It may well be that
a properly programmed Quicksort would be a valuable addition to
the Library, especially if a convincing set of speed tests were
performed. The author of this module claims that the potential
speed of Quicksort cannot be obtained if he has to conform to
our presenting coding standards, but although that may be true for
him, it may not be true for others. We feel that it is beyond the
scope and authority of this committee to decide whether this
module should be rebuilt, or just thrown away and forgotten. We
also think it is not our job to decide who should be given the job
of rebuilding, if that is decided. But we are unanimous in rejecting
this module as it now stands for any use whatsoever.

Pat Littlewood Pat Littlewood, Leader

Bud Slyver   Bud Slyver, Recorder

SAMPLE

AN ISSUE LIST WITH POSITIVE COMMENTS

ISSUE LIST FROM REVIEW 5.6.2.1   14 June 1978

There was only one issue standing between this User Manual
and acceptance with minor revisions:

1. As presently arranged, the User Manual seems an excellent
text for first-time users, but because the topics fall in teaching order, rather than in logical or alphabetical order, it
was deemed <u>hard to find information</u>.

The difficulty of finding material was tested by review members
choosing topics which other review members tried to find. We
did not test this difficulty on people who had not read the
entire manual, but we assumed it would be even harder for such
people to find material in a short time.

Although this difficulty was unanimously deemed to make the User
Manual unacceptable, the review committee expressed serious
concern that certain methods of solving this problem could
create other problems just as serious. In particular, the
committee wanted to point out that the strongest point of this
manual--putting it head and shoulders above all previous User
Manuals produced by this shop--is its excellent organization as
a teaching text, or for self study.

One way to solve the reference problem, for example, would be
to reorganize the material in the same logical order our other
manuals are organized, but the committee wanted to state that
they would find this reorganization unacceptable, now that they
have seen what a teaching-oriented organization can do.

The committee didn't want to state solutions to the problem
of quick referencing, but wanted to go on record as stating
that something equivalent to a comprehensive index would
probably satisfy that requirement without prejudicing the
outstanding teaching qualities of the present work.

2. A number of small errors in the examples were noted on
a master copy for correction.

3. Examples 4.3, 4.4 and 6.1 were deemed misleading, and
should be clarified.

Harriet Moresby   Harriet Moresby, Review Leader

John Henry Johnstone   John Henry Johnstone, Recorder

Technical Review
Related Issue Report

Do You Recommend a Special Form for Reporting on
Related Issues Raised During the Review?

Some people find it surprising in view of the position we take on the Issues List format, but we *do* recommend a special report form for distributing information on related issues raised during the review. The exact form isn't important. What's important is that it be a *special* form.

The reason for using a special form can be understood in contrast to the ordinary Issues List. The producers of a piece of work under review *expect* to get a list of issues. They know they will have to respond to the list if they are to pass review, so they need no particular motivation to pay attention to the list, regardless of its form. Indeed, they may be somewhat fearful of the list, so an informal presentation can tend to make the communication more friendly and to put them more at ease.

A Related Issue Report, on the other hand, descends like a bolt from the blue on some people who may not even have known a review was taking place. If it isn't communicated in some standard, official form, they may not even recognize it. Therefore, if we want to keep Related Issue Reports from passing directly into the wastebasket, we've got to give them *some* official status.

The mildest approach is to have a standard *transmittal sheet,* identifying the source of the material and attached to the actual communication, which may take any convenient form. Some installations prefer a formal followup system that requires that each Related Issue Report must receive a reply within a few days or one week. Another approach is to send the Related Issue Report through the appropriate manager, leaving any action or follow-up decision on the management level.

Because the Related Issue Report is, by definition, a deviation from smooth product development, there is really no way to develop a standard practice for handling all situations, especially when related issues can range over such matters as:

1. A typographical error in a related document,
2. A hidden assumption in the specifications that makes part of one module obsolete, or
3. A flaw in the original problem statement that makes the entire project plan invalid.

If an organization cannot handle case (1) without alerting the management chain, it's probably in as bad a shape as an organization that handles case (3) *without* alerting the management chain. The problem, of course, is with the middle cases, such as case (2). Such cases have always been troublesome, but with reviews in place, we reduce their number, and when they happen in spite of our best efforts, we notify *someone* who ought to be in a position to do something about them.

Do the Related Issues Become Part of the Documentation of the Work Unit?

It is probably a good idea to keep the transmittal sheet, at least, as part of the permanent or semipermanent documentation of the work unit—at least until it is clear that the issue has been resolved and no longer can affect the work unit. The Summary Report is, of course, a permanent part of the historical record, as is the master list of issues, if not the actual issues themselves. After all, the Summary Report will ultimately be the "diploma" of the work unit, so it ought to be right on top of the pile of documentation. Otherwise, readers won't know if they're looking at a graduate or a dropout.

Who Should Be Responsible for Preparing the Related Issues Report?

If the review committee decides as a whole to prepare a Related Issues Report, the responsibility for seeing to its preparation resides with the review leader. The leader could either supervise the preparation or actually write the report. In any case, the leader is responsible for following through on the report.

Sometimes, a subset of the review committee, or maybe only one member, will feel that a supplementary report is needed. In this case the responsibility should be taken by that member or subset.

Wait a Minute, I Thought the Review Committee Had to Agree by Consensus?

Absolutely, the review committee must come to a consensus decision about the product. They must all agree that the product is ready to move to the next phase in its life cycle. But related issues are different. They are usually items which do not pertain to the immediate product, but the product review brought them to mind. The committee might well agree that the product is fine, but something could be done to make it much better or to improve future products. These would be related issues and reported separately.

Does that Mean That Anyone Who Wishes to Can Write a Related Issues Report?

Yes, anyone can write anything they wish about the review (within company standards, of course). The key is that all reports issued by the committee are public information. This prevents people from politicizing the process. It eliminates memos to the file stating that "although I went along with the review, because of political pressure, I really know that the product is no good, and I want to cover myself in case of trouble. . . ." There is little danger in people expressing their ideas publicly; it's also a First Amendment guarantee.

SAMPLE

RELATED ISSUE REPORT

FROM: Review Committee #SP-1098

TO: Standards Committee; Claudia Craft; Nelson Bosch III

SUBJECT: A common standard for presentation of item format
layouts for screens.

DATE: June 6, 1976

In the course of review #SP-1098, the committee found that
there were three different formatting methods currently in
use for specifying the formats of items on screens. There
may be more in use, but these three were found in the one
review.

The methods seem to follow the programming language preference of the specifier, for they seem to be related to

     a.   FORTRAN, as in F6.2

     b.   COBOL, as in PICTURE IS Z(4)V99

     c.   PL/I, as in PICTURE'(3)Z9V.99'

These differences in format greatly confused and prolonged
our review. We would like to suggest that you investigate
the possibility of some solution to this problem. Perhaps
you could allow all forms to be used as long as they were
each translated into a common language, for documentation
purposes.

t. sinatra

Tyrone Sinatra, Review Leader

Other members of the review committee were Bill Bob Smith,
Jeremiah Smith, Alice Franklin (substituting for Penny Fried),
and Moishe Fierro. They or I would be happy to discuss the
matter further with your committee.

SAMPLE

TO: Pierre Rubenstein, Education Development Manager

FROM: Bartholemew Lincoln, Leader of Review ED-319 *BL*

SUBJECT: Incomplete Review

DATE: October 14, 1977

Although a few minor issues were raised, plus a few questions
about the subject matter, the review of this self-study unit
was proceeding quite well until we had a slight accident.

In order to work one of the exercises, Nadia Alvarez borrowed
a battery from Carl Cavello's hearing aid to operate her
calculator. In replacing the battery, Carl broke the hearing
aid. Since he was Recorder, we decided it was essential that
he participate fully in the rest of the meeting.

I therefore decided to adjourn the review until Monday,
October 17, at 10 a.m., as this is the first time we can
bring the entire committee together again.

SAMPLE

TECHNICAL REVIEW SUMMARY REPORT

REVIEW NUMBER ES-001-ED   STARTING TIME *8:30 a.m.*
DATE   1 September 1978   ENDING TIME *10:02 a.m.*

WORK UNIT IDENTIFICATION EXECUTIVE SEMINAR--BASIC CONCEPTS
PRODUCED BY COURSE DEVELOPERS--KINIWKEIN GROUP
BRIEF DESCRIPTION OVERVIEW OF BASIC COMPUTER CONCEPTS FOR HIGH LEVEL
                EXECUTIVES

MATERIALS USED IN THE REVIEW: *(check here* ✓ *if supplementary list)*
    IDENTIFICATION   DESCRIPTION

  OUTLINE   OVERVIEW THREE DAYS
  FOILS   COPIES CLASS NOTES
  MATERIALS LIST   PHYSICAL MATERIAL FOR COURSE
  EXERCISES
  EXPLANATION OF EXERCISE
  SUPPLEMENTARY READINGS

PARTICIPANTS:
      NAME   SIGNATURE   I.D.
LEADER J. MARBLEHEAD   *Jerry Marblehead*
RECORDER P.T. EVERLING   *Wally Overbeck*
3. WALLY OVERBECK   *Pat Everling*
4. S. MAY   *S. May*
5. G.M. WEINBERG   *Gerald M. Weinberg*
6.
7.

APPRAISAL OF THE WORK UNIT:
ACCEPTED *(no further review)*   NOT ACCEPTED *(new review required)*
 ✓ as is   major revisions
     with minor revisions   rebuild
                             review not completed

SUPPLEMENTARY MATERIALS PRODUCED: DESCRIPTION AND/OR IDENTIFICATION
     ISSUES LIST
 ✓ RELATED ISSUES LISTS (2)
     OTHER

RELATED ISSUE REPORT

SAMPLE

FROM: WALLY OVERBECK & P. T. EVERLING,
        Participants in Review ES-001-ED

TO: V. C. Warren, Education Manager

SUBJECT: Justification of this course for high-level executives

DATE: 5 September 1978

Although we both thought this was an excellently prepared course,
there was considerable doubt in our minds whether this audience

   1. will be able to spare 3 days on this subject

   2. wants to know this much on the subject

We really doubt that you'll be able to get them to attend, and if
they do, to get them to feel that they've spent their time
properly.

Perhaps we don't know the work that has gone on behind the scenes
to justify this course, but none of that shows in the documentation.
We realize that this is a bit late to bring this up, but this
review was the first time we knew that such a course was in
preparation. We think it would be better to ask a few questions
now than to hurt the reputation of data processing by having
top executives go through a course that gives them much more than
they want to know, or have time to learn, about computers.

The other members of the review committee didn't agree with our
fears, and our consultant wouldn't say anything, one way or the
other. He said he was prepared to discuss the matter with you
and give you some idea of the arguments on both sides that came
out in the meeting.

RELATED ISSUE REPORT

FROM: REVIEW COMMITTEE # ES-001-ED

TO: Course Developers--Kiniwkein Group

SUBJECT: Instructor's Course Log Book

DATE: 5 September 1978

During the review of the Executive Seminar in
Basic Computer Concepts it was suggested that
an instructor's course log book be developed
along with every educational package. We note
that our current practices do not suggest this
document. We are suggesting this idea for your
review and development (if you so choose).

This instructor's course log could contain helpful
information. For example:

>   Timing instructions for exercises

>   Weak spot in the material--for improvement in
>   next addition

>   Errors

>   Points which need particular emphasis

>   Class reactions and evaluations

System History	SECTION 5

*In the General Discussion of Reports, You Mentioned the
Usefulness of Having a Historical Record, but We Find
That People Seldom Go Back to the Review Reports Unless
Some (Usually Bad) Event Triggers Them. Wouldn't It Be
Better to Have Some Systematic Reporting Scheme?*

We agree that it's bad to use history only when there's
obvious trouble. In the first place, there may be trouble
brewing long before it starts to boil over. Second, if the
reports are only used in times of trouble, people begin
to think of them as a means of recrimination, which might
start to affect their accuracy. There are, on the other
hand, problems with too formal a triggering mechanism.
The biggest problem is that it can become a routine passing of data, without understanding or thought. The best
trigger is a good manager establishing the habit of leafing
through the system history file once a month, with open
eyes and open mind. Still, we don't rule out the regular
extraction of reports, as some of our clients have done.

What Is the System History File?

The system history file contains every review report—Summaries, Technical Issues Lists, and Technical Related Issues Lists. The history file may contain supplementary information such as memos and other correspondence, but a complete report record is the minimum requirement.

Information in the system history file should be public information and available to anyone involved in the project. It represents the first place anyone would look to find the current state of a particular piece of work. If the product or subproduct is complete, the summary report reflecting this information will be found in the system history file. If the product has been reviewed and requires further work and review, this too will be reflected in the system history file. A product that has not yet been reviewed would be reflected by the absence of information in the file.

If a product or subproduct was scheduled to be completed at a certain time, but there are no reports in the system history file, it is an indication that the product is behind schedule. This information is useful to management as an indication of a schedule slippage, but is also useful to people working on related pieces of the project. They too know that there may be difficulty in schedule and that this difficulty may have an impact on their work.

How Long Should the System History File Be Kept?

Any useful software system undergoes changes throughout its lifetime. A change in the business environment may render part of the system inappropriate. A user may request added functions or enhancements. The original producers may have made errors that are detected as the system is used.

For whatever reason, changes in software systems are inevitable, and these changes are costly to the producing organization. If it were possible to ascertain where the changes were coming from, it might be possible to alter the design and implementation process to anticipate some of these changes and thereby minimize their cost. The system history file can provide this information.

Reference to the system history will help separate those changes that were truly an increase in function from those in which the function was supposed to be in the original system and then forgotten. This information would lead to improvement in the analysis and design of software. The system history file represents a chronological or archeological record of how the system was developed. It can show where early assumptions led to final conclusions and where early problems were not manifest until late in the system life cycle.

To us, the "system life cycle" includes the entire time the system is "alive," not just the time it is under "development." Therefore, we recommend that the system history file be kept as long as the system is kept, as part of the system. To keep storage space manageable, perhaps these records could be microfilmed after they are three years old.

Doesn't the System History File Give Management a Way to Check Up on People's Errors, Something That Might Damage the Review Process?

The system history file allows management to get detailed technical information about the project without *direct* interference with the review process. Since the system history is public to all members of the project, management may refer to it for information. Having management *seek* required technical information is more desirable than having management receive *all* technical information.

We have noted that management's desire for information has adversely affected the review process. Technical people are often reluctant to point out technical problems in management's presence. Rightly or wrongly, technical people often feel that management will interpret technical problems as an indication of the inadequacy of the producers and that this interpretation will be reflected in salary and promotions. The system history file can serve as a mechanism to provide needed information without the direct implication that all errors will be sent to management.

Won't That Be Just As Inhibiting As a Manager Sitting in the Review?

Generally not. We have plenty of experience with clients to show that face-to-face contact leads to inhibition, but once things have been carefully written down and filed, the inhibition seems to lose its sting.

This isn't to say that a vindictive or stupid manager couldn't make a "case" on somebody using the information in the system history file, but if your management is that vindictive or stupid, you've got bigger problems than reviews will solve.

Can You Recommend Any Regular Reports That Can Be Extracted from the System History File?

Our clients have tried many ideas and have learned from all their trials. One thing almost all have learned is:

Don't count issues.

Counting issues only affects the way people write issues. Typically, if having many issues is considered bad, then people will protect the work of their peers by lumping many issues into one or omitting minor issues and telling the producers personally. These things defeat the purpose of the system history and of the reviews themselves. It's better not to lose the information. Besides, issues vary so much in importance that simply counting them has little meaning.

The *outcomes* of the review are more amenable to extraction of information. For instance, management can gain a pretty good overview of the review process itself— and the development process—by a report such as the one shown in Figure D.5.1. The different types of review are tabulated against the outcomes, keeping track of whether the review was the first, second, or later review of the same type for the same product.

High numbers of major revisions or rebuild decisions indicate that more attention may be needed to the way work is being done in that phase, as is the case of design in the extracted report.

The report shows that many test plan reviews are not being completed on the first and subsequent passes. This may indicate that the test plans are too large or too poorly organized to be reviewed all in one piece. It could also mean that the discipline for reviewing test plans needs to be reconsidered.

The pattern under specifications is also revealing. If a decision is to rebuild or to make major revisions, we would expect that a good review process would turn up this fact early, not after one or more reviews had already been done. Management may want to investigate why such major issues are slipping through early spec reviews undetected. Perhaps the appropriate people aren't attending the early reviews and only turn up when the material is reviewed again to check on minor revisions.

Outcomes	Accept			Minor			Major			Rebuild			Not Complete		
Type of Review	1	2	3+	1	2	3+	1	2	3+	1	2	3+	1	2	3+
Spec							5	5	4	12	10	9			
Design	3	5	8	8	12	15	12	3	0	17	0	0			
Test Plan													43	17	29
Code	31	12	5	11	3	1	1	0	1	0	0	0	2	0	0

FIGURE D.5.1

Or perhaps the specification writing is so poor that major problems turn up in almost every attempt. The report gives an indication that something bears investigating, but it cannot substitute for the investigation itself.

The pattern for code reviews looks very healthy, and hopefully most of the report will look like this most of the time. But if so, perhaps management will want to ask, Could it be *too* healthy? If so many modules are being accepted on their first review, with no issues raised at all, it could mean that reviews are superficial. That fact can be checked by studying the error history of the modules after acceptance.

But even if the error history is exemplary, there could be a problem. Possibly the code reviews are tackling too small a chunk of work at a time. As the reviews progress in an organization, the power to code and the power to review both mature. Thus, we may want to adjust the amount of code we write in one module or the number of modules we attempt to review at one time. There's no sense bringing people together too often for five-minute reviews, if it can be avoided.

Any Other Reports?

Some other useful reports we've seen are:

1. Review running time versus type of review,
2. Review running time versus review leader, and
3. Type of review versus people attending.

Report (1) can show the need for improved technique in reviewing a certain type of material or in preparing that material for review.

Report (2) can show which review leaders need further review leader experience or training.

Report (3) can show whether people are getting appropriately broad experience at different types of review. It may also show if some people are being overused as reviewers or if some are underused—perhaps because their work is not valued in the review or perhaps because they simply aren't noticed.

You've Said "Don't Count Issues," but Can Useful Information Be Extracted from the Issues Lists?

Yes. Of course, the entire inspection method depends on systematically recording the issues under a classification of types and reporting summaries of those issues so that steps can be taken to improve reviewing and improve development (see Section E.3, Inspections). You don't have to be doing "inspections" to benefit somewhat from this kind of feedback. Issues Lists from various reviews can be studied after the fact and the issues classified under one scheme or another. For instance, one client was considering the purchase of a data dictionary package. The study team looked through Issues Lists from design and code reviews to estimate how many issues would have been affected by the package.

Coding the issues during inspections is useful, but may get rid of information that would be useful to answer questions that you don't think of in advance. Just reading the Issues Lists for a project gives a newcomer a quick introduction to the typical problems this project has encountered and often suggests ideas concerning what might be done in the way of prevention.

Another interesting use of the Issues List is to extract examples of well and poorly written issues for training purposes. By posting a few bad examples each week in a public place (perhaps disguised as to origin), an installation can quickly raise the level of issue writing.

Writing Issues	SECTION 6

We Have a Lot of Trouble Writing Issues Clearly and
Without Bias. Can You Give Us Some Guidelines?

Here's an article based on an exercise we use in our workshop on "Implementing Technical Reviews." This is a training workshop for review leaders, and one of the most commonly asked questions concerns how to train people to write good issues for both the Issues List and the Related Issues Report. By doing the exercise, future review leaders not only learn better writing, but also learn how to make up examples on which to train their own people.

Taking Issue

"If it's not written down, it doesn't exist."

Clients often ask me, "What's the difference between a *formal* and an *informal* technical review?" To me, the essential difference is that the results of the formal review are *written down* and available to management as an aid to managing. Informal reviews may be conducted in exactly the same manner as formal reviews, but their output is for the workers only, to help them improve their products. The results of the informal review *may* be written, but the formal review always produces a Review Summary Report for management plus an Issues List for the workers. The Review Summary Report is highly formal, in order to bridge the communication gap between technical workers and management. The Issues List, however, takes a narrative form and leaves a lot of room for creative writing. On the other hand, when we leave room for doing good, we leave room for mistakes. Lately, I've come to realize that some people need to be trained to write effective Issues Lists. I've developed the following test which you may use to see how much you know about writing technical issues.

The test consists of 10 statements taken from Issues Lists or similar pieces of documentation. Look at each item and quickly note what, if anything, is wrong with it as a written technical issue for an Issues List emerging from a review of some technical product. If you like, suggest a way to improve it. When you're finished, check your ideas against my ideas, which follow. If you disagree with me, drop me a line and I'll raise your grade.

1. Some of the explanations of user commands were misinterpreted by members of the review committee.

2. A maximum of 10 values may be specified even though none of the standard system ABEND codes has been made not eligible.

3. The referenced table of constant values was not part of the review packet.

4. The method used for maintaining the message queue seems to solve a severe performance problem we've been having with the production version of the RKY system.

5. The price/performance table should be sorted using either Quicksort or Shell sort.

6. The three diagrams drawn by Harold Mitter are not in the standard format (DS-109) required for such diagrams in our installation.

7. The committee was unable to understand the significance of paragraph 3.1.

8. The bubble sort used for sorting the table of price/performance figures is a stupid approach if the table should grow any bigger than the present 20 entries.

9. If the BY NAME option is not used, the structuring of the structure operands must be equivalent to the structuring of the structures in the arrays of structures.

10. Frieda Sonntag has no computer science background, and her experience with PL/I is nil. She should never have been assigned the coding of this module.

Explanations of Test Issues

1. Not specific enough. *Which* explanations were misinterpreted? Don't make the producers guess, or do unnecessary work, or change something that's already perfectly clear.

2. In writing, clarity isn't the most important thing — it's the *only* thing. If you don't want to be not understood, don't never use no double negatives. Another thing—what is the issue, anyway? Is the maximum too low? Or too high? Or is it that some of the codes should have been made not eligible? Or eligible? Be direct.

3. Always give the most direct reference available. There could be more than one table, now or in the future. Why make the producers search the entire document for the reference, even if there is only one?

4. This is an interesting observation, clearly and directly stated. But what does it have to do with the product under review? It might be worth millions, so we don't want to lose it, but it doesn't belong on the Issues List for this product. For issues such as this, we have a Related Issues List. By making a separate list of related issues, we don't lose their value, but we won't waste time in this review or confuse the producers about what we're trying to say to them. For all they know, the method isn't even appropriate in their system, but only in RKY!

5. Lacopi's Law states: "After food and sex, man's greatest drive is to tell the other fellow how to do his job." Raise issues, but avoid all temptation to give advice in the Issues List. They won't be welcome if they come in that form, so if you really must give advice, find some unofficial vehicle. Take the producers to lunch, or out for a beer, before you share your vast experience on matters of sorting. If your idea isn't worth the price of a beer, why not forget it?

6. This point is nicely specific, but why do we have to mention poor Harold? We are reviewing the product, not the people. Find another way to identify the diagrams and leave people's names out of the Issues List.

7. Nothing's wrong with this one. It's specific about which paragraph is under discussion, and it says the committee doesn't understand it. Who can argue with that? Yet, surprisingly, people seem afraid to express issues this way—"We don't understand...." Don't worry about being thought stupid. If you don't understand it, it's at least a potential issue in documentation.

   And besides, once in a while, lack of understanding means there's something dreadfully wrong. So when you're afraid to express your uncertainty, remember Firestone's Law of Forecasting: "Chicken Little only has to be right once."

8. The word "stupid" doesn't add anything at all and might antagonize the producers. Take it out. Then try to express factually and quantitatively why the method is inappropriate for larger tables. And if the approach *is* stupid, what of it? As Arthur C. Clarke expressed it, "It has yet to be proved that intelligence has any survival value."

9. This wasn't really taken from an Issues List, but from an old PL/I manual. Still, I've read real issues that were almost as obscure. I'd advise you to follow the KISS axiom ("Keep It Simple, Stupid!"), except that I would be contradicting my own advice from the previous question. Oh, well, as the great philosopher once said, "If you never contradict yourself, you're not very smart."

10. It's none of the business of the review committee who management has assigned to particular jobs. The committee's business is to review the product and tell what state it's in. How it got to that state is another issue—and not for the Issues List. Who is responsible is even less of an issue, and raising it is sure to be ineffective. When tempted to attribute blame, remember Spark's Law of Problem Solution. "The chances of solving a problem decline the closer one gets to finding out who was the cause of the problem."

So there's your little test. Give yourself 10 points for each question you honestly tried to answer, because all that's needed to improve your performance as a reviewer is an honest effort. And for one extra point, Whose law heads this essay? I couldn't remember the name, so I looked it up in my various books of laws. Although I didn't find the author, I found lots of interesting maxims to spruce up the answers.

Which all goes to demonstrate Mayer's Law: "There's all the difference in the world between a wrong issue and a sterile issue." So don't hesitate to express yourself in an Issues List. Just hesitate to express yourself badly.

PART E

Varieties of Review Disciplines

Why There Are So Many Review Variations

Why Do So Many Different People Use So Many Different Variations on the Technical Review Idea?

The practice of technical review differs from place to place for a variety of reasons, the principal ones being:

1. Different external requirements, such as government contract provisions;
2. Different internal organizations, such as the use or nonuse of teams;
3. Continuity with past practices.

Continuity is probably the strongest reason. When it comes to social behavior, people tend to be very conservative about changing what they already know, even if it doesn't seem very productive in today's environment. In many installations, formal technical reviews have been introduced as a new "form" of some old practice, perhaps because it was felt easier to get reviews introduced this way.

There's nothing wrong with establishing continuity with past practices, as long as the underlying task of the review is accomplished. Usually, there is no similar function being practiced, though there may be numerous meetings on a variety of subjects related to product quality. If an organization generally has well-led, productive meetings that are regarded by everyone involved as worth their time, it's a good idea to associate the formal technical review with this tradition. On the other hand, if the word "meeting" sets everyone's teeth on edge, it may prove better strategy to emphasize the formal technical review as something different from past practices, something with it's own complete set of social behaviors.

What Are the Most Common Variations of the Formal Technical Review as You've Described It?

One of the most common variations is some kind of attempt to "cover" a greater quantity of material in the review. For example, the "inspection" approach tends to focus on a much narrower, much more sharply defined, set of questions. In some cases, an inspection consists of running through a checklist of faults, one after the other, over the entire product.

Another way to try to cover more material is by having the product "walked through" by someone who is very familiar with it—even specially prepared with a more or less formal presentation. Walking through the product, a lot of detail can be skipped—which is good if you're just trying to verify an overall approach or bad if your object is to find errors of detail.

In some cases, the walkthrough is very close to a lecture about the product—which suggests another reason for varying the formal review approach. We have emphasized the educational qualities of reviews, but as a byproduct of the quality assurance function. In some cases, rapid education of large numbers of people may suggest some variation of the formal review.

In some situations, formality doesn't seem appropriate. For instance, when members of the same team are reviewing each other's rough work, prior to finishing it for formal, external review, an informal version of the formal procedures may be more comfortable. As the procedure gets less formal, however, there is the danger of drifting away from its central purpose. Therefore, many teams adopt some sort of algorithm for pacing themselves through an informal review. They may walk through a procedure, or perhaps they play "musical chairs"—to give each person a chance to explain or examine one part or one aspect of a product.

Another dimension for variation is the amount of stability in the staffing of the review committee. At the one extreme, each review has a unique group chosen for it alone, but there are many variants that provide for some degree of permanence by having a group of people perform related reviews. At the other extreme, there are permanent *review teams*, devoted to a specific product, class of product, or type of review.

In the following sections, we'll try to explore a few of these variations in some detail. When reading about these review disciplines, keep in mind that there's no way we can run through all existing variants of the formal technical review, even if we knew of all of them. Instead of looking for detailed ways of doing reviews, look upon these descriptions as guides to *thinking about* other ways of reviewing. As you plan your own review procedures, try to apply similar modes of thinking to them.

You Speak About the Educational Value of Technical Reviews. Is There Any Quantitative Data?

We are collecting data ourselves that are not yet based on large enough and diverse enough samples. Some of the articles in the bibliography give qualitative data, but very little has been done to quantify *any* data-processing education—or any education at all, for that matter.

One recent article seems to have some bearing on the question. Fisher et al. surveyed a group of 362 computer professionals to establish their "continuing education patterns." Programmers were given a series of topics and asked to assess where they learned most about them. Among the choices were professional meetings, manuals and books, employer-supplied education, universities, vendor-supplied education, company standards and materials, and other programmers. The following summary results can be applied to the question of reviews as an educational experience, although there was no indication of what experience any of these people had with reviews:

Source of Information	Programmers	Nonprogrammers
Other programmers	29.1%	17.4%
Shop standards	14.6%	12.9%
Books and manuals	12.3%	10.8%
Seminars	4.5%	6.5%

We're not certain what it means for nonprogrammers to learn from "other" programmers, but learning from others is by far the highest category in both groups. These findings were no surprise to us or to our clients who have been involved in technical reviews or team programming. We've said that working for one year on a programming team, or attending reviews regularly, is the educational equivalent of working alone for three years. What teams and reviews do is harness this natural tendency for people to learn most and best from other people. A person who regularly participates in technical reviews will have many more and diverse opportunities to learn from other people than does the isolated programmer, who in spite of the difficulties of asking for help or of seeing the work of others is learning twice as much from others as from any other source.

The best measure of this learning power is obtained simply by *asking* people who do reviews. We're doing that now, formally, and hope eventually to tabulate the results.

The Walkthrough

What Is a Walkthrough?

First of all, the term "walkthrough" has been used in the literature in a variety of ways. Sometimes it has been used as a synonym for any kind of formal technical review. In other cases its description has been highly specific to a particular installation's practices, down to the last detail. As we will use the term, we refer to a number of variations, all of which are characterized by the producer of the reviewed material being present and *guiding the progression of the review.*

In its most usual form, the walking through is done on the basis of a step-by-step simulation of a procedure, as when walking through code, line by line, with an imagined set of inputs. Indeed, the name "walkthrough" derives from this procedural approach. Nevertheless, the term has been extended to the review of material that is in no sense procedural, such as data descriptions, reference manuals, or specifications.

What Is the Difference Between a Structured Walkthrough and Any Other Walkthrough?

The addition of the word "structured" to the name.

What Are the Advantages of the Walkthrough?

With a walkthrough, because of the prior preparation of the presenter, a large amount of material can be moved through rather speedily. Moreover, since the reviews are far more passive than participating, larger numbers of people can become familiar with the walked-through material. This larger audience can serve educational purposes, but it also can bring a great number of diverse viewpoints to bear on the presented material. If all in the audience are alert, and if they represent a broad cross-section of skills and viewpoints, the walkthrough can give strong statistical assurance that no major oversight lies concealed in the material.

Another advantage of the walkthrough is that it doesn't make many demands on the participants for preparation in advance. Where there are large numbers of participants, or where the participants come from diverse organizations not under the same operational control, it may prove impossible to get everyone prepared for the review. In such cases, the walkthrough may be the only reasonable way to ensure that all those present have actually looked at the material.

It Sounds as if the Walkthrough Might Be Very Useful to Us in Some Situations. What Else Can You Tell About the Way It Is Conducted?

If the number of participants is small (less than seven), the procedures need not be very different from what we have described for any formal technical review, with the exception that the process starts with the walking through—as a supplement or substitute for advance preparation. Some people insist that the presentation be uninterrupted, in which case it acts as a prologue to an ordinary formal review, but without putting material in everybody's hands. This can be an advantage when the walkthrough is used informally, for you can just start whenever you find a group of listeners and a room.

If interruptions are allowed, the walkthrough may represent the entire review, expect for the decision at the end. Issues are raised in the order they are encountered in the walkthrough, which is the order dictated by the presenter.

With a larger number of participants, some method must be used for capturing the issues without completely disrupting the flow of the walking through. Participants may simply take notes and make individual or group reports after the review. These reports may or may not be consolidated into a single report by a review leader. A recorder can take down issues brought up in open questioning, but large numbers of people are easily bored by this approach. A common method is to allow questions that seek clarification of the *presentation,* but to prohibit the raising of issues except in written reports.

What Are Some Problems with the Walkthrough, in Practice?

The problems of the walkthrough spring rather directly from its unique advantages. Advance preparation is not required, so each participant may have a different depth of understanding. Those close to the work may be bored and not pay attention. Those who are seeing the work for the first time may not be able to keep up with the pace of presentation. In either case, the ability to raise penetrating issues is lost.

A well-prepared presentation by a skilled presenter can relieve these problems somewhat, but a skilled presenter creates other problems. For example, after a skilled presentation, we don't know how much of our understanding is based on the material and how much on the presentation. If the work is used by others in the future, they are unlikely to have the presenter at their beck and call to clarify difficult issues. Therefore, although the walkthrough assures that the product *can* be understood, it doesn't assure that it's *likely* to be understood without the presence of a skilled presenter. If we are certain there will be continuity of responsibility for the product, we may not need assurance that it can stand on its own, in which case the skilled presenter doesn't hurt.

On the other hand, an inarticulate advocate might cause the review group to reject a high quality, worthwhile product. This situation is part of a more general problem of being able to separate the presentation from the material. The problem exists even when reviewing documentary material in the usual way, but is made more acute when the presentation whizzes by and cannot be studied at leisure. Some installations videotape the walkthrough to get around this problem, and some of these use the videotapes for educational purposes later on. Many of the videotape problems associated with other formal reviews are minimized in the walkthrough, insofar as it is primarily an uninterrupted lecture.

Doesn't the Presenter's Ego Get in the Way of a Proper Evaluation?

Yes, a high degree of ego involvement by the presenter can be the most serious problem of all with the walkthrough. When informally walking through code with trusted and trusting teammates, the problem doesn't arise. In the formal review, however, the presenter is placed in front of a room of more or less strangers and told to explain a product that is personal work or, even worse, the work of teammates. Under these circumstances, it's hardly surprising that the producer often confuses explanations with justifications. Justifications tend to lead the walkthrough into discussions of style, motivation, and politics—all of which are fascinating, but not appropriate material for a product evaluation meeting.

Having a producer present—during *any* technical review—may lead to irrelevant discussions and defenses. Without strong leadership, these controversies easily turn the review into a destructive adversary proceeding, rather than a positive cooperative examination of the product.

In the walkthrough situation, the leader is relinquishing even more control of the meeting to the individual who is making the presentation. Unless the leader is particularly strong and experienced, the presenter not only presents the product but also leads its review—too much power to be placed on one person if we are to assure reliability of the product.

For example, if the presenter is more comfortable with one section of the product than another, the walkthrough presentation may be paced—consciously or unconsciously—so there is little time to review the questionable sections. Even when the astute leader detects this situation, controlling it is another matter. A hurried presenter tends to feel persecuted—not given a fair opportunity to represent the product. These feelings supply a built-in rationalization for rejecting any unfavorable outcome or issue raised by the review.

Conversely, some presenters skim over material they personally know well, thus lulling the review committee into passing on questionable matters. Again, the review leader may be able to lessen the problem, but possibly only at the risk of seeming to persecute the presenter.

Well, Enough of Advantages and Disadvantages! Do You Recommend Walkthroughs or Don't You?

It's always pleasant to be able to give simple yes or no answers to complex questions, but we can't bring ourselves to do it here. In considering the use of some form of walkthrough in your own situation, you will have to weigh the desirable characteristics against the questionable aspects.

The walkthrough discipline should guarantee that each line of the product is examined, but the presentation may lead people astray, so that the examination isn't uniformly reliable. The reviewers might accept a verbal statement of the presenter that could force the reviewers into the same (possibly incorrect) mental set of the presenter. Viewed from an incorrect perspective, almost any error can be made to seem correct—whether the perspective is introduced intentionally or by oversight.

One way to view the walkthrough is as part of a spectrum that has *lectures* on one end and *simple formal reviews* on the other. In the extreme case of the lecture, with no questions or comments allowed, the presumption is that the lecturer knows everything worth knowing about the subject, cannot make an error, and is facing an audience that has nothing to contribute about the subject. At the formal review end of the spectrum, the assumptions are somewhat reversed. There is no lecturer, but it is assumed that the producer could indeed make errors— the finding of which is the purpose for convening an "audience" of such knowledgeable people. To decide how much walking through to do, appraise your own situations according to how they fit these assumptions.

For instance, there may be a small team of producers in your installation that works in a language that other teams don't use. In order to get an objective code review committee, you'll have to select people who don't know the language in which the code is written. In this case, a number of installations have found a walkthrough most advantageous—though, of course, it can't be expected to provide the kind of detailed language level criticism that a more expert review group would produce.

Even in this case, the members of the review committee will gradually acquire a certain knowledge of the foreign language. At the same time the code will tend to become simplified to the point where it can be understood by nonexperts. Not only are these both excellent results in themselves, but they may lessen the need for walking through future code.

Aw, Come On! Give Us a Real Yes or No!

Okay, we give in. Any competent professional programmer should know how to conduct a walkthrough, know how to participate in one, and know enough to recognize when one might be valuable or dangerous, or both. If you haven't tried it, try it! If you haven't tried anything else, try doing without it!

Inspections

What Is an Inspection?

An inspection is a method of rapidly evaluating material by *confining attention to a few selected aspects, one at a time.* For example, the inspection could be used with material that is thought to be correct in detail, where the intention is to ensure that no global aspect has been overlooked. One might inspect an entire system design to assure that no major feature has been overlooked. The details of the design may well have been reviewed already by a small number of people, but the inspection is conducted to add the insurance of statistics of a large audience.

Inspections are quite commonly used as part of a feasibility study. For instance, one extremely large three-year project was implemented in several pieces at several locations around the world. After six months of work, representatives from each location gathered for an inspection/review. Each one brought only *completed material,* which they spent two weeks inspecting. This completed material was representative of the work thus far completed, so the review was an inspection in *two* dimensions.

Only selected aspects of a selected sample of all the pieces of work were examined.

Based on the findings of this series of inspections, the group reevaluated its plans and cost estimates (which turned out to be within one week of the ultimate delivery date and just within budget). The inspection had revealed what rate of rework and reliability the different producers could reasonably expect, so the six-month reestimate could be based on measured, rather than conjectured, information.

Are You Implying That Inspections Are Used Only for High Level Pieces of Work?

Not necessarily. The distinguishing characteristic is the *selection of aspects,* not which aspects are selected or what type of work is inspected. Inspections can be carried out on code, documentation, or any other level or type of material. For example, a small software house is producing an application for a valued client. The client has multiple installations and is very sticky about portability across different FORTRAN compilers on different machines. The client, therefore, insists that all purchased software meet a list of criteria that will provide, with assurance, the needed portability. A standards inspection, based on these criteria, is implemented as a supplement to the ordinary reviews the software house conducts to ensure correctness. The limited focus allows the participants to concentrate on one aspect of the material, which enables them to deal with more material in the same period.

How Is the Inspection Conducted?

Although some installations do not practice it, we recommend some form of advance preparation, if only to assure the stability of the material being inspected. The preparation will consume some time, but need not be to the level of depth and breadth of the ordinary formal review. By the time the inspection starts, each participant should at least be familiar with the overall structure of the product—otherwise the inspection is slowed down by a lot of fumbling and page turning. Each participant should also be informed of the primary area of concern— standards, modifiability, portability, coding errors of certain types, and so forth. When possible, the participants should be supplied with a checklist of items to be on the lookout for.

Inspections can last much longer than ordinary reviews, because only one aspect at a time can be completed and dismissed from consideration. When people are brought together from remote locations, there is an obvious advantage in being able to continue inspecting for several days at a time—or even weeks.

But CAUTION! No *session* of the inspection should be longer than the concentration span of the members. Inspections are difficult and exacting technical work, so a break every hour or so wouldn't be unreasonable.

What Kind of Report Does an Inspection Generate?

If a checklist is used, there may be a standard format in which to record issues. If not, the report should use some format that mentions each specific aspect that was addressed, even if no issues were raised on that point.

Most of the rules for an ordinary Review Summary and Issues List apply to an inspection. They should be drafted promptly, and all participants should be identified. Signatures are needed, as well as a consensus, but a separate consensus may be taken on each aspect. Participants are not accepting responsibility for the product as a whole, but only for the selected aspects being inspected.

Naturally, the report should be delivered while the

information is still timely. In a long inspection, it may be beneficial to issue reports day by day on aspects covered so far.

What Is the Role of the Leader in an Inspection?

The leader has the same responsibilities as in any formal technical review, but the emphasis may be more on interpersonal skills than technical skills. Because the inspection is more structured—following a fixed agenda of aspects to inspect—the leader may not need much technical ability. On the other hand, an inspection *may* consist of many more people than an ordinary review, so a good deal more conflict management may be required. For the same reason, very particular attention must be paid to the advance preparation of the physical arrangements; otherwise the inspection may run aground on details of personal inconvenience.

Round-Robin Reviews

What Is a Round-Robin Review?

In a walkthrough, the process is driven by the product being reviewed. In an inspection, the list of points to be inspected determines the sequence. In a plain review, the order is determined by the flow of the meeting as it unfolds. In contrast to these types, the various kinds of round-robin reviews emphasize a cycling through the various participants, with each person taking an equal and similar share of the entire task.

What Are the Advantages of This Approach?

Round-robin reviews are especially useful in situations where the participants are at the same level of knowledge, a level that may not be too high. It ensures that nobody will shrink from participation through lack of confidence, while at the same time guaranteeing a more detailed look at the product, part by part.

For the most part, round-robin reviews are an excellent way of raising the knowledge level of a relatively inexperienced group, especially one that lacks even one strong person who could "teach" the others. Therefore, they are often used in "bootstrapping" situations and also in various kinds of classroom work—when the instructor is wise enough to admit to ignorance.

Another advantage of round-robin reviews is that they avoid endless arguments about how the work should be split up for review, since in most cases any arbitrary method works well.

Can You Give an Example of a Round-Robin Review?

The most common round-robin review is similar to the child's game of musical chairs, though it's practiced in different installations under a variety of names. The "missing" chair is the leader's chair, which each person takes a turn occupying. In one variation, applied to code reviews, each person would take one line of code, or one paragraph, or some other small but arbitrary unit of work. If there are more than enough units to go around, the process is repeated until all units are assigned.

Each person in turn then goes to the front of the review and "walks through" the line or section of code. The entire group then reviews that unit, raising issues and recording them as in any other review. When that unit is finished, the next person takes the chair and the first joins the other reviewers. The process continues until the entire work has been reviewed.

Although the procedure may sound frivolous, the procedure encourages each participant to know some part of the product in detail and to learn programming skills through the process of in-depth analysis. If there is something that any participant doesn't understand, the round robin ensures that it will be explained during the review— or else raised as an issue. The principle at work is that the best way to learn about something is to try to teach others about it.

What Are Some Other Round-Robin Variations?

Musical chairs can be played with other division principles in place of the walkthrough idea. *Musical chairs inspections* can be carried out with each person taking one point of the checklist and becoming a specialist in the application of that point to the product. After a number of such sessions, each person should have had a chance to be a specialist in each checklist item—another fine educational tactic.

Another method of division for musical chairs is based on the idea of "feature chiefs." This is similar to the musical chair inspection in that the division is made on the basis of function, rather than form. In this case, though, the division is by *correct* function, rather than by possibly erroneous ones. The various features in a specification are allocated among the participants, each of whom must demonstrate how the work at hand contributes to that feature or leaves that feature unaffected, if that is its role. In a large, complex project, relatively permanent feature chiefs can be appointed, so that through time they become experts in their functional part of the specification. A feature chief review can always be used to supplement other reviews, if desired.

Isn't It a Disadvantage of Round-Robin Reviews That a Single Person Is Responsible for One Part, Functional or Otherwise?

It can be, which is one reason the reviews must be held in public. It's *not* a round-robin review if, for instance, we send each feature chief a copy of the design document and ask for acceptance of the design for that feature. In that quite commonly practiced method, we have no way of knowing whether the signer put in fifty hours of work or simply initialed the cover letter without examining the contents. In the round-robin review, each reviewer must present a reasoning process that will *convince* the others that the particular part or function is of acceptable quality.

Nevertheless, it *is* dangerous to depend too much on a single mind. It's awfully easy to convince people of an incorrect method of reasoning, which is why several forms of *redundant round robins* are used.

What Are Redundant Round Robins?

One example is what Harlan Mills calls a *speed review*. The work is divided into equal parts in some fashion, after which each individual spends a short time—say three minutes—studying each part and making notes of issues. At the end of the interval, the work units are passed around the room, with sufficient intervals being scheduled to give the desired level of redundancy.

In Mills' original description of the speed review, each participant reviewed each piece of work—in that case, one proposed solution to some classroom exercise. The object there was to feed back to each producer a series of independent impressions of the individual's work, but a speed review is very useful for certain other tasks.

For instance, suppose we want to find out if a particular module is easily understandable for maintenance. By dividing the module into pieces and speed reviewing each piece, we can collect the first impressions of half a dozen people. These impressions, taken together, will give us a much more reliable estimate of the readability of the code than we could get from any one person. Speed reviews of this type are also very effective at detecting certain types of bug—the kind that, if it isn't seen in the first glance, will probably never be seen, once the mind gets set in a certain way. With five first glances, there's five times the chance of one of them catching it.

On the other hand, speed reviews are obviously superficial if used for certain kinds of analysis. In the general type of review we have been portraying, everyone is supposed to have examined the material rather deeply before the review. This is also a round robin, in a sense, with essentially no time limit. The problem with an untimed round robin is that people, in the press of events, may devote widely different amounts of time to the review task. In many cases, a substandard preparation will be exposed by a competent review leader.

Another form of round robin controls the devotion of time to the review by keeping the reviewers within sight of one another in one place for the entire period of studying the product. This "big room" technique is often used for design reviews, especially high level reviews of large systems. Many organizations seem to have invented this technique independently, giving it names such as "circus," "war room," "merry-go-round," and "nobody leaves the room." A large, comfortable room is dedicated to the review. All the design documents are posted on the walls of the room in some meaningful sequence. In one worldwide network, the walls represented the four quadrants of the globe, so that reviewers could go around the world by walking around the room.

Participants are "locked in" the room to wander about studying the system in any manner they choose. The locking in can sometimes be quite extreme, with food brought in and bathroom passes being issued only one at a time. This circus technique, as we will call it, can be especially good at exposing systemwide dependencies or oversights. Participants freely discuss issues with one another, with no attempt to have everyone in the same discussion. In some circumstances, as many as twenty-five or thirty reviewers can be in the room at one time. Eventually, each participant presents a list of notes, which are discussed and consolidated into an issues report.

With large numbers of people, there will certainly be a diversity of points of view, but it may be wise to combine the circus with some explicit assignments, such as features or errors or some other checklist items. One criticism of this technique is that if a system requires such a review, it can't be very well designed in the first place. Certainly with a true top-down approach, it shouldn't be necessary to have so much complexity at any one level. It would be too bad, though, if the technique disappears, because it's an awful lot of fun.

Instead of putting a single design through the circus technique, we can use another variant of the big room technique to make a simultaneous review of several alternate designs or specifications. As in an art show, the reviewers circulate freely, examining the alternatives in any order or manner they desire. At the end of a preset time, or when all agree, the reviewers consolidate their views in some fashion and render a judgment on the alternatives. In some "art shows," the purpose is to pick a "winner," but more often the art show is better used to gather a great deal of information in a concentrated period—information that will be used in a later, calmer meeting to reduce the number of alternatives under consideration.

It All Sounds Rather Chaotic to Me. How Can It Be Kept Under Control?

It's important that the rules of the particular round robin be understood by all participants. If they are, the chaos is to some extent only an illusion. A tremendous amount of information is being processed in a concentrated period, which keeps the level of excitement and interest high. Some people would argue that the effectiveness of round robins is merely an artifact of this excitement, fun, and humor. They could be right. On the other hand, only a few trolls would object to having a good time, if the job gets done effectively as a result.

Let's assume that the time is acceptable. We still have the problem that most people *hate* to sit all alone in their offices studying the details of some thick document. It's boring—as well as being error prone and slow. In our opinion, the major contribution of round-robin reviews is the creation of an atmosphere of interest and enthusiasm for the review work. Once that atmosphere is established, we've got to get better reviews than those produced by the circulation method.

Review Teams

What Is the Distinction Between a Review Committee and a Review Team?

The distinction is the same as between any team and committee. Fundamentally, a team is a group of people who

1. Have worked together with common responsibility in the past;
2. Continue to work together with common responsibility at present—and that responsibility is their *major* responsibility; and
3. Have a reasonable expectation of continuing to work together and share responsibility in the future.

Typical committees deviate from these characteristics in several ways. There may be no past experience with one another to draw upon, so that many interpersonal games have to be worked out during the committee

251

meetings or avoided through the use of some "rules of order"—hence, one of the major reasons for *formality* in reviews. When it happens that the members of a particular committee *have* worked together extensively in the past, they may begin to take on some of the characteristics of a team. For instance, their meetings may become less and less formal, without losing effectiveness by getting tangled up in games.

On the other hand, a team just starting out doesn't have this past. They're really a team in name only, unless and until they get past the game-playing stage. Even so, they have something that most committees don't have. First of all, their common goal is of major importance to them, rather than being a side issue to their main job. This shared sense of importance, once it truly is shared, adds a seriousness of purpose to the team that is frequently lacking in committee work.

In many ways, it is the shared *future* that most distinguishes a team from a committee. Team members realize that they are going to have to live with one another after the present business is ended. This realization smooths over numerous interpersonal problems that can prove so disruptive when the members don't care what happens tomorrow. On the other hand, team members sometimes *delay* true team formation by excessive politeness—but that's another story for another book.

Is a Quality Assurance Group an Example of a Review Team?

It can be, if it meets the criteria given above. One of the most commonly practiced types of review is conducted solely by personnel from quality assurance, reviewing the work of others. If the quality assurance group is large, however, members may find themselves collected in a different combination for each review, which may prevent true team formation.

What Are the Advantages and Disadvantages to Having a Permanent Team Devoted Solely to Reviews?

The principal advantages are specialization and teamwork. With the amount of practice a specialization team gets, they rapidly develop strong instinctive skills as well as effective explicit procedures. As they work together as a team, they learn to build upon each person's strongest points, compensate for each person's weakest points, and educate themselves in areas where the entire team is weak.

The principal disadvantages are directly related to these advantages. All the experience the review team is getting is *not* being shared with anyone else, which eliminates a valuable advantage of reviews. As the team develops a team spirit, a we-they dichotomy may develop that can prove most destructive to project or installation goals. This division will be made all the stronger when there are people whose work is reviewed by others, but who never do any reviewing themselves. Even worse, more than a few full-time reviewers lose their empathy with producers and assume a stance of superiority.

We feel that this last disadvantage is the worst of all and bad enough to disqualify full-time reviewers as a recommended procedure. The principle to follow is this:

> **Avoid using technical reviewers who are themselves "above" review.**

Then What About Users Acting as Reviewers?

The user is not a "technical" reviewer, in most instances. The reviewer participates as an "expert" in what the user wants, a role it would be hard for anyone else to fill. The important thing is to avoid creating a "reviewer class," which will tend to place itself "above" the people whose work is being reviewed. When this happens, those reviewed start discounting the worth of the review, which is exactly why we got managers out of the review cycle to begin with.

*Yes, But Our Particular Customer Is a Government
Agency, with Its Own Technical People. Part of Our
Contract Says That They Will Review the Technical
Material at All Levels and Have the Right of Disapproval.
What Can We Do About That?*

What you can do is not take on such contracts. In our experience, outside technical people are an incredible pain in the lower anatomy. Why? Not because they are government employees, but because they are in a position of authority with no responsibility whatsoever. In individual cases, such a reviewer may be so personable as not to be utterly discounted by the producers, but the position is almost impossible to fill properly. If you're nice enough not to be resented, you probably won't say anything bad about the product, no matter how bad it is.

To make such a relationship work, the user must accept the responsibility for specifying *what* is to be done, but *not how* it is to be done. Otherwise you're courting unceasing trouble of the nastiest kind throughout the life of the project.

*I Can See the Principle, But Our Client Is Going to Take
Over the Software Maintenance Responsibility After We
Deliver It. Doesn't That Give Them the Right to Review
How It Is Done as Well?*

Don't mistake our meaning. The customer has the *right* to criticize *any* part of the work. On the other hand, you have the right to walk out on such a customer or refuse to do business in the first place. Try taking your car into a garage for a tuneup and standing over the mechanic criticizing every step being done. Then you'll understand the reaction to criticism coming from someone who's above criticism.

If the customer is going to take over maintenance, it would be wise to integrate *some* of the would-be maintenance personnel into your development effort. They can learn more this way than in any amount of formal training, especially by participating in reviews. Because they will be, in some sense, part of the development group, they will also be subject to reviews of their work, which should short-circuit the resentment.

But We Can't Do That with Our Customer, Yet They Still Insist on Reviewing Our Technical Work as We Do It. What Do You Suggest?

We really don't know how to handle that situation in any foolproof way. You've set up a very, very touchy situation, so the best we can advise is that your review leaders receive special training in handling interpersonal squabbling. You may survive. Others have, but it's never been especially pleasant.

Yet Elsewhere in This Handbook You Recommend Reading the Code from Purchased Software. Doesn't That Make You the User on the Other Side of the Fence?

Not really, because you are not sitting in a review with the producers. They've already made their product and believe it to be ready for the open market. If you reject it, that's a problem for them, but not for you. It's already done, and the producers will probably ignore any of your opinions fed back to them.

If you're *contracting* for custom-built software, that's another matter. You should choose your vendor carefully, using reviews of their existing work to help you assess their professional standards. But once you decide they're up to the level you require, then you're going to have to trust them to do the work to your specifications. Be sure that you *specify* such things as maintainability in measurable ways, so you can review explicitly whether or not the work meets the specifications. See *Software Metrics* (Gilb, 1977) for some ideas on how this can be done. But don't hang over their shoulders, or they'll get back at you in some way you won't appreciate.

If Your Opinion Is Correct, Then How Can We Have Review Teams?

There are lots of other approaches besides having a group of gurus spending all their time criticizing the work of others. You can have specialists in reviewing who don't spend *all* of their time at it, so they have time to produce work that others can review. As we've suggested elsewhere, it may be most beneficial to have a team of review *leaders*, especially when getting started. Just don't let them get into the business full time on a permanent basis. As soon as a substantial number of leaders are trained, keep the review jobs circulating so everyone benefits and everyone accepts the judgments of the review committees.

If you refer back to our definition of what makes a team, you'll find nothing about the team having to be together full time, but only that they share a major responsibility. After football practice, and out of season, the members of a football team aren't usually together in one gang. Their team activities are part of their total activity, but not their only activity. Similarly, we can form long-lived review teams whose members have other major commitments elsewhere, yet still are sufficiently committed to the review task to become a true team.

Can You Give an Example of Such "Part-Time" Review Teams?

One very effective approach is to select a team of reviewers for each project at its inception. The review team can be all "outsiders" to that project or a mixture of outsiders and producers. These outside reviewers are producers on *other* projects, so that although being a reviewer is a major responsibility, it's not their *sole* responsibility.

This type of review team brings the advantage of continuity to the project, as they move from specification reviews through design reviews to code reviews. They can develop the effectiveness of a team, yet retain some of the broad view and objectivity of outsiders. Many installations tend to gravitate to this pattern simply because it seems sensible to pick people for a design review who already know the specifications and someone for a code review who has previously become familiar with the design. Crossman (1977) describes how his bank adopted this pattern explicitly, as an adaptation of several other review techniques, including inspections, with measured results comparable to other approaches. It's difficult to tell from his data, however, whether the one serious potential danger of this approach has been manifest—whether or not the inspection team (or other review team) gradually becomes too closely identified with the product to provide fresh insights in successive reviews.

A Collection of Review Tactics

What Do You Mean by a Review Tactic?

Tactics are understood in contrast to strategies. A strategy is the grand plan, whereas tactics are the smaller plans that may contribute to the achievement of the grand plan. The walkthrough and the inspection are overall strategies for conducting reviews, but so is the idea of conducting the review under no special advance discipline. Within each of these strategies, there are a number of useful tactics that can be applied optionally. In the remainder of this section, we shall list a potpourri of such tactics that we have gathered in reviews all around the world.

The Devil's Advocate

John Stuart Mill, in his essay *On Liberty*, had this to say about the idea of "the devil's advocate":

The most intolerant of churches, the Roman Catholic Church, even at the canonization of a saint, admits, and listens to, a "devil's advocate." The holiest of men, it appears, cannot be admitted to posthumous honors, until all that the devil could say against him is known and weighed.

The enshrinement of a program, say, in the installation library, has much in common with the enshrinement of a saint in the Church Hagiography. In particular, it's especially difficult for someone to stand up and say negative things without those things being ascribed to his or her character, rather than to the character of the product under review.

To overcome the natural reluctance to criticize certain saintly products, some people find the "one positive and one negative" tactic inadequate. In such instances, it may prove useful to adopt the concept of the devil's advocate. One person is assigned the task, when the review materials are passed out, of making the strongest possible case *against* the product. The devil's advocate doesn't have to be "fair," "compassionate," or "nice" in any way, but it's understood by all that it's the devil speaking, not the person, so no stigma is attached to having produced an argument that didn't hold water.

In the review, the devil's advocate argues the devil's case. The rest of the review group, like the College of Cardinals, must convince themselves on each negative point raised by the devil's advocate: Is this a real issue or not? Their decision becomes the review decision, with the devil's advocate not participating in the consensus.

The devil's advocate tactic can be particularly useful when the greatest danger is not in a collection of small errors, but in some "systemic" flaw in the overall approach. In those cases, an accumulation of individual negative points may simply not address the underlying problem. To do that, a well-reasoned argument must be constructed in advance covering the product as a whole. By commissioning a devil's advocate, we increase the chance that such a systemic problem will be turned up and argued effectively. Most often, the tactic is found in design reviews or in code reviews where major design decisions have been left to the programmers producing the code.

Be cautioned that the devil's advocate approach is not the easiest tactic to apply. The major problem is forgetting that the advocate is merely *pretending* to be an agent of the devil. Sometimes it is the review group that forgets the pretense and accuses the advocate of impure motives. Worse, though, is when the advocate forgets or actually *has* impure motives. Be sure to select someone who has no possible self-interest in either a positive or a negative outcome of the review, who is a good actor, and who has a thicker than normal skin.

Bebugging

The question of evaluating the reviews themselves has always been a nagging one. The *bebugging* tactic (Weinberg, 1971, Gilb, 1977) is a way of testing the reviewers as they are testing the product. The usual bebugging procedure is for the producing team to leave some number of known problems (bugs) in the product submitted for review. The producers make a list of these known problems and seal the list in an envelope, which is placed on the table in plain sight as the review begins. When the review is finished, the leader opens the envelope and compares the producers' list with the Issues List generated by the review. If the reviewers have caught all these issues, there is some evidence that the review was thorough. If some issues went undetected or were dismissed as not serious, then the quality of the review may be questioned.

In order to achieve naturalness in the bugs, it's usually best for the producing team to save certain problems they have found during their informal reviewing. It turns out to be very difficult to create "natural" bugs that aren't trivial to find in a review. If the producers think they can do it, though, you have to let them try, so they'll learn for themselves how hard it is.

The bebugging procedure, if it uses natural bugs, serves an important educational function. In actual training, several independent reviews of the same bebugged product can be performed, after which all Issues Lists are compared with one another and with the bebugging list. The important result is learning why issues were missed, not discovering who's the "best" reviewer.

To keep the procedure honest, sometimes the producers should "bluff" by putting a blank sheet of paper in the envelope. When the process is carried out in the right spirit, everyone looks forward to opening the envelope as a time of laughter and good natured kidding. Be careful, though, if you see any sign of resentment on either side. The bebugging technique, practiced in this way, is far from precise enough to be used as a way of evaluating the review group in a single session. It's main use, we feel, is as a motivator. Everyone likes to show up well when the envelope is opened.

The Money Bowl

Another common review problem is the producer who can't keep quiet during the review. One solution is to keep producers out of the review, but that's not always feasible or desirable. When troubled by a talkative producer, some installations have used the *money bowl* tactic. At the start of the review, or as soon as the problem is recognized, a small bowl or cup is placed in the center of the conference table. Each time that the producer—in the judgment of the leader—speaks out of turn, the producer must pay a predesignated fine to the bowl. (A quarter is a typical amount in the United States, but with inflation, who knows what will be appropriate in the future.)

At the end of the review, there may be a substantial sum in the bowl. In Australia, the custom is to take the money down to the local pub and buy reviewers and reviewed beers until the money runs out. Then the reviewers buy the rest of the beers for the producers. In other places, some other libation might prove more suitable, but the spirit should be the same—a friendly gathering after the review with medicinal potions to heal any wounds of the review.

The use of the bowl, of course, helps the leader control the defensive tendencies of the producer by making the producer aware of any tendency to interrupt when not asked a direct question. Some leaders prefer to use the penalty on *anyone* who speaks out of turn, if general control of the meeting is a problem. The amount should be large enough to pay for a meaningful amount of liquid refreshment, but not so large as to pose a personal hardship. If you have an independently wealthy producer, the system may break down, for the producer may see the penalty merely as the price of an on-stage ticket. Mostly, though, the money bowl acts as a humorous nudge to the producer's conscience, so a good time is had by all.

The Alarm

Review leaders often have difficulty enforcing time limits on speechifying. It's difficult to interrupt somebody who's all wrapped up in a presentation, but sometimes it has to be done to keep the review flowing. A good technique for timid leaders or aggressive speakers is to use a small alarm.

The little alarms that are sold for timing parking meters are quite satisfactory for this purpose. So are kitchen timers, if they don't tick too loud. The group agrees on time limits for various presentations or comments before the reviewing starts. The leader then sets the alarm at the beginning of each person's contribution. When the alarm goes off, the person must stop within, say, thirty seconds—a limit that is also set into the alarm.

The alarm technique works because everyone realizes that the alarm is impersonal and fair. Without the alarm, a long-winded speaker cannot believe that three minutes have already elapsed because "it didn't seem like three minutes to me." Be sure, though, to set the alarm again for the windup period. Some speakers have been known to take half an hour to do a thirty-second wrapup.

Issues List Bloodhound

It can be a pain to reconvene a review just to go over an explicit list of issues that were to be resolved. On the other hand, if it falls on the review leader to follow through on the Issues List without review, there can be problems, such as:

1. The leader may not want the responsibility, and thus press for another full review; or
2. There will be nobody to check up on the leader's checking up on the issues list.

A useful tactic for avoiding these problems and sharing the workload is to appoint an Issues List bloodhound whenever the review group decides that there shouldn't be need for a further review to check the issues. The bloodhound should be a person who is as knowledgeable as possible about the product, but shouldn't, of course, be from the producing team. In effect, the review group is choosing the bloodhound as their representative, delegating the full powers and responsibility of the group.

After the review, the bloodhound does whatever is necessary to ensure that the Issues List is completely and correctly handled. The leader should follow up on the bloodhound and also provide whatever political punch the bloodhound may need to fulfill this mission. As a last resort, if the bloodhound cannot get the issues handled, the leader should reconvene the review, with a report to management on the changed review status.

The Stand-up Review

Everyone knows the review member who cannot stop talking. Sometimes a whole department is inflicted by this disease, and reviews go on interminably. Even if you come together to review the minor modifications to a previously reviewed product, you can't seem to get out in less than a full two hours.

One of our clients adapted a technique from an African tribal council. Anyone can speak as long as that person remains standing on one leg. In the adaptation, the entire review was conducted in a room without table or chairs. People quickly tired of listening to harangues when they couldn't use the time to catch up on sorely needed rest, and review times plummeted.

We're not sure the original African idea isn't worth trying, too, for anyone who wants to make a speech. It would be particularly useful for preventing a walkthrough from becoming a "walkover." We call this approach the "hopthrough."

Tables

Some of our clients swear that round tables prevent reviews from becoming dominated by the person who happens to be at one head or the other. Other clients swear by the U-shaped arrangement, with the recorder stationed in the opening in the U and the leader at the base. We even have some clients who refuse to use tables in a review and require that each participant face the other unprotected by a barricade.

Informal Reviews

Is There Ever an Advantage to Reviewing Code
Informally, Rather Than Going Through All These
Procedures?

Of course there is. It takes time (and usually costs money) to bring people together for a formal review, so any process that removes problems more cheaply in advance of the review is going to be worthwhile. Ideally, the formal reviews would only very rarely raise serious problems. That's the way they function best, as a check on the actual production procedures. If too many problems reach the review, it will begin to cost more to review than to produce.

How Are Informal Reviews Conducted?

Because they *are* informal, there's no set way to do them. Perhaps the best we can do is give you some guidelines we developed with one client who wanted something to put in a procedures manual. We've extracted some relevant sections from the heading *Team Programming: Informal Code Reading.*

1. Conditions

The rule here is "earlier is better than later." Offering programs to be read only when there is an insoluble "bug" is an inefficient, anxiety producing, and not very effective procedure. Our objective is to have the major benefits of informal code reading before code reaches the computer or even gets into machinable form.

When WRITER (see below) has the *paper program* ready for transcription into machinable form, that is the time for informal code reading. After transcription, there is already an "investment" in the code which will make it harder to modify.

The size of the code is determined not by some number of lines, or some number of specification pages, but by the amount of *effort it takes to review it.* The WRITER should pass to the reviewer a "chunk" of code that can be reviewed critically in *no more than one hour of concentrated work.* For difficult code, this could be 5 lines; for easy code it could be 100 lines. For inexperienced readers, the amount will be smaller than for experienced readers, but do not take advantage of the chance of having a *very* experienced reader. Don't exceed the one-hour capacity of the average programmer who will have to read it when it is finished and in maintenance.

2. Team Member Roles: PROGRAM WRITER

The writer's job is to create the original version of the *paper program,* starting from the specifications transmitted by the Leader. After producing the paper program, the writer waits for the *Reader* to perform an informal review, after which they meet to produce an agreed upon version of the paper program—or to agree to disagree. If there is disagreement, the writer's job is to continue meeting with subsequent readers until agreement is reached or the approach is scrapped.

The following are some guidelines to follow when acting in the role of writer:

1. You must not accept a writing job if the specifications are incomplete or unclear. In this case, you must first

request completion or clarification of the specs before accepting the role.

2. If clarification or completion of specifications is required, you may work informally with the source of the specifications to resolve the problems. The same informal conferencing should take place concerning specification problems that turn up after the job is accepted.

3. Although the conference with the spec writer may be informal, the results of the conference *must* be written into the spec and signed by interested parties. Otherwise, you should *not* accept changes to the spec.

4. In some situations, the spec may be passed to you through a formal specification review. In that case, you must sit as a member of that review group.

5. Once an acceptable spec is obtained, your job is to produce a paper program that meets the objectives in the spec. Be sure that you understand the relative importance of different objectives! Don't take it for granted that "efficiency" must be in every program, or that it must not. If you have to trade off objectives, and objectives are not clearly weighted as to importance, call a conference with the source of the spec.

6. Your paper program is to meet the standards of the installation and the project. It is your job to know those standards.

7. Your paper program must be delivered by the set deadline, or else you must inform the Leader as far in advance as possible that you will not be able to produce it.

8. There is no reason to keep your problems to yourself. *Ask* questions rather than guess at answers. If you feel you need a better way to do something, ask someone on the team. If you are unsure of the spec, ask the Leader or the source. If you are unsure of a standard, look it up or ask someone who knows—but don't take their guess for an answer.

9. When you deliver the paper program to the Leader, it should be—as far as you know—correct and demonstrably correct, using the program structure and the test packet you have developed. Any additional documentation must help the reader understand its

correctness, but in general, strive for a program that is self-documenting.

10. When the paper program is turned over to the Leader, you and the Leader should pick a *Reader* to make the informal review. In general, the Reader will be someone on the team whose skills, experience, and thinking patterns are complementary to yours, so as to give the program the best possible test.

11. While the Reader is working on the paper program, you are to be as helpful as possible—but try not to argue for the program where it should argue for itself. You and the Reader are part of the same team, and any problem caught in this stage is not going to be known by anyone but you two. Remember, this is the cheapest and most effective time to catch problems.

12. When the Reader has finished, the two of you meet informally and hammer out a consensus version of the paper program. If you two can agree on this version, it becomes the program of *both* of you.

13. If you cannot agree on some points, you must confer with the Leader, who together with you two will choose a *Rereader* to review the code once again. At the end of the rereview, the three of you will meet and try to create a consensus version.

14. If the three of you cannot agree on a consensus version, the Leader will take the job away and reassign it, or go back to the source to decide if it should be changed or withdrawn.

15. Once there is a consensus version, it becomes the work of the *entire* team. Other team members may wish to review it in addition to the reviews specified here, and they should be encouraged to do so, since they might be held responsible for its quality. The review process specified here is to be considered as a *minimum* informal review, and not to prevent other interested team members from helping produce reliable programs to the specifications.

16. Once the paper program has been accepted by the team, responsibilities of the Writer cease, as such. The Writer *may* be chosen as a *Tester,* but not necessarily.

3. Team Member Roles: READER

READER is chosen by LEADER and WRITER to make a critical review of the paper program produced by WRITER. READER'S responsibilities may be summarized by saying that after the review has been completed and the paper program has been accepted for Transcribe and Test, READER and WRITER should be indistinguishable as far as being "author" of the code. If READER cannot accept responsibility for the paper program at the conclusion of the review process, then Reread is dictated.

Specific activities of READER to meet this goal include:

1. checking for completeness of the paper program
2. checking for conformity to specifications, standards, and general stylistic practices
3. listing (informally) all potential difficulties discovered in (1) and (2)
4. working independently of WRITER as much as possible as if this were maintenance some years later when WRITER was not available
5. not following (4) *too* rigidly, but noting which questions could not be answered without recourse to WRITER
6. *not* rewriting the code to hand to WRITER and say "this is the way *I* would have done it!"
7. meeting with WRITER to resolve questions raised in the review—*this* is the time for any rewriting to be done

Once this point is reached, READER and WRITER become equivalent, and READER participates in points (8), (9), and (10) of WRITER'S responsibilities as an "alter-ego." If READER and WRITER cannot agree at this point, their disagreement is precisely equivalent to *indecision* on the part of a single programmer—so Reread is indicated.

4. Team Member Roles: LEADER

LEADER is the person responsible to the outside for transmittal of the specification and return of the eventual working program. LEADER could be a "chief programmer" or a leader chosen by the team, or any other sort of person able to fulfill the following responsibilities:

1. communicate with the people supplying the specification in cases where it is found inadequate or unclear (though WRITER or READER may do this informally once authorized by LEADER)
2. select WRITER and transmit specifications
3. monitor the passage of time in case WRITER loses track of time available
4. select (with WRITER) the person to be READER
5. meeting with READER and WRITER to discuss the final result of the informal review
6. deciding (with READER and WRITER) on the next step to be followed—Reread or Transcribe and Test.
7. if Reread, selecting (with READER and WRITER) the REREADER
8. if Transcribe and Test, signing the necessary authorizations so that the paper program may pass into machinable form and get test runs.

Informal Reviews Sound Like a Good Idea for Our Installation, but Should We Start Them Before or After Formal Reviews?

If you start formal reviews first, informal reviews will undoubtedly spring up in some form at just about the same time. Once people know their work is going to be public property, they usually decide they'd like to have friends look at it before strangers. Our own preference is to start formal reviews with the full understanding and consent of all levels of management. What goes on *within* the programming team, on the other hand, is the internal business of the team, so they may start informal reviews whenever they want. If the reviews are indeed informal, there won't be any way to enforce any particular practice of them anyway.

On the other hand, if management for some reason is slow to take up the idea of formal reviews, the team shouldn't wait for them. Quality is useful at any time.

What Should We Look For in Informal Reviews?

Pretty much the same things you would look for in formal reviews, to the extent that you are qualified to do so. Some parts of the formal review may require the participation of a technical expert, a user, or some other special person who would be hard to get into an informal review. On the other hand, if you have some definite question for such a special person, there's no need to wait for a rejection in the formal review to get your information. The idea of the formal review is *not to prevent* people from communicating outside of the review itself, but merely to *assure the quality* of the communication that *has* taken place.

You may find the checklists supplied in Part F useful for informal reviews as well as for formal reviews, though they might be interpreted differently.

Do You Mean That the Informal Review Is Pretty Much a Rehearsal for the Formal Review?

Not at all, although we have seen it used that way when some manager decided to sit in on formal reviews to "see who was doing the bad work."

Then What's the Real Difference Between Them?

There are many differences, so we're not sure which one is the "real" difference. For one thing, the informal review is among "family," so the formal rules and regulations shouldn't be needed—though good manners help even in family matters.

A second difference, of course, is that the results are not reported out to anyone from an informal review, which lowers the level of tension considerably.

A third difference is the "presumption of guilt."

In a formal review, the "expected" state of affairs must be an essentially correct and good piece of work. Otherwise, it wastes everyone's time. The only things wrong with the work should be such things as:

1. Small standards violations;
2. Big oversights caused by insufficient project overview;
3. Clerical errors, as in transcription of documents; or
4. A very few direct blunders, if any.

In an informal review, on the other hand, the reviewer is expected to be a *reviser,* actively participating in getting the thing to the state suitable for a formal review. The formal review can thus be looked upon as a check or review on the informal review process, which itself is more of a revision process. The programming cycle thus involves a series of repetitions of the cycle of WRITE-REVIEW-REVISE. The informal review comprises both REVIEW and REVISE, while the formal review is REVIEW only.

PART F

Types of Materials Reviewed

Varieties of Reviews and Their Origins

SECTION

1

We've Heard About Code Reviews, but Are There Other Materials That Can or Should Be Reviewed?

It's not surprising that most of the public discussion of technical reviews has thus far focused on the varieties of code reviews, rather than on reviews of other materials. In the early history of the software development business, we were primarily concerned with code accuracy, because the coding seemed to be the major stumbling block to reliable product development. As our coding improved through the use of more reasonable programming languages, structured programming, top-down implementation, organized testing techniques, and especially through code reviews, we began to see other problems that had been obscured by the tangle of coding errors.

At first we noticed that many of the difficulties were not coding errors but design errors, so more attention has come to be devoted to reliable design techniques—including *design reviews*. As these techniques begin to be effective at clearing up design problems, the whole cycle starts again, for we notice that design is no longer the major hurdle.

In many of these cases, we never clearly understood the problem the design was attempting to solve. We were

277

solving a *situation,* not a problem. Currently, increased emphasis is being placed on the analysis process, which becomes the next area of application of technical reviews—specification reviews. When we institute these reviews, we find that the user may not understand the problem and has no way of communicating what is clear or vague about the problem statement.

After Design and Specification Reviews, Are There Further Stages in the Review Process?

First of all, if your system development cycle involves several *levels* of specifications and/or designs, then there should be several levels of specification and/or design reviews. The specifications and the design represent the various *forms* the system takes at different points in its life cycle. So does the code, which we also review. If we want to pass from initial conception to final implementation without allowing the system to escape from the control of our review process, then each and every form of the system must be reviewed.

System *documentation* is certainly one important form the system takes. Although it may include all or part of specifications, design, and code, these portions will not usually comprise the entire set of documentation. Consequently, additional parts of the documentation will have to be put through to *documentation reviews.* Moreover, it may be necessary in some instances to review specifications, design, or code in terms of their adequacy as system documentation, as opposed to their adequacy as working documentation during development.

We Write Code in a High Level Language. Do We Have to Review the Object Code as Well as the Source Code?

Because the translation from source to object is a *mechanical* process, we may be able to rely upon the compiler for accurate translation and therefore not review the object code. On the other hand, some projects (such as compiler development projects) are forced to perform *manual* translations from source to object. In such a case, it would be foolish to review specifications, designs, and source code and then neglect to review the error-prone translation to object code.

In between error-free compilation and error-prone manual translation lies the usual reality—a compiler that may, on occasion, display some erroneous behavior. Certainly, if a project involves using a compiler with which the installation is not familiar, it would be well to review *some* of the translations the compiler makes from source to object. This principle can be extended to any *software tool* whose performance may influence the performance of the system itself, as we shall discuss under the subject of *Tool Reviews*.

What Role Do Test Data Play in Each of These Reviews?

Test data (as well as test results, and test plans generally) play a double role in reviews. Each form of the system will ordinarily be accompanied by some sort of test plan that forms a part of the system at that stage of development. This test plan will therefore be reviewed along with the rest of the material. As the system moves from one form to another, the role of the test plan is to assure that the translation is correct. For instance, does the design satisfy the specifications in all details or has something been overlooked? The test plan accompanying the design is supposed to be an adequate proof, when used with a review of the internal structure of the design, that the design has indeed satisfied the specification.

Therefore, the test plan is part of the review of each form of the system and must also be reviewed *itself* for its own adequacy, as we shall discuss under *Test Plan Reviews*.

So Far, All You Have Discussed Is Reviewing Products
Directly Connected with the System. Are There Other Items
That Should Be Reviewed?

Our feeling is that the review is the most powerful—and ultimate—quality assurance method for anything that is bound for human consumption—especially in the software area. Therefore, we suggest that *anything people are going to use* during the software development-installation-maintenance cycle be reviewed for clarity and accuracy.

For instance, educational materials are a prime candidate for review, as we shall discuss under *Reviews of Training Materials*. Numerous systems that have looked good on paper have failed because the people involved were not adequately trained—something much less likely to happen when training materials are explicitly reviewed as part of the system development cycle.

Yes, But Even Educational Products Are Products. Are
There Nonproducts That Are Reviewed?

We appear to be having some trouble communicating over the word "product." Every worthwhile thing that is produced has at least one user. Therefore, in one sense of the word, everything is a product. Can you provide an example of a nonproduct, in your sense of the word?

Yes, I Was Actually Thinking Explicitly of Standards,
Which Seem to Float Somewhere in the Air Above
Everything Else. Do You Consider Standards to Be
Products, and Therefore Reviewable?

Most certainly yes, though we can see some part of the confusion. Standards, like test plans, are at least *implicit* in every other review, so there is some question as to whether they need to be reviewed in their own right, in separate and distinct standards reviews. The answer depends on the particular circumstances, as we shall discuss under the topic of *Reviews of Procedures and Standards*.

How About Software Packages That We Buy from Outside Vendors?

Obviously, these are products too. Some of these are *tools,* while others are partial or complete application systems in themselves. To the extent that they are tools or systems, what we say about reviewing internally produced tools and systems will apply. On the other hand, there are special considerations in reviewing purchased software (or training, or any other product, for that matter). These will be discussed under the heading of *Tool and Package Reviews*.

I Think I'm Beginning to Get the Idea—Just About Anything Can Be Reviewed.

Right. If it's tangible, it can be reviewed. Hardware engineers have known this for years. They conduct formal reviews of hardware design and extend the principles of these reviews to other facets of the hardware development cycle.

The same concepts apply to software development. All tangible goods produced during the software effort should be reviewed. All such goods introduced into the cycle from outside should be reviewed, to assure equal quality with internally produced goods, since any weak link may destroy the chain. Of course, we have been talking at all times about *technical* reviews. Some parts of the system development process, such as vacation schedules, dress codes, or salary policies, do not have a significant technical component. Although such items can benefit from reviews, they *may* require only management participation. In such reviews, *political* considerations are often dominant, so entirely different disciplines are needed to keep the reviews productive. Although the participants in these *management reviews* might benefit from studying the disciplines used in conducting *technical reviews,* there is not much in common between the two activities, other than that in both reviews people gather together in a room to discuss a topic.

I'm Not Sure That I, or My Management, Understands the Difference Between Technical and Management Reviews. Can You Give Further Examples of the Distinction?

Ideally, the *technical* review concerns itself with establishing *facts,* while the *management* review merely uses such facts as input to a decision involving the application of *values.*

As one specific instance, consider the scheduling of vacations during a project. If vacations are to be scheduled wisely—so as not to disrupt a project by having critical people absent at critical times or by having critical people collapse from exhaustion at critical times—management must balance a variety of value-charged issues. All such discussions will be theoretical, however, if they aren't based on reliable, factual information about the current state of the project—the kind of information that management should have been receiving continuously from *technical* reviews.

Consider, for instance, the project that hasn't been reviewing the technical product, but merely issuing vacuous "All's Well," messages to management at regular intervals. Management will be unaware of what is critical—or even that anything *is* critical—and is likely to schedule vacations generously right at critical times. Through such examples, we can see that management reviews *involve* technical information, though they cannot be relied upon to *generate* it. That can be done only through properly conducted *technical* reviews of the products themselves—

reviews in which the technical expertise of the technical staff is used to create *fact in place of conjecture.*

Aren't There Some Areas in Which It's Difficult to Separate Management (Value) Issues from Technical (Factual) Issues?

Yes, absolutely. This difficulty places an important burden on project management to make the separation properly. It is all too easy to use the facade of a technical review to make values look like facts. Suppose, to take one of the most common cases, a project is nearing its deadline without nearing actual completion. The project manager, or some lower level manager, may be in serious trouble if the project, or subproject, is late. In *hopes* of having the project on time—because it is so important (a value)—the manager schedules a "technical" review of the status of the product. The manager sits in the room while the "review" is being conducted and chastises anyone who tries to indicate some fact that is not in accordance with the most optimistic view of the product's status. Soon, all flow of factual information is stilled, except for facts that support the manager's hope that the product is in good shape. The review report then provides the manager with a way of keeping upper management at bay a bit longer. When the day of reckoning finally arrives, the manager can use the review report to place the *blame for failure* on the technical staff. If only they had given some warning, the manager argues, steps would have been taken to ensure success, but if the technical people are going to cover up their failures, what can the poor manager do?

A strong manager can achieve this kind of job protection without actually attending the reviews, though it takes a little longer. All that is needed is consistent "punishment" of review groups that produce true, but unfavorable, review reports. After a while, the technical staff gets the message and stops reviewing properly.

A *good* manager, on the other hand, will always

want to have reliable information from the reviews, no matter how unpleasant that information may be to the manager's personal plans and desires. Using this information, the manager may decide on any one of a variety of courses, based on *values* applied to the facts, such as— come clean with upper management and plead for more time; conceal the facts and hope that something happens to extend the deadline; reveal *some* of the facts in hopes of getting more time and/or resources; use the facts to put pressure on the staff to increase their efforts; offer to resign; or simply retire to a monastic life. The *wisdom* of each choice is not a technical matter but a management matter, unless that choice is based on faulty technical information.

Functional Specification Reviews

*Why Are Specification Reviews Necessary, Since Our
Analysts Are Very Experienced at Writing Specifications?*

No matter how experienced your analysts or users may be, they are still human beings. In the past, specification problems may have gone unnoticed, concealed among the numerous design and coding problems. If you decide to undertake code reviews and design reviews without functional specifications reviews preceding them, you will probably experience what many of our clients experienced.

As they began to review designs, they had occasion to compare the designs with the original specifications. In doing so, they would notice a number of problems with the specifications themselves. Some failed to deal with all possible cases. Conversely, there were many "don't care" cases that were specified as if they were of primary importance. Designers were in the habit of guessing what was meant by ambiguous statements in the specification— sometimes correctly and sometimes not. Many specifications contained inconsistencies, with two or more parts contradicting one another.

As a result of these design reviews, such problems began to be brought to the attention of the users or analysts who checked with users. The results inevitably proved interesting, even when it was the design review that proved wrong. What had appeared illogical in the review was logical because of a constraint in the user's application. In such cases, the review process led to clearer supporting material for unusual circumstances in the specification.

In other cases, the analyst had misinterpreted what the user wanted, or the user had misinterpreted what was to be received from the system. In either case, it was a problem area that couldn't be resolved by the designers. In fact, we observed several cases where a specification review made the user aware of an inconsistency in the old system's way of carrying out the application. Long before receipt of the new computer system, the procedure was changed, resulting in a significant improvement in the user department's efficiency. What this example illustrates, of course, is the way that a review may turn up issues concerning some aspect of the system not currently "under review." We always allow for a Related Issue Report from any review, in order to capture this unexpected information bonus.

Who Should Attend a Specification Review?

The primary concern of the review is that the specification represents the desired system. Whoever has created the specification should have been either from the user organization or in close touch with that organization. In either case, the user should have a representative on the review committee. In the end, only the user can judge whether the system is satisfactory. When the analyst is attached to the data-processing function, someone else— actually from the user organization or at least totally familiar with user operations—should attend the review.

Similarly, someone on the review committee should represent the people who will *receive* the specification—

the designers. This representative will be needed to raise issues about parts of the specification that may prove too costly to implement or operate.

Other than these two sides—user and designer— the review committee should be made up of people as knowledgeable as possible about systems "similar" in some way to the system under review. This similarity could be in terms of function or in terms of the contemplated design approach or approaches. The important thing is to have a committee capable of raising issues overlooked in the specification.

In the Systems We Develop, There Are Multiple Users, with Different and Sometimes Contradictory Points of View About What the System Should Do. Who Gets Invited to the Review?

Before considering whom to invite, we should lay down some general principles. First of all, you must prevent, insofar as possible, the *technical* review from becoming a *political* review—that is, an arena in which the various user factions wrestle for control of the system. Keeping the review on track in this situation often involves invoking all the disciplines we have previously discussed. In particular, the review should concentrate on *errors*, because these are the least controversial aspect of the specification. If the various users cannot even agree on what is an error, it will indicate to the review leader that the specification is not ready for technical review. The review should then be adjourned and the specification passed back to the originators for resolution of the *political* problems.

Of course, not every issue can be clearly marked "political" or "technical." For instance, someone may assert that a particular function will be "too expensive" to implement. The review leader must press for a separation of the parts of this issue, as by:

1. Getting explicit estimates of the expense, along with the technical foundation for these estimates;

2. Recording "expense unknown" as an issue, in case there is controversy over the expense or in case an estimate would involve work outside the scope of the review;

3. Getting explicit statements of the value of the function to the users and then including these statements in the specification; and

4. Recording "value unknown" as an issue when users cannot immediately state the value of a function.

In this way, the leader breaks down the vague, qualitative statement, "too expensive," into an explicit comparison between cost and value. Or if the explicit comparison cannot be made, appropriate issues are raised concerning the specification.

That Seems Reasonably Clear, but You Still Haven't Said Who Gets Invited.

Sorry, but before discussing "who," we had to clarify the major problem to avoid—the political situation. Obviously, if some user faction is *not invited* to a review of the specification, then we cannot be sure that their point of view is represented, even as concerns "what is an error?" On the other hand, if there are more than a few user factions, we will have too many people in the review, and it will degenerate into name calling, apathy, or worse.

In some cases, not all users will have equal interest in all parts of the system or its specification. In that case, the material can be divided so that each user need deal only with relevant parts. Be careful, though, not to make premature judgments for the users as to *which* parts are relevant. The worst sort of specification error is to overlook a user's significant interest in some part of the system.

Where the division of interest is not *absolutely* clear, it may prove worthwhile to call a meeting of all user representatives to plan the review pattern—who is interested in what. In the end, it is the *user* who must decide what is of interest and what is not. It never pays, in the long run, to leave someone out who expresses an interest in some aspect of the system.

Satisfying the most suspicious users may involve some additional review time, but it's well worth the extra effort. *Never* try to save time by putting "just a couple more people" in the review.

I'm Not Sure I Understand What You Mean by a "User" or by a "User Faction." Can You Elaborate?

First of all, don't make the mistake of thinking that the *customer*—the one who's paying the bill—is the only user. The head of the affected department may sign the authorizations, but the clerk who will have to operate the terminals qualifies in many more ways as a user, particularly as concerns the specifications.

By "user faction," we mean a group of users whose interests are so similar that the entire group can reliably be represented by a single person or by a small group. It shouldn't be necessary to review the specifications with every one of the 250 input clerks, but it would certainly be wise to review the input portions with someone representative of this faction.

How Do You Identify All the Users and User Factions?

This is one of the most difficult questions encountered in specification writing. If the writers forget someone with a significant interest in the system, their forgetting indicates a part of the specification sorely in need of review. One good precaution is to circulate and post a memo announcing the scheduled reviews, with a request that omitted factions get in touch with the review leader.

Within one organization, it should be possible to develop a checklist of some of the user factions that might

otherwise be overlooked. Some of the common ones we
have encountered are:

1. Legal department—when there are government regulations involved, or contract dealings with suppliers
   or customers, or union affairs;
2. Auditors—almost any time money or other items of
   value are involved;
3. Safety engineers—whenever there is new equipment
   involved or new ways of using old equipment;
4. DP operations—whenever the size of the application,
   or the scheduling, or the configuration required, or
   the special procedures or forms, or any other factor
   suggests possible implications for the operations area;
5. Security officers—when security or privacy of information is at issue;
6. Data base administration—in almost any circumstance;
7. Vendors—when the system will depend on specific
   equipment, software, or services to be supplied from
   an outside source;
8. Other installations—when portability is desired.

The rule is, TOUCH ALL POSSIBLE BASES. It's
much better to waste a bit of time asking someone who
isn't interested than to omit someone who is. It's also a
good idea to get them to sign their names saying they're
not interested, for exactly the same reason they sign their
names in a review—it elicits more responsible behavior
from busy people.

*Well, I Agree It's a Fine Idea to Get the Users Involved in
Reviews, but How Can We Get Our Users to Cooperate
and Communicate with One Another?*

First of all, the reviews by themselves will *not* solve the
problem of uncooperative users. The review is a *checking*
procedure, not a procedure for writing specifications.

Often, however, we find that a great deal of heat and animosity among users and between users and data processing can be traced back to *unchecked specifications.* Oh, there may have been some *show* of specification checking, but without formal review procedures, the checking was ineffective at best and a place for name calling and politicking at worst. The *earlier* your development finds errors, omissions, and misunderstandings in specifications, the less heat will be generated among your users, so reviews can help to that extent, anyway.

Second, you don't have to get the users to cooperate with *one another,* but only with the review leader in a very limited and well-structured situation. Moreover, it is a situation that—by virtue of its formality and openness—tends to prevent people from acting in immature and destructive ways. If someone is unwilling to help in an effective procedure for finding *errors,* there's something wrong with that person, not the procedure. You'll have to solve that problem to have an effective development, perhaps by getting rid of or refusing to work with that person.

Third, we do often find that the reviews present an opportunity for people to learn that they *can* work together. By gaining success in the rather formal procedures of a review, people gain confidence to try working cooperatively in less structured situations, like writing the specifications in the first place. The simplest way to get them to cooperate in the reviews is to ask them—politely. Assuming you are just instituting review procedures or have already used them with success in other areas, they will have no reason to distrust the procedures. Explain the possible benefits and the potential value of the user's contribution. Very few people will refuse to contribute, though many will refuse to take help from others.

Once you have the user at the review, you must demonstrate that you are interested in the user's opinion. Be sure that any issue the user raises without resolution is recorded on the Issues List. Wherever possible, be sure that the presentation of the specification will not embarrass the user, who might not understand something technical. The specification is a document that is supposed to form a bridge between the user and the technical staff. If the user doesn't understand, it must be considered a fault in the specifications, not in the user.

What About the User Who Wants to Institute Changes When the Specification Is Reviewed?

Everyone must be reminded that the purpose of the review is to raise issues, not to resolve them. The user may indeed suggest some change as an issue, to be taken up outside the review. If you think that it's better to keep the specification away from the user to prevent raising such ideas, you're in for a shock, sooner or later. Many of these changes would eventually be brought up. Otherwise, the user will not be satisfied with the produced system. The sooner in the process you note the need for change, the less will be the cost of instituting the change. That's what specifications are for, after all!

You Don't Know Our Users. They Never Stop Making Changes, Once You Give Them a Chance. How Can We Stop Them at Some Reasonable Time if We Let Them Review Everything?

First of all, they're not reviewing *everything*, but only the specification. Second, in our experience, the endless change syndrome is almost always found in installations that don't have a formal review procedure for specifications. Once your user has signed off on a review of the specifications, you have something solid on which to base future work. Changes after that point will have to be made formally, at considerable bother and possible expense to the user, which should discourage arbitrary change. Moreover, many of the "arbitrary" changes won't be needed on a specification that was carefully reviewed.

On the other hand, if the user is never able to pass on the specification in a review, then there's nothing to worry about. Until there's an agreed upon specification, there really *is* no project. It's the user's problem, not yours.

Our Users Would Like to Get Involved in Reviewing Specifications, but They Have No Common Language with the Producers. What Can We Do?

This is a major problem in some installations, but it can and must be solved. If your users and producers really don't have a common language, how do you write specifications now? With no noticeable means of communication, how do you produce what the user wants? By telepathy? By luck?

It is essential to develop a common language for communication at the specification level. To some extent, you may have to develop explicit training for your users and/or your technical people. Don't put all the burden on the users—they were there first, long before all this DP jargon was developed. But no matter how much effort you put into formal training, gaps will exist in your communication. It is precisely these gaps that the formal review of specifications is designed to catch—and catch early. The review itself will prove the most effective training ground—or at least the most effective ground for discovering how great the need for training is.

What Specifically Should the Specification Review Committee Look for in a Specification?

One of the best checklists of criteria we know was supplied to us by Boeing Computer Services. We present it below in unmodified form, because we feel that it should provide a sound top level basis for reviewing specifications (or "requirements") in almost any installation environment.

The BCS Requirements Checklist

The following criteria apply to the Requirements Document.

5.1 *Complete*
All items that are needed for the specification of the requirements of the solution to the problem have been included.

5.2 *Correct*
Each item in the requirements specification is free from error.

5.3 *Precise, Unambiguous, and Clear*
Each item in the requirements specification is exact and is not vague, there is a single interpretation of each item in the requirements specification, the meaning of each item in the requirements specification is understood, and the specification is easy to read.

5.4 *Consistent*
No item in the requirements specification conflicts with another item in the specification.

5.5 *Relevant*
Each item in the requirements specification is pertinent to the problem and its solution.

5.6 *Testable*
During program development and acceptance testing, it will be possible to determine whether the item in the requirements specification has been satisfied.

5.7 *Traceable*
Each item in the requirements specification can be traced to its origin in the problem environment.

5.8 *Feasible*
Each item in the requirements specification can be implemented with the techniques, tools, resources, and personnel that are available within the specified cost and schedule constraints.

5.9 *Free of Unwarranted Design Detail*
The requirements specifications are a statement of

the requirements that must be satisfied by the problem solution, and they are not obscured by proposed solutions to the problem.

5.10 *Manageable*

The requirements specifications are expressed in such a way that each item can be changed without excessive impact on other items.

Changes to the completed requirements specifications can be controlled. Each proposed change to the specifications can be traced to an existing requirement and the impact of the proposed change can be assessed.

Can Any of These General Headings Be Further Refined into More Detailed Checklists?

Yes, there are a variety of approaches to testing these specification criteria, though a full listing of techniques known to us would be beyond the scope of this manual. For example, if requirements are written in some formal language and put into machine-processible form, cross-reference listings can be used to check for consistency in the use and meaning of data items. Such a formal language might be tied directly to a data dictionary of some sort, thus permitting further checking. Cross-referencing can also help in checking completeness and traceability.

With machine processing—or by establishing manual procedures—we can accomplish much in the way of checking for correctness and precision, at least on a syntactic level. Much work is afoot, especially in universities, on formal testing of specifications, so that over the years we will certainly see an accumulation of techniques available to the practitioner. Nevertheless, we can hardly imagine how some of the checklist characteristics could ever be checked automatically, so specification reviews will remain the principal arena for assuring the adequacy of requirements specifications for the foreseeable future.

Can You Give Us Any Checklists for Specification Checking?

Yes, we have a checklist that has been accumulated over years of working with specifications that ultimately led to trouble for installations because of ambiguity. By using these actual ambiguities as a key, inspectors can mark up a document for return to the writers. Even more important, writers can trap the ambiguities before they go out the door.

Be sure you understand that this is *not a checklist of English grammar*. While it is true that ungrammatical forms almost always lead to trouble, the converse cannot be asserted with assurance. A statement may be perfectly clear and unambiguous according to the rules of grammar, yet still be read in several ways by different readers. For instance, consider the sentence we used above:

> **Writers can trap the ambiguities before they go out the door.**

In a test of this document, some people thought that "they" meant the writers, not the ambiguities. English grammar clearly shows that "they" refers to the closest preceding noun that agrees in number, but this rule doesn't prevent people from making a mistake. In writing a specification, it's better to be understood than to be grammatically perfect but potentially misunderstood. For instance, we could revise the above sentence to read:

> **A writer can trap the ambiguities before they go out the door.**

Now that "writer" is singular, nobody will mistake the referent of "they." Well, almost nobody. After all, a tired or careless reader could miss and supply the "s" and ignore the grammar.

To produce "fail-safe" specifications, we have to penetrate the mind of the person who read the specification incorrectly. In this sentence, we might ask:

> What makes the reader tend to associate
> "they" with writers rather than with
> ambiguities?

Upon examining the sentence, we might hypothesize that the reader feels more comfortable semantically with people (writers) going out a door than with "ambiguities" going out a door. With that insight, we could rewrite in fail-safe form:

> **A writer can trap the ambiguities before
> they are written down.**

A reader would have to work exceptionally hard to associate this "they" with "a writer."

Unfortunately, in making the sentence fail-safe, we've changed the meaning, since we don't mean to imply that writers will be able to catch ambiguities that early. A better choice for rewriting might have been:

> **A writer can trap the ambiguities before
> they are sent to review.**

In other words, though we can give you a checklist to help you spot trouble areas, we can't provide sure-fire rules for correction. But then, the job of the review isn't to correct, but only to raise issues. For that job, the checklist should do a service.

This checklist can alert the reader to a *potential* ambiguity in a specification. Even if the reader should personally understand the sentence, it may need clarification for other readers. In reviewing the specification, then, the object is to flag all possible ambiguities as issues, asking that they be resolved by fail-safe writing.

Any checklist of this sort is based upon experience. Different experiences will produce different checklists. Don't take this list for gospel, but consider it to be a dynamically growing entity. Any time you detect an ambiguity not on the list, try to spot the general rule and add an entry of your own. The result of this procedure will be an increasing clarity in your English language specifications.

Keyword	Example	Might be read as
A (or AN)	The dataset will contain an end of file character.	There will be one and only one end of file character. Some character will be designated as end of file character. There will be at least one end of file character.
AFTER	The control number comes after the quantity.	The value immediately following the quantity is the control number, which is thus defined by its position. If there is a control number, it comes somewhere after the quantity.
ALL	All files are controlled by a file control block.	One control block controls the entire set of files. Each file has its own control block. Each file is controlled by a control block, but one control block might control more than one file.
ALL	The field will be all nines.	The file will be '99'. The field will be '9999999'. Whatever the length of the field, each character will be a '9'.
ALL THE TIME	The interrupt status is set to "optional" all the time.	The interrupt status is initially set to "optional" and is never reset. The interrupt status is set to "optional" every time a routine that might have set it is terminated.
ALSO	The exception information will be in the XYZ file, also.	Another place the exception information appears is the XYZ file. Another type of information that appears in the XYZ file is the exception information.

298

AND	The sequence ends on a flag and an end of file.	The sequence ends on a flag, and the sequence also ends on an end of file—that is, the sequence ends on either a flag or end of file.
		The sequence ends on the double condition of flag plus end of file.
BOTH	Both files are controlled by a file control block.	One control block controls two files—i.e., both files.
		Each file is controlled by a control block—i.e., there are two control blocks for the two files, one for each.
CURRENT	The control total is taken from the current record.	The control total is taken from the record that is current in the accounting sense.
		The control total is taken from the record that is currently being considered by the program.
EVERY	Every list updates a table.	One table is updated by every list.
		Each list has its unique table to update.
		Each list has a table to update, which may not be unique.
FOLLOWING	The checksum is on the following summary card.	The checksum is on the next card, which is the summary card.
		The checksum is on the first summary card that follows, which may be many cards away.
FROM	The registry numbers start from 100,000.	The registry numbers start with the number 100,000.
		The registry numbers start with the number 100,001.

299

Keyword	Example	Might be read as
LARGEST	The field will be set to the largest possible value.	The field will be set to '††††' (where '†' is taken to represent the last character in the entire collating sequence). The field will be set to '2000' (which happens to be the largest value expected in this application).
LAST	The control total is taken from the last record.	The control total is taken from the record at the end of the file. The control total is taken from the latest record. The control total is taken from the previous record.
LATEST	The control total is taken from the latest record.	The control total is taken from the record that is currently being processed. The control total is taken from the record with the latest date.
MAY	The return code may contain an integer or a blank.	The return code must contain either an integer or a blank. The return code may contain an integer or a blank, but it might also contain something else that's not defined here.
ONLY	Digits can only be in the part number list.	Only digits can appear in the part number list. The only list in which digits appear is the part number list.
OR	The sequence ends on a flag or an end of file.	The sequence ends on either a flag or an end of file, or on both. When the sequence ends, one and only one of these conditions will hold—flag or end of file.

SAME	All customers have the same control field.	All customers have the same value in their control field. All customer control fields have the same format. One control field is used for all customers.
SHOULD	The operator should mount the designated disk pack.	The operator must mount the designated disk pack, otherwise the system will simply repeat the request. The operator ought to mount the designated disk pack, but if not, the system has alternative actions.
SMALLEST	(See LARGEST)	
THEIR	A family unit consists of a mother and father and all their children.	A family unit consists of a mother and her children and a father and his children. A family unit consists of a mother and a father and all the children whose two parents are that mother and father.
THEY	(see example in preceding text)	
TO	(see FROM)	
TOO	(see ALSO)	
UNTIL	Elements are added until the element with the present date has been added.	The adding of the elements will always stop with the element with the present date. The adding of the elements will stop with the element with the present date, if not stopped otherwise, as by terminating the list.

Keyword	Example	Might be read as
WE	We will create an operator's guidebook.	The user (who wrote this spec) will create an operator's guidebook. The user and the developer (who are the readers of this spec) will create an operator's guidebook.
WHEN	The terminal session ends when the signoff command is issued.	The only way to end a terminal session is with a signoff command. If a signoff command is issued, the terminal session ends; if not, there could be other ways of terminating.
WHEN	The counter is set to zero when the subroutine is invoked.	The counter is set to zero by the time the subroutine is invoked. The counter is set to zero the first time the subroutine is invoked—and only then. The counter is set to zero whenever (each time) the subroutine is invoked.
WILL	The pointer will be set before the data value is set.	Someone will have set the pointer value before the data value is set. The pointer value must be set before anyone attempts to set the data value.

The checklist is broken into two parts. The first part contains ambiguities that turn on a single keyword taking on two or more meanings. You can use this list simply by scanning for the keywords—a job that can be done mechanically on some specs—and checking each potential trouble spot.

The second part of the checklist requires a bit more trouble when scanning the specification, although there are often triggering words or phrases. In the second list, there may be many more than two or three alternative meanings.

Some Methods of Transforming Specifications to Reveal Ambiguities, Errors, and/or Misunderstandings

1. Vary the stress pattern in a sentence to reveal possible alternative meanings:

    The exceptional cases are handled by the terminal operator.

    The exceptional *cases are handled by the terminal operator.*

    (implying that these are the only cases handled this way)

    The exceptional cases are handled by the terminal operator.

    (as opposed to some other operator)

2. When a term is defined explicitly somewhere, try substituting that definition in place of the term.

    The current status file becomes the old status file.

    The direct access file containing the current status of all active accounts becomes the sequential file of accounts carried over from the previous period.

    (The replacement indicated several potential trouble spots because of disparities in the definitions of the two files.)

3. When a structure is described in words, try to sketch a picture of the structure being described.

    All files have a control block.

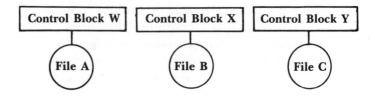

When this picture was sketched, the writer realized that the spec should have said:

> *Each file has a control block, which may or may not be unique*

It was also considered appropriate to supplement this description with a sketch like this:

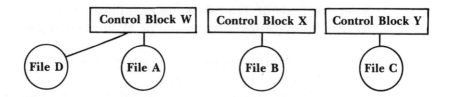

4. When a structure is described by a picture, try to redraw the picture in a form that emphasizes different aspects. The second picture in (3) above was redrawn like this:

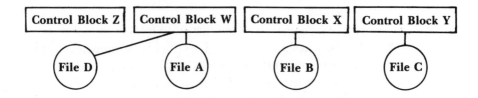

This redrawing raised the issue of whether there could be a control block with no file.

5. When there is an equation, try expressing the meaning of the equation in words.

$$I = P \times R$$

> *Interest (I) is computed as the product of Principal (P) and the Rate (R) for one period, if the interest is for the*

same period as defined by the rate. The more general formula would involve the number of periods, but the simpler formula can be used because we are dealing with a single period at a time.

6. When a calculation is specified or implied in words, try expressing it in an equation.

   True interest rate for a single period is the ratio between interest paid and the actual money received, which is the difference between the face amount and the interest deducted in advance (the discount, r).

   $$R = \frac{F \times r}{F - F \times r} \quad \text{which simplifies to } R = \frac{r}{1 - r}$$

7. When a calculation is specified, work at least two examples by hand and give them as examples in the specification.

   If the discount (r) is .06, the true rate, R, is .06/(1 − .06) = .0638. . . .

   If r is .10, R = .10/.90 = .111. . . .

8. Look for statements that in any way imply CER-TAINTY and then ask for proof.

   There can be no more than fifty lines per invoice.

   Ask: "How do you know there can be no more than fifty lines per invoice?"

   Words such as ALWAYS, EVERY, ALL, NONE, and NEVER are useful clues to indicate unproved certainty.

9. When you are searching behind certainty statements, PUSH THE SEARCH BACK as many levels as are needed to achieve the kind of certainty a computer will need. Suppose you hear, in answer to your question in (8), the following:

   Our invoice form has only fifty lines. If a second form is used, it has to have a different invoice number.

   Your next question might be: "May I see some actual invoice forms?" In the original example from which this case was drawn, we discovered that when a salesperson has just a few more line items than will fit in the fifty lines of the form, he or she writes two line items on one or more lines of the form to save having to start another sheet!

10. Be on the lookout for words that are supposed to be PERSUASIVE, such as CERTAINLY, THERE-FORE, CLEARLY, OBVIOUSLY, or AS ANY FOOL CAN PLAINLY SEE.

    Clearly, the dataset control pointer will be set before any data value is set.

    This turned out to be a statement of requirement, rather than of fact. It cost about $850,000 to learn the difference.

11. Watch for VAGUE words, such as SOME, SOME-TIMES, OFTEN, USUALLY, ORDINARILY, CUS-TOMARILY, MOST, or MOSTLY.

    Exception processing will be required for some of the line items.

    In cases such as this, try to get a number or per-centage. The word "exception" tends to make us think of a small percentage, but in one application, "some of the line items" turned out to be over 90 percent that required exception handling—thus de-stroying the design that had assumed less than 10 percent.

12. When lists are given, but not completed, make sure that there is a complete understanding of the nature of the subsequent items. Watch out for ETC., AND SO FORTH, AND SO ON, or SUCH AS.

    The permitted inputs are 'A', 'B', 'C', etc.

    There are any number of ways this list could be completed. Here are a few examples, though the list is open ended:

    The permitted inputs are 'A', 'B', 'C', 'D', 'E', 'F'.

    The permitted inputs are all single characters from 'A' through 'Z'.

    The permitted inputs are 'A', 'B', 'C', 'AA', 'BBCBA', or any other string starting with 'A', 'B', or 'C'.

13. In attempting to clarify lists, as in (12), we sometimes state a rule. Be sure that the rule doesn't contain unstated assumptions, as in:

    The valid codes range from 100 to 1000.

The rule seems to imply integers, but does it? It seems to imply numbers only, but is this true? Are the endpoints included? Are there invalid codes in the same range?

In the specification from which this rule was taken, the exact statement could have been expressed as:

The valid codes contain exactly three digits (100 to FFF, inclusive) or three digits and one fraction digit (100.1 through FFF.F). "Digits" includes the hexadecimal digits, 0123456789ABCDEF. Within this range, it is invalid to have a code of the form XXX.0—this code must be expressed as XXX, suppressing the point and the non-significant zero.

Is that the list you assumed from the first statement?

14. The above problems (11, 12, and 13) might have been caught by looking for lists WITHOUT EXAMPLES or examples that are TOO FEW or TOO SIMILAR to each other to explicate the rule. Consider the following statement from a specification:

    Invoices with a self-identified field starting with % carry the discount in that field.

    Upon further clarification, the rule was found to be more precisely expressed as:

    Invoices with a self-identified field starting with % carry the discount in that field, such as %12 meaning 1.2% discount, %100 meaning 10% discount, and so forth.

    It was easy enough to correct the code, but only after the loss of much money and customer goodwill.

15. Beware of vague verbs, such as HANDLED, PROCESSED, REJECTED, SKIPPED, or ELIMINATED. There may be oodles of processing concealed beneath a statement such as:

    Unmatched detail records are to be rejected.

    Find out just what has to be done on a reject.

16. PASSIVE VOICE constructions are also traps. Since the passive voice doesn't name an actor, it's easy to overlook having anybody do the work, as in:

    The parameters are initialized.

Find out who, if anybody, initializes them. In this example, nobody did, so they went uninitialized—at a cost of about $45,000 worth of debugging.

17. Be especially on the lookout for COMPARATIVES WITHOUT REFERENTS. Always ask, "Compared with what?" in such cases as:

   The headings are taken from the EARLIEST control card.

   The final total is to be placed in the NEW file.

   Overload reports require SPECIAL handling.

   What's "earliest" depends on what other things are compared with it. What's "new" depends on when you ask, for yesterday's new file is today's old file. What's "special" to you isn't very special to the people who deal with it every day. So look for -EST words, -ER words, and thousands of others that inject an implicit comparison.

18. PRONOUNS are often clear to the writer and not to the reader. Key on the occurrences of IT, HE, SHE, THEY, HIS, HERS, ITS, THEIR, WE, US, OUR, YOU, YOUR, and try to find the referent and state it explicitly.

   Consider this case:

   The array will be initialized with your regular rate table.

   In this case, there were hundreds of user clerks employing rate tables, many of which contained small differences from the basic table. Because YOUR was not spelled out to the level of specific persons, the analyst took a table from a clerk chosen at random. It was the wrong table.

Design Reviews

How Important Are Design Reviews? Aren't Most Errors
in the Code, Rather Than in the Design?

Where most errors are found depends on the state of the art at the installation. Where no reviews at all are practiced, even informal code reviews within a programming team, most errors are at the coding level. Even then, though, the design errors may prove more *serious*, on the average, than the coding errors. They are, on the average, harder to detect, harder to pin down once detected, and require far more extensive and costly modifications to set right. For instance, in a TRW study (Boehm, McClean, Urfirg, 1975), the diagnostic time for design errors averaged 3.1 hours as opposed to 2.2 hours for coding errors. Correction time averaged 4.0 hours against 0.8 hours—a five to one ratio that seems congruent with our own experiences.

The general rules seem to be:

1. Errors made earlier in the development process tend to have wider implications, so specification errors are potentially more devastating than design errors, de-

sign errors are potentially more devastating than coding errors, and so forth.

2. Without reviews, earlier errors tend to *show up* later.

3. The later an error shows up, the more work has to be done to find its cause among many possible causes.

4. The later an error is diagnosed, the more parts of a system are likely to be changed by a correction, so that even when a single part has to be changed, many parts have to be *examined* to be sure they don't have to be changed or aren't changed implicitly.

Where code reviews have already been in practice, we may find that a large majority of errors are design and/or specification errors, since many of the coding errors are eliminated before system testing. In the same study, TRW found that as many as 75 percent of errors found at system test were design errors. Since design errors were about 7/3 more costly to diagnose and correct, we can infer that, in these systems, *seven times as much was spent* dealing with design errors in system test than in dealing with coding errors.

Finally, there are those systems in which the design errors prove so gross that no system test is ever reached—the system collapses of its own developmental weight before integration is achieved. How many of these does it take to justify the institution of design reviews?

We Employ a Two-Stage Design Process. First There Is a High Level, or Preliminary, Design, Followed by Detailed Design to Elaborate on This General Approach. Which of These Two Levels Is the Better Choice for Reviews?

Neither. Or both. If you fail to review the high level design, your detailed design work will be partially devoted to elaborating the design of errors. If you fail to review the detailed design, you'll waste a lot of time coding the errors of that phase. Why not review both designs?

The general principle is simple. *Whenever* the system becomes embodied in a new form or passes from one hand to another, there should be a review to ensure that nothing has been lost, gained, or done wrong in the transformation. If you have *seventeen* levels of design, then there should be *seventeen* levels of review.

We Don't Use High Level and Low Level Designs, but Rather a Concept of Logical Design and Physical Design. How Does This Approach Affect Design Reviews?

According to the principle, you should naturally have two kinds of review. This separation of logical and physical designs can prove helpful in partitioning the review and maintaining proper size and interest on the review committee. A user might be extremely interested in some aspect of the logical design—such as the boundary between the human and automated parts of the system—yet have not the slightest interest in sorting algorithms or storage devices used in carrying out the process. Such a user might well attend the review of the operator protocols—a review that might be of little interest to systems programmers. As always, the important thing is to have all—and only—relevant people at the review.

I Find It Hard to Understand How You Can Review Designs? Code May Be Clearly Correct or Incorrect, but Isn't That Much More a Matter of Opinion with Designs?

It is true that design is still considered more of an art form than is coding. Indeed, design will probably always be more intuitive than rigorous. Nevertheless, there are "rules" of good design and, more important, rules for recognizing bad or flawed designs.

For example, if two designs carry out an equivalent function, the simpler one is the better choice. Though "simple" may be a complex attribute to recognize in some situations, in most cases it will be easy for the review committee to agree on which design is simpler, on whether two designs do in fact carry out equivalent functions, and on whether a certain design is too complicated in any case.

Another example of a broad and powerful design principle that can be used effectively in reviews is that a good design should consider and anticipate future changes. An adaptable design, in other words, is recognizably superior to one that is rigidly tied to present circumstances.

A third example of a deep design principle is that a design that accepts more user variation without being disturbed is superior to one that requires strict adherence to a nonhumanized format. And who else can better recognize a humanized format than human beings, sitting in review?

There are now several worthwhile books on system and program design available to design reviewers. None are cookbooks, but each can contribute to the reviewer's wisdom—and, consequently, to a better evaluation of the trade-offs involved in any design decision. Designs *can* be evaluated, not necessarily in the abstract, but certainly when specific alternatives are discussed under review discipline in the context of the environment in which they are supposed to operate.

Is It Possible, Then, to Develop Checklists for Design Reviews?

It is not only possible but desirable—as long as you don't get carried away and start believing that mechanical application of a checklist can do all the work of the review. For example, we present below two examples of design checklists. The first covers "preliminary" or "high level" design as practiced at Boeing Computer Services. The second is a checklist in the form of an inspection report as used at IBM Kingston to guide the review of detailed module design, as reported by Michael E. Fagan (1976).

The two checklists comprise a nicely contrasting pair—the BCS checklist being more open and intuitive, as appropriate for high level design, and the IBM checklist being very highly structured, as would be more appropriate as the design creeps closer and closer to the actual code. Following the BCS and IBM checklists, we've added a "design misfit" checklist based on the work of Don Gause. The categories of this checklist are designed to cut "across the grain" of many other checking systems. After you've asked your usual questions about the design, try asking these.

The BCS Preliminary Design Document Review Checklist

This checklist suggests things that a reviewer should expect to find as results of the Preliminary Design task. These results are all presented in the Preliminary Design Document. This is not an exhaustive list, and the reviewer is encouraged to look for other items as results of Preliminary Design.

1. Are the preliminary design objectives clearly stated?
2. Does the Preliminary Design Document contain a description of the procedure that was used to do preliminary design or is there a reference to such a procedure? Such a procedure should include the following:
   a. A description of the design technique used.
   b. An explanation of the design representation.
   c. A description of the test procedures, test cases, test results, and test analysis that were used.
   d. A description of the evaluation procedures and criteria that were used.
3. Is there a list of the functions that are to be provided by the computing system?
4. Is there a model of the user interface to the computing system? Such a model should provide the following:
   a. A description of the languages available to the user.

    b. Enough detail to allow you to simulate the use of the computing system at your desk.

    c. Information about the flexibility/adaptability/extendability of the user interface.

    d. Information about tutorials, assistance, etc. for the user.

    e. A description of the functions available to the user and the actual access to those functions.

    f. An appreciation of the ease of use of the computing system.

    g. The detail required to formulate and practice the user procedures that will be required to use the computing system.

5. Are there models and/or descriptions of all other interfaces to the computing system?

6. Is there a high level functional model of the proposed computing system? Such a model should be accompanied by the following:

    a. An operational description.

    b. An explanation of the test procedure, test cases, test results, and test analysis used to ensure that the model is correct.

    c. An evaluation of the model with respect to the requirements to ensure that the requirements are satisfied. (Preliminary Design does not provide detailed results that allow for detailed qualitative and quantitative analysis.)

    d. A discussion of the alternatives that were considered and the reasons for the rejection of each alternative.

7. Are the major implementation alternatives and their evaluations represented in the document? For each of these alternatives you should expect to find the following:

    a. A complete, precise, and unambiguous model that identifies the modules, the input and output sets of the modules, the operational sequences of the modules, and the criteria for the execution of each operational sequence in the model.

    b. An evaluation of the model that ensures that the requirements will be satisfied. Some of the things to look for in this evaluation are:

> ? performance
> ? storage requirements
> ? quality of results
> ? ease of use
> ? maintainability
> ? adaptability
> ? generality
> ? technical excellence
> ? simplicity
> ? flexibility
> ? readability
> ? portability
> ? modularity
>
> An examination of these models should include both the functional model and the associated data models.

  c. Estimates of the costs, time, and other resources that will be required to implement the alternative. These estimates should be accompanied with the following:
> ? a description of the estimating technique used
> ? the source of the data used in making the estimates
> ? the confidence factor associated with each estimate

  d. An identification of the modules that will be implemented as hardware and those that will be implemented as software. (Some will be a combination of hardware and software.) This should also include recommendations to buy, buy and modify, or build each module. Each recommendation should be accompanied with supporting information.

8. Is there a recommendation from the Preliminary Design team to implement one of the alternatives?

9. Is the recommendation of the Preliminary Design team adequately supported?

10. Does the information presented in the Preliminary Design Document and during the Preliminary Design Review give you confidence that the computing system can be implemented to satisfy the requirements to such an extent that you would use the proposed system?

THE IBM DETAIL DESIGN REPORT

MODULE DETAIL

MOD/MAC: _____ SUBCOMPONENT/APPLICATION _____

SEE NOTE 1 BELOW

PROBLEM TYPE:	MAJOR*			MINOR		
	M	W	E	M	W	E
LO: LOGIC						
TB: TEST AND BRANCH						
DA: DATA AREA USAGE						
RM: RETURN CODES/MESSAGES						
RU: REGISTER USAGE						
MA: MODULE ATTRIBUTES						
EL: EXTERNAL LINKAGES						
MD: MORE DETAIL						
ST: STANDARDS						
PR: PROLOGUE OR PROSE						
HL: HIGHER LEVEL DESIGN DOCUMENTATION						
US: USER SPECIFICATIONS						
MN: MAINTAINABILITY						
PE: PERFORMANCE						
OT: OTHER						

TOTAL:

REINSPECTION REQUIRED? _____

*(A problem which would cause the program to malfunction; a BUG)
(M = Missing; W = Wrong; E = Extra)
Note 1: For modified modules, problems in the changed portion versus problems in the base should be shown in this manner: 3(2), where 3 is the number of problems in the changed portion and 2 is the number of problems in the base.

Design Misfit Checklist

1. Boundary Oversights
   a. Is anything going to fall between the cracks of "mine" versus "yours."
   b. Is anything going to be claimed by two or more parties?
   c. Is each input, function, and output specifically addressed by a specific, identifiable part of the system? Can you prove it?
   d. Is there any misinterpretation of the person-machine interface—either by person or machine?
2. Overadaptation
   a. Has any portion of this design received more emphasis than it seems to deserve? Can you explain why that happened, and what effects it has had?
   b. Is the design overly constrained, perhaps by paying too much attention to one part at the expense of others?
   c. If you could relax any single constraint, which would it be? How would the design be affected?
3. Afterthoughts
   Examine the last three things added to the design and answer the following questions for each:
   a. What has been crammed in?
   b. Could someone tell that the change was not part of the original conception—that it is a patch to the design?
   c. What wasn't considered when this change was made?
   d. What would happen if this change were undone and left out of the final design?
4. Vestiges
   a. What things are in the design because "we've always done it that way?" Why are you doing it that way?
   b. Does the design reflect the machine on which it will operate? If so, why?
   c. Is your design independent of the programming language that will be used? If not, why not?
   d. Do you have a place to hold the buggywhip?

5. Mistakes
   a. What have you forgotten?
   b. What has been done wrong?
   c. Did you dot the i's?
   d. Did you ever go back and correct that problem you found when you were busy with something more important?
   e. Do you have any notes on scraps of paper?
6. Insensitivity
   a. Have you remembered the people who will have to use this system?
   b. Have you remembered the people who will have to operate it?
   c. Have you remembered the people who will have to repair it?
   d. If you were one of these people, what *one* thing would you change in the design to make your life easier? Why wasn't that change made?

Can We Use a Design Review to Compare Two or More Contending Designs?

No, you can't use *a* design review to compare two or more designs, but you can use *two or more design reviews* to compare two or more designs.

Do You Mean That One Design Review Should Be Restricted to Reviewing One Design?

Yes. When you try to do two designs at once, the review becomes a yelling contest for the advocates of the various alternatives. The proper way to compare designs is as follows:

1. Prepare for each design a statement of its performance on each major goal of the specifications.
2. Conduct a review of each competing design/spec statement from (1). The output of each review is a state-

ment that this design does in fact do what the statement says or an Issues List detailing the points in doubt (see examples).

3.   Once each design has a reviewed and accepted design/ spec statement, the statements can be compared to choose the design that will be used. This choosing is *not* done in a review, but is based on the reviewed statements.

What Form Should This Design/Spec Statement Take?

Various forms have been used. We prefer the form to be as clear, simple, and quantitative as possible. For this purpose, we have found Tom Gilb's Goal-Limit Specification to provide an excellent basis (see form on page 322).

The Goal-Limit Specification is essentially a grid. Down the left side are the attributes the system is to have. Across the top are column headings detailing the contents of the column. The figure on page 323 shows a typical Goal-Limit Specification filled out as part of the specification process. The design/spec statement uses the same attributes and metrics, but the column heads are somewhat different, as shown in the figure on page 324.

For each design, the METRIC, PLANNED, WORST CASE, and %WEIGHT columns are copied from the Goal-Limit Specification. Then a DESIGN PERFORMANCE column is filled out for the design. Based on a comparison between DESIGN PERFORMANCE and PLANNED and WORST CASE, a GRADE is filled in for that attribute. The GRADE ranges from 0.00 to 1.00. Then the GRADE is multiplied by the WEIGHT, and the results are summed, giving a score for the design.

Do You Choose the Design with the Highest Score?

Management chooses whatever design they wish, regardless of its score. But if they decide to choose a low scoring design, then it would be a good idea if they adjusted the figures in the Goal-Limit Specification to reflect their true feelings about the importance of things. This method is essentially the MECCA method, described by Tom Gilb in several of his books, including *Software Metrics*. The purpose of the MECCA method is to bring these decisions out in the open, so everyone can examine and understand the process. It allows you to make decisions that will be understood, so that future work can anticipate the way decisions will be made.

Once the process stabilizes, you will often choose according to the highest score. Here's a simple example to illustrate the method. (See Tom Gilb's books for much more detailed explanation.) Suppose there were just three attributes considered important—Reliability, Cost per Invoice, and Performance. Suppose these three attributes were posted onto design/spec sheets and the designs A, B, C, and D were graded as shown on pages 325–328.

The job of the four separate reviews would be to judge whether these four design/spec sheets were, in fact, correct for the given designs (see Issues List on page 329). Once the reviews have established that the design/spec grade sheets are correct, management can use the sheets to make a decision on the designs. Obviously, a real design has many more components, but pretending that these were complete, management might reason as follows:

1. Design D grades at .49, much lower than the others, and can safely be rejected.

2. Design C seems to grade higher than the others, at .80, but it *fails one of the criteria*—performance. Management might decide that they actually don't care that much about performance, when they see the nice cost of design C. In that case, the whole design question should be reopened, as designs A and B might well have been able to give lower cost at reduced performance levels. Even D might have to be reconsidered or some other alternative that didn't make it this far. What management has done is to change the rules during the game, which is their right—even their

duty, in some cases. But when the rules are changed, then with this method, everyone can see that they've been changed and adjust designs accordingly, which could result in a much better system.

3. The difference between A (.745) and B (.750) is too small to be decisive, for the method can't be *that* precise. Perhaps management will ask that these two designs receive further work, or perhaps they will decide to adjust the weights or ask that the grades be reconsidered. If grades are reconsidered or designs are changed, then new reviews must be performed.

4. Management could also decide arbitrarily on the basis of "intangibles" between A and B or could decide to have both implemented. They do so in the knowledge that the review assures that they have used reliable information on the technical issues.

GOAL - LIMIT SPECIFICATION

REFERENCE_____ DATE_____

CHARACTERISTICS OF ATTRIBUTE / NAME OF ATTRIBUTE	METRIC UNITS	BEST CASE (no value for better)	PLANNED (quite satisfactory)	WORST ACCEPTABLE CASE	% WEIGHT	MORE IMPORTANT THAN	REMARKS or REFERENCES

GOAL – LIMIT SPECIFICATION
REFERENCE Accounts Payable--Invoice and Inquiry   DATE 12 November 1980

CHARACTERISTICS OF ATTRIBUTE / NAME OF ATTRIBUTE	METRIC UNITS	BEST CASE (no value for better)	PLANNED (quite satisfactory)	WORST ACCEPTABLE CASE	% WEIGHT	MORE IMPORTANT THAN	REMARKS or REFERENCES
R RELIABILITY	Errors to client/ Invoices	1/ 5000	1/ 5000	1/ 500	15	M	STD-RE-131
M MAINTAINABILITY	% of bugs identified in period of time (hours)	90/1 95/5	90/1 95/5	50/1 80/8	15	A	STD-MA-101
A AVAILABILITY	% up / office day	100	98	95	10	-	
C COST	$$ / invoice		0.90	1.32	15	P	
P PORTABILITY	% of original development cost as salvage value to anyone's COBOL		97	90	5		
S SECURITY	Customer breaches per year	0	1	2	5		
PR PERFORMANCE	Response under maximum load (time/% achieved) (seconds / %)	2/99	2/95	5/90	5		
L LEARNING EASE	Time to safe solo use by new hire (hours)	4	8	16	15	R	STD-TR-OF33
MA MARKET APPEAL	% of clients who judge equal or better than old	100	98	95	15	R	

Form design Copyright 1976 Tom Gilb (may be copied for private use

323

DESIGN/SPEC GRADE SHEET

REFERENCE_____ DATE_____

NAME OF ATTRIBUTE / CHARACTERISTICS OF ATTRIBUTE	METRIC UNITS	PLANNED	WORST ACCEPTABLE CASE	% WEIGHT (W)	DESIGN PERFORMANCE	GRADE (0-1) (G)	G x W

DESIGN/SPEC GRADE SHEET

REFERENCE___*Design A*_____   DATE___*10/10/78*____

CHARACTERISTICS OF ATTRIBUTE / NAME OF ATTRIBUTE	METRIC UNITS	PLANNED	WORST ACCEPTABLE CASE	% WEIGHT (W)	DESIGN PERFORMANCE GRADE (0-1) (G)	G x W
R Reliability	errors to client/ invoices	1/ 5000	1/ 500	30	1/ 1000	.40	.12
C Cost	$$ / invoice	0.90	1.35	50	0.93	.95	.475
PR Performance	Response under maximum load (time (secs))/ % achieved	2/95	5/90	20	2/90	.75	.15
							Overall grade .745

DESIGN/SPEC GRADE SHEET

REFERENCE _____Design B_____   DATE _10/10/78_____

CHARACTERISTICS OF ATTRIBUTE / NAME OF ATTRIBUTE	METRIC UNITS	PLANNED					
			WORST ACCEPTABLE CASE				
				% WEIGHT (W)			
					DESIGN PERFORMANCE		
						GRADE (0-1) (G)	
							G x W
R Reliability	errors to client/ invoices	1/ 5000	1/ 500	30	1/ 5000	1.00	.30
C Cost	$$ / invoice	0.90	1.35	50	1.10	.50	.25
PR Performance	Response under maximum load (time (secs))/ % achieved	2/95	5/90	20	2/95	1.00	.20
							Overall grade .750

326

DESIGN/SPEC GRADE SHEET

REFERENCE _Design C_   DATE _10/10/78_

CHARACTERISTICS OF ATTRIBUTE / NAME OF ATTRIBUTE	METRIC UNITS	PLANNED	WORST ACCEPTABLE CASE	% WEIGHT (W)	DESIGN PERFORMANCE	GRADE (0-1) (G)	G x W
R Reliability	errors to client/ invoices	1/ 5000	1/ 500	30	1/ 5000	1.00	.30
C Cost	$$ / invoice	0.90	1.35	50	.85	1.00	.50
PR Performance	Response under maximum load (time (secs))/ % achieved	2/95	5/90	20	5/70	FAIL	FAIL (0)
							Overall grade FAIL (.80)

DESIGN/SPEC GRADE SHEET

REFERENCE _Design D_   DATE _10/10/78_

NAME OF ATTRIBUTE / CHARACTERISTICS OF ATTRIBUTE	METRIC UNITS	PLANNED	WORST ACCEPTABLE CASE	% WEIGHT (W)	DESIGN PERFORMANCE	GRADE (0-1) (G)	G x W
R Reliability	errors to client/ invoices	1/5000	1/500	30	1/1000	.40	.12
C Cost	$$ / invoice	0.90	1.35	50	1.10	.50	.25
PR Performance	Response under maximum load (time (secs))/ % achieved	2/95	5/90	20	2/80	.60	.12
							Overall grade .490

In reviewing the design/spec grade sheet for alternative
design C, we raised the following issues:

1. The estimated performance of 95% of responses within 2
seconds under full load is not justified by the analysis.
We believe there is a computational error in evaluating
the load/response formula. Term 3 requires the <u>square</u> of
the number of active terminals, and it seems that in making
the calculation, this number was not squared. Our rough
recomputation shows that the 95% level for this design would
be achieved at around 20 seconds, but we recommend that the
entire calcuation be redone.

The committee felt that this issue was sufficiently important
to require a decision of NOT ACCEPTED for the design/spec grade
sheet, with MAJOR REVISION required.

There were two other minor points.

2. An arithmetic error in the cost calculation seems to have
given $0.87 per invoice instead of $0.85.

3. When the number 1/5000 was transcribed from the calculation
sheet to the design/spec grade sheet, it seems to have been
written as 1/500.

These two minor errors, together with the major error (1), seem
to indicate that the design/spec grade sheet was filled in
hastily. Its rough appearance also supports that view.
Although we found no other errors, we are suspicious of the entire
computation, and suggest that it be redone, slowly and carefully,
before the review is reconvened.

Wilma Judge ___ Wilma Judge, Review Leader

S.T. Halle _____ Sam T. Halle, Recorder

Code Reviews

Why Has the Code Review Received So Much Attention in
the Literature? Is It More Important Than the Other
Kinds of Review?

Because *any* error can lead to the downfall of a system,
it's hard to assert that one type of review is more important
than another. Probably the reason code reviews have received so much attention lies in the relative position of
coding in the development cycle. Since coding is the last
constructive step before testing, there is a tendency to
blame errors on that step. When something is found to
be wrong, the temptation—and usual practice—is to correct the code without cycling back to the design, let alone
the specification. Therefore, most people think that most
errors are in coding and that those errors are the most
important ones. Although the coding errors, in a particular case, may indeed be the most important, there is no
reason to believe this to be true in general. But because
coding is the step in which we usually find a lot of errors,

it's the first place we think of once we get the idea of
reviews.

Then You Think That Code Reviews Aren't the Ideal Place to Start, If We're Just Instituting Reviews for the First Time?

On the contrary, we might as well take advantage of the
feelings that people have concerning coding errors. Like
the doctor who is going to have to perform a painful
procedure on a patient, we may need the patient's pain
as motivation to get the procedure accepted. The principle, in general, is this:

**Start the reviews where the perceived pain is
greatest.**

In most installations, this will mean code reviews.
More particularly, it may mean code reviews in *maintenance,* where the cost of error is so great, so immediate,
and so obvious even to those outside of DP.

But Won't All That Pain Put Too Much Pressure on the Early Reviews?

That's a definite possibility that we must watch out for.
We mustn't lead people to expect that reviews of one small
part of the programming process will magically correct
two decades of muddled work in every conceivable area.
Nevertheless, the results from code reviews are most likely
to be readily translated into facts that many people will
be able to appreciate. If those leaders responsible for instituting reviews will take the trouble to bring these facts
into the open, they will gain a substantial measure of early
support for the review idea. Because it's easier to do this
with code reviews, they've tended to be initially more
successful.

What Do You Mean by "Bringing These Facts into the Open"?

In most installations, there are few, if any, measures of how well or how poorly programming is being done. Lacking any past perspectives, it's difficult to demonstrate that reviews—or any new procedures—are doing any good. Of all the things we *might* measure, *coding errors* and some of their consequences are the easiest, least controversial, and most dramatic.

For instance, when a client of ours was able to demonstrate that before code reviews, 55 percent of all one-line maintenance changes were incorrect on the first production run, there was strong motivation for code reviews in maintenance, even of "trivial" changes. After instituting code reviews, under 2 percent of all one-line maintenance changes were incorrect on the first production run. Furthermore, over 95 percent of *all* maintenance changes were correct the first time, as opposed to *under 20 percent* before code reviews. And when there were errors, they tended to be far less serious than previously. With that kind of evidence, it was easy to convince management to continue the maintenance code reviews, to extend them to all production coding, and to extend the concept to other forms of review. In fact, the major problem was to keep management enthusiasm under control.

Other clients have used different ways of measuring error impact before and after reviews. One showed a 77 percent reduction of production crashes during the first six months of life of postreview development projects. A software house compared field trouble reports from products developed before and after reviews and found a factor of six reduction—something that was immensely pleasing to their marketing people, not to mention their clients.

One of our clients supplied us with the following table of their experience with COBOL programs produced just before and just after formal code reviews were instituted. Errors are those detected in production runs during the first sixteen weeks of each program's production experience. The same people worked on these programs. Indeed, the programs were written over very much the same period of time—the only difference being that the first six were the last programs completed by this group *before* reviews were instituted, while the last six were the first completed *after* reviews were instituted. As the table shows (and showed to their management), the reduction of errors per line of code was 5.5 to 1—big enough for anyone to appreciate.

Experience with COBOL Programs Done Before and After Code Reviews

WEEK	SIZE*	ERRORS†	E/100 lines
−9	463	19	4.10
−7	198	7	3.54
−7	146	4	2.73
−4	880	41	4.66
−3	426	19	4.46
−2	712	37	5.19
Total	2,825	127	4.50
+2	117	2	1.13
+3	134	1	0.75
+6	664	7	1.05
+6	484	4	0.82
+7	379	3	0.79
+8	580	3	0.52
Total	2,418	20	0.82

* Size includes all cards in a COBOL deck, but not job control.
† Error counting might not be entirely accurate, since it is sometimes difficult to count whether a thing is one error or two.

But Why All This Emphasis on Error?

Primarily because "error" is the least controversial thing to measure. Not that it's always simple to tell when there is or is not an error, but at least it's simpler than telling whether or not a particular piece of code is "modifiable" or "portable." To be sure, these attributes *should* be measurable, too, but at the present state of the art, few installations are prepared to measure them, let alone provide a past history of measurement. (For a valuable survey of measurement approaches, see Gilb 1977.)

Besides, if the software doesn't work properly, what's the use of measuring other aspects of its performance?

We Lack Historical Data on Errors. Would It Be a Good Idea To Go Back in Time and Accumulate Some?

Not if it's going to be a major effort to be undertaken before you start reviews. We've seen too many installations that use the gathering of historical data as a delaying tactic. There should be some relatively gross figures scattered about for you to use, like trouble reports in operations or statistics on number of debugging runs. If you're not using reviews now, chances are that the improvement will be so dramatic that anyone with a fair mind will acknowledge its existence.

How About Counting the Errors Found in the Reviews?

Counting the errors—even classifying them for feedback into the production process and training—is a common approach to evaluating reviews. One danger, however, is that the counts will be used for evaluating the producers in a negative way. If that happens, the reviewers can easily start wallowing in endless debates over just what an error is, whether a case is one error or two errors, or in which category an error should be placed.

In our opinion, it is best to *emphasize the positive results* of the review—not the large number of errors removed, but the small number of errors remaining.

But You Yourself Have Stated That the Feedback of
Educational Information Is One of the Most Important
Functions of the Review. How Can We Feed Back That
Information If We Don't Count and Classify Errors in the
Code?

If reviews don't get started at all, they won't be of any use for educational purposes. Therefore, we want to start them in such a way as to maximize their chance of successfully taking root in the organization. If we start right out by counting everybody's errors, we're going to generate a lot of resistance.

Our approach is to start with a measure of quality of the product *after* the review—or if that can't be obtained, with no explicit measure at all. The producers, by sitting in on reviews and by being reviewers themselves, will get the most important initial feedback—namely, that they might as well think of quality when they produce the code, rather than waiting for the review to show them up.

In addition, the most glaring and frequent of the error types will be immediately obvious to everyone participating in reviews, so substantial improvement of pre-review code will soon be seen. Reviews will go more smoothly because there are fewer errors and because the reviewers will be more experienced. At that point, you may want to consider the introduction of explicit tabulations of error types for educational feedback. Just be careful you don't keep the statistics by individual programmer or team. Follow this modification of the old army procedure:

It's only a mistake if it gets out of the review.

Can You Give Us Some Guidelines for Reviewing Code?

There are even more sets of guidelines for code review than for design and specification review, so we'll provide several covering a wide range. The first is a set of questions

developed by us originally for informal reviews and later
found useful for preparing for formal reviews as well as
guiding them.

General Questions to Keep in Mind When Reviewing Code

These questions can be grouped under three general categories—function, form, and economy—ranked in order
of importance.

Function
1. Is there a concept, an underlying idea, that can be
   expressed easily in plain language? Is it expressed in
   plain language in the implemented code?
2. Does the function of this part have a clear place in
   the overall function of the whole, and is this function
   clearly expressed?
3. Is the routine properly sheltered, so that it may perform its function reliably in spite of possible misuse?

Form
1. Whatever style is adopted, is it clean and clear when
   taken as a whole?
2. Is it meaningful to all classes of readers who will see
   it?
3. Are there repeated code segments, whether within or
   between routines?
4. Are comments useful or are they simply alibis for poor
   coding?
5. Is the level of detail consistent?
6. Are standard practices used?
7. Is initialization properly done, and does the routine
   clean up after itself?

Economy
1. Are there redundant operations for which there is no
   compensating benefit?
2. Is storage use consistent, both internally and with external specifications?

3. How much will it cost to modify? (Consider the three most likely future modifications.)
4. Is it simple?

Those Questions Seem Very Broad. Can They Lead to an Adequate Review?

Not by themselves, but it's a good idea to have some large-scale questions in mind as you approach a piece of work—questions that aren't so detailed you have to refer to the list for each line of code. We suggest looking once through the code with the Function questions in mind, forgetting all other considerations. After answering those questions to your satisfaction, scan for Form. Only after you feel you've completely answered the form and function question should you turn to questions of economy.

Naturally, you can't prevent your mind from seeing something on one list while you're supposed to be scanning for something else. Don't worry about that—just jot down the briefest note and continue your scan.

And be sure to write things down. Otherwise, you'll never remember everything for the review. And write it down *each time* it occurs. Indeed, when you find one fault, interrupt your scanning and scan the remainder of the code for that one fault. The most likely error is a repeat, in some guise or another, of the one you've already found.

Having done these general things, you may be ready to scan for very particular kinds of problem, such as those expressed on the following COBOL checklist from IBM.

We Did a Formal Code Review as You Suggested, and It Was Terrific. Unfortunately, Nobody in Our Management Was Interested in the Report We Issued. What Should We Do?

Usually we expect formal reviews to be instituted top-down, with informal ones being initiated bottom-up. What you're doing, in fact, is an informal review that follows the format of a formal review. It doesn't become a formal review until your management is interested in using the resulting report to help them manage your development effort. If they don't need it, fine and dandy. But send it to them anyway. Eventually they'll see the light. Many places have started formal reviews like that. Since the benefits to your team are there for you to see, any use management makes of the report is just frosting on the cake. Just hope they don't try to *stop* you from doing reviews.

IBM COBOL Program Checklist

During the second inspection the unit being inspected should be examined for the following points.

	Error Type
1. Identification Division	
Remarks Paragraph	
Does the prose in the REMARKS paragraph function as a complete prologue for the program?	PR
2. Environment Division	
Does each SELECT sentence explicitly define the external (system-dependent) specifications for the file?	SU
3. Data Division	
File Section	
Are the File Definitions (FDs) in the same order as their respective SELECT sentences in the ENVIRONMENT DIVISION?	DA
Do the record and data item names conform to their usage?	DA
Does each FD contain comments regarding:	DA
Usage of the file (RECORDING MODE, Block Size, Record Length, Imbedded Keys, etc.)?	
Amount of activity (updated how often, used every time program is run, etc.)?	

Error
Type

Interaction with other data items. (Do
its records contain objects of
'Occurs...Depending On' clauses
(ODOs); is the length of its records
dependent on an ODO object elsewhere in the program, etc.?)

Is the file SORTed or MERGEd?   EL
Are statistics kept on file activity in a
given run or series of runs?   EL

Working-Storage & Linkage Sections
Do the data item names conform to their
usage?   DA
Does each data item (except for elemen-
tary items of obvious usage-subscripts,
etc.) contain comments regarding: DA
Characteristics (Fixed- or Variable-
Length, maximum allowable length,
etc.)
Interaction with other data items. (Does
this data item contain or depend on
objects of ODOs, etc.?)
Area of use in program. (Is it used
only in a certain section, or during a
range of paragraphs, etc.?)
Are all data items with any kind of unify-
ing quality placed together according to
a particular scheme: DA
Usage (arithmetic work areas, work
areas for file records, etc.)?
Commonality of purpose. (Everything
used to process a particular file, etc.)?
Are all WORKING-STORAGE items that
are used as constants designated as such?   DA
Are data items (that are required to be
in a particular order) sequenced correctly?   DA

4. Procedure Division
Are block comments included for major
functional areas (e.g., paragraph, SEC-
TION, segment)?   CC
Is the module sufficiently commented
(enough detail)?   CC

	Error Type
Are comments accurate and meaningful?	CC
Does the code essentially correspond to the outline of the module documented in the REMARKS paragraph?	LO

Does each paragraph, SECTION, or segment have a homogeneous purpose which justifies and/or necessitates placing all the code together under such a grouping?   MN

Does each performed paragraph or SECTION document the function it accomplishes and what part of the overall logic it represents?   CC

In a segmented program, is it clear why segmentation is necessary?   MN

Does each segment stand alone or is there heavy dependence on other segments?   MN

Is the assignment of paragraphs to, and the arrangement of, the segments such that thrashing between segments is eliminated or held to a minimum?   MN

5. Format
   Throughout the module:

Are THEN/ELSE groups aligned?	MN
Are nested IFs indented properly?	MN
Are block comments and remarks effectively positioned?	MN
Are the clauses of complex verbs indented properly and clearly under the verb:	MN

    Complex arithmetic (ADD, SUBTRACT, COMPUTE, etc.?)
    SORT/MERGE?
    INVALID KEY/AT END on I-O verbs?
    File-names and options on OPEN/CLOSE?
    Complex PERFORM?
    STRING/UNSTRING?
    SEND/RECEIVE?
    SEARCH/SEARCH ALL?

6. Module Logic

Through the module, in verifying that the code matches the design, ensure that the following criteria are met:

ENTRY & EXIT LINKAGE

Is initial entry and final exit correct?	EL
Is each entry point defined correctly?	EL
Is each parameter referenced in an ENTRY statement a 77 or 01 item in the LINKAGE SECTION?	EL
Is the usage of STOP RUN/GOBACK/ EXIT PROGRAM verbs correct in this module, in the context of the whole of which this module is part?	EL

LOGIC

Has all design been implemented?	LO
Does code do what the design called for; (i.e., is the design translated correctly)?	LO
Is the design correct and complete?	DE
Appropriate number of characters within a field tested or set?	LO
In the PERFORM statement, if loop control is used, is the loop executed the correct number of times and does it access the correct addresses?	LO

Language Usage

Is the optimal verb or set of verbs used?	PU
Is the installation-defined restricted subset of COBOL used throughout the module?	PU
Is attention given to normal 'housekeeping' requirements in COBOL; (e.g., setting the length of a variable-length target field before a MOVE to that field is executed)?	PU

Storage Usage

Is each field to be initialized set correctly?	SU
Before the first use of any field, has it been initialized properly?	SU
Is the correct field specified?	SU
If storage is set and used recursively, is it 'housekept' properly?	SU

Error
Type

Is the field initialized statically; (i.e., by
means of the VALUE clause on its definition), when it should be dynamically
(by assignment), or vice-versa?   SU
Is the use of the REDEFINES clause in
the data item's definition compatible with
all uses of the data item in the code?   SU

Test and Branch
Is correct condition tested (IF X = ON
vs. IF X = OFF)?   TB
Is (are) correct variable(s) used for test
(IF X = ON vs. IF Y = ON)?   TB
Is each condition-name, used as a test of
a data item, defined as an 88-level under
that data item?   TB
Are null ELSEs included as appropriate?   MN
Is each branch target, of a simple GO
TO or GO TO...DEPENDING ON state-
ment, correct and exercised at least once?   TB
Is the most frequently exercised test leg
of an IF statement the THEN clause?   TB

Performance
Is logic coded optimally (i.e., in the few-
est and most efficient statements)?   PE
Has subscripting been used where in-
dexing logic would be more effective and
appropriate, or vice-versa?   PE
Have ERROR DECLARATIVEs been
coded for files likely to have recoverable
I-O errors?   PE

Maintainability
Are listing controls utilized to enhance
readability (e.g., EJECT, SKIP)?   MN
Are paragraph and SECTION names
consistent with the logical significance of
the code?   MN
Is each PERFORMed paragraph termi-
nated with an EXIT paragraph?   MN

Linkage Requirements
For each external call to another module: EL

> Are all required parameters passed to
> each called module?
> Are the parameter values passed set
> correctly?
> Upon final exit from this module, are
> all files closed?

Copy Facility Usage
> Is every data item definition and pro-
> cessing paragraph, standardized for the
> installation, generated in the module via
> the COPY facility?   OT
> Is there a sound reason why the RE-
> PLACE option of the COPY statement
> is utilized to change any of the names
> of data items in the COPY'd code?   OT

Note: This checklist is not an exhaustive set of prompting
questions; however, it is considered to be representative
of and applicable to most COBOL programs.

Are There Similar Lists for Other Languages?

Increasingly, you can find such lists in the better language
textbooks. In particular, there have been a number of
books devoted to style in programming, including:

- Kernighan, Brian W., & Plauger, P. J., *Elements of Pro-
  gramming Style*. New York: McGraw-Hill, 1974
- Ledgard, Henry F., *Programming Proverbs*. Rochelle
  Park, NJ: Hayden, 1975
- Weinberg, Gerald M., *PL/I Programming: A Manual of
  Style*. New York: McGraw-Hill, 1971

One or more of these books can be usefully employed in
a training program to prepare people for active participation in code reviews. It's important to read the books,
for no summary of rules can replace a sound understanding of the concepts contained in them.

Following is an example of such rules, summarized by Kernighan and Plauger and based upon FORTRAN and PL/I examples taken from textbooks.

Summary of Rules from Kernighan and Plauger

To paraphrase an observation in *The Elements of Style,* rules of programming style, like those of English, are sometimes broken, even by the best writers. When a rule is broken, however, you will usually find in the program some compensating merit, attained at the cost of the violation. Unless you are certain of doing as well, you will probably do best to follow the rules.

- Write clearly—don't be too clever.
- Say what you mean, simply and directly.
- Use library functions.
- Avoid temporary variables.
- Write clearly—don't sacrifice clarity for "efficiency."
- Let the machine do the dirty work.
- Replace repetitive expressions by calls to a common function.
- Parenthesize to avoid ambiguity.
- Choose variable names that won't be confused.
- Avoid the FORTRAN arithmetic IF.
- Avoid unnecessary branches.
- Don't use conditional branches as a substitute for a logical expression.
- If a logical expression is hard to understand, try transforming it.
- Use data arrays to avoid repetitive control sequences.
- Choose a data representation that makes the program simple.
- Write first in an easy-to-understand pseudo-language; then translate into whatever language you have to use.
- Use IF...ELSE IF...ELSE IF...ELSE... to implement multi-way branches.
- Modularize. Use subroutines.
- Use GOTOs only to implement a fundamental structure.

- Avoid GOTOs completely if you can keep the program readable.
- Don't patch bad code—rewrite it.
- Write and test a big program in small pieces.
- Use recursive procedures for recursively-defined data structures.
- Test input for plausibility and validity.
- Make sure input doesn't violate the limits of the program.
- Terminate input by end-of-file or marker, not by count.
- Identify bad input; recover if possible.
- Make input easy to prepare and output self-explanatory.
- Use uniform input formats.
- Make input easy to proofread.
- Use free-form input when possible.
- Use self-identifying input. Allow defaults. Echo both on output.
- Make sure all variables are initialized before use.
- Don't stop at one bug.
- Use debugging compilers.
- Initialize constants with DATA statements or INITIAL attributes; initialize variables with executable code.
- Watch out for off-by-one errors.
- Take care to branch the right way on equality.
- Be careful when a loop exits to the same place from side and bottom.
- Make sure your code "does nothing" gracefully.
- Test programs at their boundary values.
- Check some answers by hand.
- 10.0 times 0.1 is hardly ever 1.0.
- Don't compare floating point numbers solely for equality.
- Make it right before you make it faster.
- Make it fail-safe before you make it faster.
- Make it clear before you make it faster.
- Don't sacrifice clarity for small gains in "efficiency."
- Let your compiler do the simple optimizations.
- Don't strain to re-use code; reorganize instead.
- Make sure special cases are truly special.
- Keep it simple to make it faster.

- Don't diddle code to make it faster—find a better algorithm.
- Instrument your programs. Measure before making "efficiency" changes.
- Make sure comments and code agree.
- Don't just echo the code with comments—make every comment count.
- Don't comment bad code—rewrite it.
- Use variable names that mean something.
- Use statement labels that mean something.
- Format a program to help the reader understand it.
- Document your data layouts.
- Don't over-comment.

Documentation Reviews

*It's Not Clear Why We Need Documentation Reviews,
Since We Have a Staff of Proofreaders Who Read Our
Documentation Before It Goes Into Final Printing. Is That
an Alternative to Reviews?*

Certainly proofreading is essential for any documentation, because grammatical and typographical errors cause readers to lose respect for a document. But how do you assure yourselves that the documentation is technically correct? You certainly wouldn't consider syntax checking sufficient to ensure the correctness of code, would you?

Incidentally, proofreading is a no cost by-product of technical reviews of documentation. A master copy of the reviewed document is kept by the recorder, and typos are simply noted in passing and then sent along with the other review material.

*Just What Do You Consider "Documentation" for
Purposes of Documentation Review?*

Different types of documentation may be reviewed at different times, or even several times for different purposes, but all documentation must be reviewed at least once. For instance, commentary within the code should be reviewed at the time the code is reviewed, prior to acceptance into any system. The comments are properly considered part of the module, but are also clearly documentation. Indeed, the code itself is documentation and in some instances is reviewed separately as to its quality in the documentation role. Some installations go so far as to exclude any written documentation for code except for that actually compiled and stored with the code. In those cases, documentation reviews may be a subset of code reviews, but the documentation is still conceptually separate, in the sense of having different characteristics to be reviewed.

Specifications should ordinarily become part of the system documentation. Similarly, various design documents may serve a dual purpose—working documents for development and support material for maintenance and operation. Nevertheless, working descriptions of the system—be they specifications, designs, or code—will rarely be entirely sufficient as system documentation. Therefore, separate documentation reviews will have to be set for anything else that will be retained for use with the system after development.

Would That Include User Documentation?

By all means. User documentation is probably the most neglected of all documentation. The neglect is probably an unintentional bias on the part of the developers—who can empathize a bit with the problems of the maintainers, but not with those of the users. User documentation is often done in a rush. By the time the user documentation is developed, the product has often been shipped and installed. By the time the documents arrive, many users have struggled to develop their own, have given up on the system, or are using the system in some home-grown fashion that they were able to figure out without help from the developers.

Some of these problems can be relieved by making the user documentation part of the specifications and reviewed as such. Even so, the review will be useless unless user representatives are involved. Typical user documentation is prepared by developers who understand the system well from the point of view of someone on the inside and familiar with the technical jargon. They are in most cases quite unlike the people who will try to use the documentation.

To worsen the problem, few technical people have skill in written communication. They find writing documentation to be the least fun part of the system development cycle. They spend as little time at it as possible, as late as possible, and their heart simply isn't in it. Yes, we must definitely review user documentation.

But Just How Important Is User Documentation Anyway, as Long as the System Itself Works Properly and Is Properly Documented?

No matter how good the hardware and software of a system is, the system will fail if people cannot learn—or have difficulty learning—how to use it. Therefore, without quality user documentation, the system can hardly "work properly." And without reviews, how can we know the quality of the documentation?

Who Should Be Involved in the User Documentation Review?

The best people to review user documentation are—you guessed it—the users. They are most aware of their needs, their skills, and their motivations. In one sense, only the user can review user documentation—the user is the ultimate authority. If the user says the document is not clear, it may be the "fault" of the writers, or it may be the failing of the user, but in either case something must be done.

In another sense, though, the user must be aided in the review by people whose broader experience in data processing may provide insights not available to the user concerning how the documentation will actually function in the future. This helping function is sometimes performed by someone from the training staff who will be responsible for teaching the use of the system. Such a trainer needs to review the documentation in any case and so does double duty on the review committee. Trainers, being experts at communication, are almost always a source of valuable tips on written communication. Moreover, "documentation" in a wider sense includes, and must be related to, training programs.

There are several other groups that may have an active interest in the quality of the user documentation. For instance, someone from the marketing staff in a software firm will want a crack at the material the users will see. All too often, salespeople are the ultimate representatives to irate customers. If the documentation doesn't do its job, the salesforce will be incessantly occupied with interpreting the mystical words.

Do the Producers Have to Get Involved in Documentation Reviews?

Whatever the ultimate use of the documentation, we must not forget to involve the system's producer. No matter how clear a document is, it will be all the more dangerous if it turns out to be inaccurate. Without the producer present, we stand in danger of approving a document that effectively describes some other system.

When producing documentation for nontechnical people who somehow use the system, we have to strike a balance between telling the truth and making ourselves clear. The *whole* truth usually proves overwhelming, even to technical people; but partial truths have a tendency to come back later to haunt us. By mixing users, trainers, and producers in a documentation review, we stand a better chance of getting just that mixture of truth, half-truth, and white lies that effectively gets the point across.

What Do You Look for in Reviewing User Documentation?

The first thing to look for is *some evidence of testing.* Even with a panel of the world's greatest expert editors, we cannot really anticipate how a user will react to a document without trying it out. The writers of the documentation should provide data on tests they have conducted, exactly as a programmer would provide data on machine test runs.

If test data are provided, then the review panel need only verify two things:

1. The test procedures were valid.
2. The information in the documentation is complete and correct.

There are, of course, many ways for a test to be invalid. The people tested may not be representative of the actual users—they may know too much or too little, or perhaps their motivations are weaker or stronger. The test itself might not be thorough enough, or perhaps it emphasizes many details at the expense of a few important points that must be gotten across. The testers may have communicated much information to the user representative other than that contained in the documentation itself, thus creating an atypically helpful situation. Conversely, the test environment may be too strict and therefore unfairly critical of the documentation. Rarely does documentation stand absolutely on its own. Users have access to related documents, to other users who may have supplementary knowledge, and sometimes to experts on a consultation basis. Moreover, they may be able to solve certain problems by trying them out on the system at negligible cost or risk.

All such factors must be taken into account by the committee reviewing the adequacy of the tests. Of course, if the material is incorrect, then issues must be raised as with any other material, so the committee does double duty, just as in a code review. In most instances, reviewing the testing of some documentation is far more difficult than reviewing the testing of some code—because the environment is so much more slippery. Fortunately, that environment is also much more adaptable, so that people have a way of muddling through and getting the job done in spite of poor documentation.

But It's Really Impossible for Us to Get Testing Done on Our Documentation Before a Review. Isn't There Some Other Approach?

Of course there are other approaches, but you are skating on thin ice when you distribute untested documentation. We don't mean that the tests have to be carried out like an ironclad sociological experiment, though careful planning never hurts. What we want is that *some* people actually try to use the documentation under moderately controlled conditions.

You may have the impression that experienced writers can merely draft complete, correct, and communicable documentation sitting at the typewriter, but this is merely lack of knowledge on your part. Every good writer has developed techniques for testing written material before foisting it on the world. What you see as the writer's "work" is actually tested and revised and retested and re-revised material.

Nevertheless, we know that common practice in the industry today is to leave most of the testing of documentation to the ultimate user, on the job. Where this is the practice, we can expect 100 percent improvement just by having anybody review the material, in any way whatsoever. Get the reviewing started. Don't be put off by the requirement for other testing. Once reviewing starts, many people will become aware of the serious need for testing, so eventually things will work out.

Do You Consider Error Messages to Be Part of User Documentation?

Absolutely. Error messages often fall between two stools—considered by programmers to be user problems and by users to be programmer problems. Although error messages may be reviewed in specification or code reviews, the state of the art in writing them is so poor that it may prove worthwhile to convene special reviews for the set of error messages in a system.

Error messages are, in effect, the primary user documentation. Many users never use a manual, but all users see error messages from time to time. If the messages are the result of "clever" ideas of some of the least capable programming trainees, respect for the system can be destroyed in short order. Messages should be clear and explicit. Where consistent with these goals, they should be short—but the object is not to save computer resources.

All too often, the designers of widely used software know full well that they, themselves, will never be using the error messages. At least that's the impression conveyed by the typical set of cryptic system messages. The truth is probably that the producers never realize that the error messages are cryptic. *They* know what they mean, and they lack that rare ability to project what their error message will do to a frustrated, harassed user. Once error message reviews are scheduled, the producer's empathy with the user starts a continuous uphill climb. Of course, *testing* the messages is, as usual, the best way to prepare for the review, but short of that, the review alone will be a blessing compared with current practice.

Is There Some Sort of Checklist for Documentation?

We found it difficult to come up with one checklist that would apply to all forms of documentation. Documentation is too varied. Instead, we have a shopping list out of which various checklists can be extracted.

A Shopping List of Faults to Look for in Reviewing Documentation

1. Have all phases of the document's life cycle been considered?
   a. Is there provision for user feedback?
   b. Is there provision for making changes?
   c. Will changes in the system cause difficult or expensive changes in the documentation?
   d. Is there adequate provision for distribution of the documents?
   e. Is there adequate provision for the distribution of changes to the documents?
   f. Can documents be reproduced easily?
   g. Can copying be prevented or controlled?
   h. Are there available people to supplement documents?
   i. Do the user and creators agree on the purpose of the documents?
   j. Is there adequate provision for keeping support people current and informed?
   k. Are tools available (e.g., fiche readers, terminals) for reading/accessing/storing these materials?
   l. Have the documents been properly approved?
   m. Do these documents show where they fall in the total plan?
   n. Do the documents indicate other documents that may be used as follow-up?
2. Are the contents of the documents adequate?
   a. Coverage of topics
      i. All essential topics complete?
      ii. Have irrelevant topics been kept out?

        iii. Topics complete, but is there completeness in detail, assumptions, facts, unknowns?

        iv. Is technical level appropriate to level of document?

        v. Who is the intended reader (readers)?

  b. Correctness

        i. No errors of fact?

        ii. Are there no contradictions?

  c. Evidence

        i. Is the evidence adequate to support the presentation?

        ii. Is the evidence realistic?

        iii. Is there a clear statement of goals of the documents? Are the goals consistent?

        iv. Does the presentation sound authoritative?

3. Are the materials in the documents clear?

  a. Are examples clear?

        i. Used where necessary?

        ii. Relevant where used?

        iii. Contribute to understanding?

        iv. Misleading?

        v. Wrong?

        vi. Less effective than their potential?

  b. Are diagrams, pictures, or other visual materials clear?

        i. Used where necessary?

        ii. Relevant where used?

        iii. Contribute to understanding?

        iv. Clearly rendered?

        v. Misleading?

        vi. Wrong?

        vii. Less effective than their potential?

        viii. Appropriate amount of information?

  c. Is terminology clear?

        i. Consistent throughout all documents?

        ii. Conforms to standards?

          iii.   Is there a glossary, if appropriate?

          iv.   Are definitions correct?

          v.   Are definitions clear?

          vi.   Is the glossary complete?

          vii.   Is there too much technical terminology?

    d.   Is writing style clear?

          i.   Do paragraphs express only connected ideas and no more?

          ii.   Are larger logical units broken by subheadings?

          iii.   Is the fog index too high for the audience?

          iv.   Does it talk down to the typical reader?

          v.   Does it put you to sleep?

          vi.   Is there an abstract?

4.   Are the documents adequately supplied with referencing aids?

    a.   Is there a table of contents, if appropriate?

    b.   Is the table of contents well placed?

    c.   Is there an index, if appropriate?

    d.   Is the index well placed?

    e.   Is the table of contents correct?

    f.   Is the index correct?

          i.   Are page references accurate?

          ii.   Are there entries for the kinds of things the various classes of users will be seeking?

          iii.   Are the entries under the right titles?

          iv.   Are there alternate titles for entries that might be accessed using different terminology?

          v.   Are major and minor entries for the same terms distinguished?

          vi.   Are terms broken down adequately, or are there too many page references under single terms, indicating that more subcategories are needed?

          vii.   Are there superfluous entries?

    g. Is there a bibliography of prerequisite publications?

        i. If there are no prerequisites, is this stated?

        ii. Is the bibliography where it will be found before attempting to read the document?

        iii. Are the references complete enough to locate the publications?

        iv. Are there annotations to help the reader choose the appropriate document?

    h. Is there a bibliography of related publications which may contain further information?

        i. If this is a unique source of information, is this stated?

        ii. Are the references complete enough to locate the publications?

        iii. Are there annotations to help the reader choose the appropriate document?

    i. Does the organization of the documents themselves contribute to the ease of finding information?

        i. Is page numbering sensible?

        ii. Is page numbering complete?

I Read Somewhere About Automatic Tests for Quality of Documentation. Are There Such Tests, and Can They Be Used Instead of or in Addition to Documentation Reviews?

There's a long history of attempts to quantify the quality of written material, especially to evaluate materials for school use. The book, *The Measurement of Readability*, by George R. Klare, Iowa State University Press, 1963, surveys the work done up to that date. To our knowledge, there have been a number of attempts to automate some readability measures.

General Motors has a system called STAR (Simple Test Approach for Readability) which has had wide use. Information can be obtained from:

Colleen A. Belli
Public Relations Staff
General Motors Corporation
3044 West Grand Blvd.
Detroit, MI 48202

A program listing is available for a BASIC or FORTRAN IV program to give a variety of measures on a text.

The GM program is the only one we know of where a program is available, but it's probably not necessary to automate the measurement to make it useful for input to a review. Some simple mechanical checks that can be done by hand include (see Bibliography for references):

1. Gunning's Fog Index,
2. Flesch's Reading Ease Formula (*How to Test Readability*), and
3. The Cohen Cloudiness Count.

We've also been informed of a most interesting manual method called TEXT-RAY analysis, used by the U.S. government to try to overcome their bad reputation for muddled writing.

This method is described in a government document, issued by the comptroller general of the United States, entitled *From Auditing to Editing*. It involves graphic analysis of sentences marked according to a set of rules that could presumably be implemented on a computer system.

Information is also available from Bell Laboratories on their Writer's Workbench project. (See Bibliography for details.)

Can These Methods Be Used in Place of Documentation Reviews?

We seriously doubt that they can *replace* reviews because they treat only the clarity of written material. They don't deal with such questions as:

1. Clarity of diagrams,
2. Correctness of written material,
3. Suitability of overall organization,
4. Coverage of topics,
5. Indexing,

and a host of others treated on our checklist. But we do recommend a little manual application of one or more of these indexes to texts that form part of reviewed material. The results could point the way to improvement, without getting too involved with unmanageable questions of style.

I'm Sure That the "Astronomical" Number of Errors in (the First Edition of) this Handbook Was Intentional (Bebugging?); But if Not, You Had Better Review Your Own Work, Hadn't You?

We could pretend that we left certain errors in intentionally, since we did do that with one. For the most part, however, the typographical errors in the first edition of the handbook provide an interesting object lesson for technical reviewers.

The errors are there because of a combination of time pressure and inadequate hardware/software to support the activity. We were using an IBM Composer that had sufficient memory for only two pages at a time and had no provision for off-line storage of a page. Therefore, each page had to be reviewed while it was still in the machine, and if the reviews got more than one page behind, the keying had to stop and wait until part of the memory could be cleared. If we had not been in a hurry to get the handbook ready for seminars, the keying could simply have waited for reviewing, but we were pressed.

Knowing about these problems, we organized a floating team of reviewers for a continuing series of speed reviews. Whenever these reviews were fully carried out by the entire review team, a high level of accuracy was attained. One problem, though, resulted from the page-by-page nature of the reviews. Because we never saw more than one page at a time, there were several places where material was repeated or omitted across page boundaries. Once we paid the price of late detection of some of these boundary problems, we revised our reviewing procedure to give a page-to-page dimension.

But the requirements of having the entire team available on instant call at all times proved too heavy to apply uniformly. Sometimes people had clients to work with; sometimes they got sick; sometimes they had to leave early to handle a personal problem; sometimes the phone rang. As a result, some pages did not get the full review treatment.

Our control over the whole process was not good enough to say with certainty which pages did not receive the full review designated for the entire handbook—a failure of management control that our clients are warned not to repeat. The reason we didn't have this control is that we didn't make a separate Review Report for each and every page.

Our latest figures, using errors reported by our readers, are as follows:

Number of Errors on the Page	Number of Pages with this Number	Total Errors	Percent of Errors
0	148	0	0.0
1	32	32	40.0
2	15	30	37.5
3	6	18	22.5

Total pages = 201   percent error-free pages = 74.6
Total errors = 80

Average errors per page = .40

Some of the important error categories were
Misspelling the word "review"	11
Misspelling the word "occurred"	4
Misspelling the word "manager"	4
Missing the letter "i"	about 35
Missing a doubled letter	about 15
Wrong italization	18

With faster feedback of this information into the review process, the error rate could probably have been cut in half. Many of the above error types were found during review, but were not tabulated, so we didn't know we should make a special effort to look for these repeated offenders. In addition, special checks should have been made systematically on headings, for although errors were few in headings, they were very conspicuous.

Is It Really Necessary to Make a Separate Review Report for Each and Every Page, Just for Proofreading?

Probably not, as long as some form of written control is present. We're experimenting with the following Proofreading Checkoff sheet, which allows us to handle six pages on one piece of paper, with up to three reviewers for each page. Errors are written down, and the followup on them is written down and checked by at least one person. Working back against these forms, we should be able to spot any page that didn't receive full reviewing. Also, if some page has many errors, it usually indicates that more reviewing will pay off, as the typist was having a bad page.

The person posting the checkoff sheet should watch for signs that one or more proofreaders weren't paying attention. There should be a large overlap in the errors found, if all readers were working accurately. We give each reader a clean copy, not marked by the other readers, so we can check for overlap. This gives the independence we need to make judgments on how good a job the readers were doing.

Proofreading Checkoff for:

Page	Reader	Date	Errors	Corrected	Checked

Prepared By: *Date:*

Test Plan Reviews

Why Isn't a Test Plan Review Simply Part of the
Functional Specification Review, Since Any Good
Specification Should Contain Acceptance Test Material?

There are two reasons why the acceptance test material from a functional specification is not adequate for a final test plan. First of all, the acceptance test material in the specification is usually only given at a high level, with many details left to the design and coding phases. Second, the specification only gives the tests that the *user* will need to accept the system. Generally, such user tests will have to be supplemented by an equal or greater volume of tests that depend upon the internal structure of the system and on its relationship with the hardware and system software. There is no way the user can specify or even review such test material, nor can the developers specify most of it prior to the completion of at least the design phase.

Nevertheless, part of the test plan review will consist of relating the detailed test plan to the originally specified acceptance test criteria. If those criteria haven't been reviewed, the test plan review will lose much of its meaning.

Why Isn't the Test Plan Review Part of the Code Review, Since the Code Will Have Been Run Against the Planned Tests?

Some organizations do combine code reviews with some or all of the features of a test plan review. Our own preference is to have test plans developed and reviewed *before* coding takes place, for several reasons.

First, planning tests requires a calm atmosphere. Once the coding is on paper, everyone starts to itch for some sort of machine output.

Second, if test planning is done after coding, there is a tendency for the tests to "track" the code. When this happens, errors and oversights in the code tend to get propagated into the tests, thus making the tests less reliable. Of course, reviews will help correct these oversights, but review results will be better if fewer problems go into the reviews.

Third, actually implementing the tests might require a long lead time. Test files may have to be generated or extracted by sampling from actual files. Harness or test bed code may be needed, either on a stand alone basis or as modifications to system software or, on occasion, even hardware.

Fourth, creation of the test plan is an activity that has great benefits in its own right, especially for its impact on design thinking. If test plan creation is postponed, it cannot affect design except in an *ad hoc,* patched in manner.

But Doesn't the Code Tend to "Track" the Test Plan?

Yes, that's a definite possibility. But why should we worry about that, since that's exactly what the code is supposed to do.

*I Don't Agree with the Idea That Tests Can Be Made Up
Before the Code Is Complete. Won't There Always Be
Coding Situations That Require Special Tests, Not Related
to the Specification in Any Direct Way?*

Of course there will be some such tests, and these tests
will have to be reviewed during code reviews, as a supplement to the previously developed test plan. Indeed,
just *because* we will have to create such tests, we would like
to unburden the code review in any way we can. If most
of the tests have been planned and reviewed in test plan
reviews, the code reviews can concentrate on three kinds
of high level issues:

1. The structure of the code itself,
2. The effectiveness of the code at meeting the pre-
    planned tests, and
3. The adequacy of the supplementary tests and of the
    code at meeting them.

We should also observe that the reviewers will want
to consider very carefully any piece of code that requires
an excessive amount of these supplementary tests. If a
great many tests cannot be related directly to the function
of the code, an overly complicated approach to the coding
may have been taken. At the very least, such code will
tend to contain a great many surprises for the maintainers.

What Should a Test Plan Consist Of?

Quite simply, a test plan specifies a set of *environments* in
which the module or system is to be executed, along with
the *inputs* it will receive in each environment and the
outputs expected for each of those inputs.

By environment we mean such things as hardware
configuration, special features in use, loading factors, op-

erating system configuration, simultaneously operating tasks, and any other factors that might affect or be affected by the performance of the code, with the exception of the "direct" inputs and outputs. We can't always draw a clear line between environment and direct inputs and outputs, but that's not important. Generally speaking, the environment is that part of the input that remains relatively constant over the period of the test, plus that part of the *potential* output that is not supposed to be affected— that is, that is also supposed to remain relatively constant.

Why Are You Making What Seems to Be a Rather Artificial Distinction Between Environment and Other Input and Output?

The distinction is intended to call attention to potential influences on and effects of the code that might be overlooked in the review. By separating the environment, we are reminded to invite certain people to the review who might not otherwise even know it's going on.

For instance, one of our clients implemented a data entry application whose pattern of disk access turned out to interfere with almost every other major application running in the same multiprogramming environment. Had one of the systems programmers, or perhaps one of the programmers responsible for another major application, been present at the test plan review, a serious and costly political hassle might have been avoided. Had the possibility of interference been considered *in advance,* there were several easy methods of avoiding it. After the fact, however, the data entry people had too much invested in their particular design simply to redo the system—though in the end, that's what they were forced to do.

The principle is this: Try to think of everyone who *might* be affected by the system, especially including those who *ought not* to be affected. Get such people, or their representatives, to participate in the review of your test plans. And don't forget that in many cases, the tests *themselves* may require substantial interference with normal computer operations or with operations in the users' departments. For example, new hardware may have to be cut in temporarily while other applications are running, causing unpredictable ramifications. Or parallel operations may prove burdensome and confusing to the user and must therefore be planned and reviewed with utmost care and concern.

Who Else Should Be Invited to Test Plan Reviews?

The user is always required when reviewing those parts of the test plan that concern the face of the system seen by the user. In many cases, however, an inexperienced user may not be able to anticipate the full range of inputs. Quite commonly, the user's conception of input data is far cleaner than the user's real data turns out to be. Therefore, when the user hasn't really experienced computer input before, it's wise to put some other user on the review committee as well—one who has often felt the sting of input errors.

Commonly, a representative of the coding group is present at the test plan review—if only for educational purposes. One of the designers will be present to make sure the tests interpret the design properly. If the installation has a separate quality assurance group, one of its members will usually participate. Such testing specialists quickly learn to spot nicks, cracks, holes, and chasms in proposed test plans.

What About Checklists?

Most organizations now have some sort of standards for testing that can be used as the initial basis for a checklist. Beginning on page 371 we give a comprehensive checklist published by Laura L. Scharer (1977) on system testing. You may want to eliminate some of the items in order to create a more compact checklist for your own use. Before doing so, however, you should consult the original article for the reasoning behind this particular choice of items. Another source of checklist material is one of the several good books on testing, such as given in the bibliography.

System Testing Checklist

I. Test Preparation

   1. Test team members given assignments.

   2. Final operating environment defined.

   3. All conditions to be tested, identified, and documented.

   4. Test files created for execution of all system functions.
   - **a.** file sequences correct
   - **b.** meaningful starting values established
   - **c.** all record types included
   - **d.** file volume large enough to demonstrate control groups, totals, page breaks on reports
   - **e.** meaningful time period established

   5. Test transactions developed to demonstrate all test cases.
   - **a.** unit testing criteria satisfied
   - **b.** system testing criteria satisfied
   - **c.** transactions created for at least two cycles of system execution
   - **d.** end-of-period (month, year) system options demonstrated

   6. Test results predicted and documented for later comparison with computer output.

   7. Parallel system output identified for standard of correctness.

   8. Acceptability and accuracy standards established and documented for later assessment of results.
   - **a.** core availability in production mode
   - **b.** timing constraints in production mode
   - **c.** if 100% accuracy not required—justify

II. Test Operations

   1. Test transactions entered by data entry department using standard procedures.

2. Tests executed by operations personnel without programmer supervision.

3. Transaction listing obtained before text execution.

4. File dumps obtained prior to program execution.

5. System executed to demonstrate all test cases. (May require multiple executions of the system or of individual modules.)

6. All hardcopy (reports, control totals) obtained.

7. Transcription of console messages (and timing information) obtained.

8. File dumps taken after test execution.

9. Output from parallel run available.

III. Unit-Test Evaluation

1. JCL executes program without errors or unnecessary operator intervention, and file labels are correct.

2. JCL-defined file capacities adequate, assuming moderate expansion.

3. Execute time acceptable according to preestablished standards.

4. Sufficient core available for execution and moderate expansion of program size.

5. Input data accepted as formatted without data exception.

6. All logical paths executed correctly.

   a. all invalid data trapped
      • troublesome transaction combinations discovered
      • edit messages all forced
      • no-match or invalid-key conditions forced
   b. program-controlled terminations before normal EOJ tested
   c. no-file case executing
   d. empty-file case (file exists, but has no member records) executing
   e. file updating accurate, complete, according to specifications
      • first-record processing accurate

- addition of a record prior to the first record executes correctly
- multiple-file match logic working
- last-record EOF processing accurate
- addition of a record after the last record executes correctly
- fields updated as specified: quantity replacement, quantity addition, etc.
- record deletion, addition executes correctly
- multiple transactions per master record all execute correctly
- changes to keys handled accurately

  f. all report breaks demonstrated
- page overflow
- detail, minor and major control breaks, final control break

7. Created files conform to design specifications.
8. Field sizes in files adequate: no unexpected truncation, loss of significant digits.
9. Mathematical accuracy, rounding.
10. Reports conform to designed layout.
11. Report information contents agrees with titles, headers.
12. Report page numbering accurate.
13. Spelling correct on report titles, headers.
14. Field sizes on reports adequate.
15. Audit trails (control totals) accurate.

IV. System Test Evaluation

1. JCL executes system without errors or unnecessary operator intervention, and file labels are correct.
2. JCL-defined file capacities adequate, assuming moderate expansion.
3. Execute time acceptable according to preestablished standards.
4. File sequences (sort specs) accurate throughout system execution.
5. No-file case executing throughout all system steps.

6. Empty-file case executing throughout all system steps.

7. Available means for cross-checking system results exhausted.

   a. different reports with same or derivative information

   b. file contents vs. report values

   c. control break totals vs. final totals

8. Interfaces working accurately.

   a. between programs

   b. between subsystems

   c. between other computer systems

   d. with existing manual systems

9. Files closed at EOJ (normal or due to error).

10. Execution sequence (system flow) accurate and workable.

11. Audit trails (control totals) accurate.

12. Error-correction procedure loops work.

13. System restart procedures satisfactory.

14. File recovery procedures satisfactory.

15. Files and reports conform to output from parallel test, if applicable.

16. Output accurate after more than one execution cycle.

17. End-of-period output accurate, and period-totals reset to zero.

V. Acceptability Test.

1. User review of output.

2. Judgment of acceptability according to predetermined standards.

3. Services provided by the system conform to originally stated user requirements.

4. Changes in user requirements since original statement.

5. System testing judged complete.

6. User sign-off on output.

Tool and Package Reviews SECTION
7

Should We, as Consumers of Software Packages, Review Them After We Buy Them?

It would be better to review them *before* buying them, but we realize that many software packages are purchased by people who have purchasing power rather than technical knowledge. Nevertheless, the major cost of a bad piece of purchased software is rarely the purchase or lease price, but rather, the infinitude of costs incurred when trying to use it or in consequence of its use with our own software.

All the old remarks about judging a book by its cover or a car by its paint job apply to the purchase of software. It's pure folly to assume that you can tell the quality of a software product based on the prospectus or the salesperson's pitch. You have to get beneath the often slick surface. At the very least, you have to review the user's manuals for form and content.

Some of the Software We Purchase Doesn't Have User's Manuals, So How Can We Review Them?

If there are no user's manuals, your review should be short and sweet.

Isn't It Enough Just to Review the User Documentation, Rather Than to Delve into the Innards of the Software?

In most cases, in spite of any claims to the contrary by the salespeople, you will wind up having to maintain the software in some way or another. There may be no maintenance contract, or your use of the system may require changes that fall outside the scope of the maintenance contract or even nullify the contract. In these cases, it is of critical importance to review the insides of the product, not just for accuracy and function, but particularly for maintainability. Besides, if your own people are going to have to work with it, the review process is as good a way as any to start their education.

What If We Have an Ironclad Maintenance Agreement?

First, there's no such thing, in practice, because once the vendor has you hooked into using the system, you're no longer in a position to push certain "rights" specified in the contract.

Second, even if the contract were ironclad, a peek inside the product will give you a most effective way of predicting what sort of experience you're going to have with the product in the future. Cheezy code will cause trouble, whether you wrote it or someone else wrote it. At least when you write it, you have more control over getting it to work when the going gets rough. A maintenance contract isn't worth toothpicks if the product is not maintainable.

Yes, But Our Vendor Simply Will Not Let Us Examine the Insides of the Software, to Protect Their Investment. What Can We Do Then?

In our experience, there are a number of simple solutions to that problem. Number one solution is to find another vendor. The software market is sufficiently competitive that no vendor can afford to maintain a holier-than-thou attitude, unless they have something to hide—such as the inferior quality of their work.

The vendor has a legitimate interest in preventing plagiarism and theft of their trade secrets, but there are ways to inspect code without compromising these interests. As consultants, we commonly look at code and other information our clients consider confidential. If necessary, this confidentiality can be made explicit in a *nondisclosure agreement* signed by both parties before material is exchanged.

For instance, the agreement can contain a clause saying:

> *Each party acknowledges that all material and information which has or will come into the possession or knowledge of each in connection with this contract or the performance thereof, consists of confidential and proprietary data, whose disclosure to or use by third parties will be damaging. Both parties, therefore, agree to hold such material in strictest confidence, not to make use thereof other than for the performance of contract, to release it only to employees requiring such information, and not to release it to any other party without the written consent of the other party. Each party agrees not to release such information or material to any employee who has not signed a written agreement expressly binding himself not to use it other than for the purposes of the present agreement, nor to disclose it except as under this clause.*

Most organizations employing consultants have such a standard clause of their own, as do most established software vendors. It's been our experience that vendors who won't agree to such a relationship are not worth dealing with. What they're hiding usually turns out to be best left hidden.

A second approach is to sample the code, as well as other supporting materials. In any case, you won't usually want to review the entire system. One of the principal advantages of purchasing software is that you shouldn't have to review all of it. You can usually assume a relatively consistent level of work by the vendor—something you can't assume in your own shop. Unless the sample is chosen in a phoney way to fool you, it should suffice to protect you against the truly bad software on the market. It's amazing how much you can learn about what you're getting into with a piece of software, just by spending a few hours with a sample of the code.

It Would Be Very Difficult for Us to Review Our Vendor's Software Because It's Written in a Language We Don't Use. What Can We Do Then?

Again, consider first what you're getting into if you have to do maintenance. Second, learning a new language isn't that big a deal, especially learning it well enough to review, rather than write. And the review will once again be good training.

But suppose that for any one of these reasons you can't or won't review some part of the interior of the product. In that case, you *must* protect yourself by insisting on meetings with several present users of the software. The information gathered from these meetings will constitute the reviewed material. If the vendor can't supply you with names of satisfied customers, you can simply postpone the decision. There's no need to be first on the block.

When you do find satisfied customers, you should obtain sufficient information to be sure that their situation is applicable in your environment. For instance, they may have many assembly language programmers to maintain the product, whereas your shop is strictly COBOL oriented.

*It Seems to Me to Be an Awful Lot of Trouble. It's Also
Potentially Insulting to Someone Who Offers to Give You
Some Piece of Software Free.*

There ain't no such thing as a free lunch, and there ain't
no such thing as free software. Time after time, our clients
have discovered that the most costly pieces of software
are those they were given for nothing. Yes, there are times
when you get something really good—for nothing; but
usually you get something good for nothing. And if the
product is truly good, you'll find that its producers are
proud to have it reviewed, so that others can see what a
fine job they've done.

*I Can See the Value of Reviewing Purchased Tools and
Packages, but I Anticipate Difficulty Selling the Idea
Around Here Because Everyone Is So Busy. Any Ideas?*

Some of our clients have *begun* the practice of reviews by
taking a crack at purchased (or gift) items. Because they
were reviewing work of outsiders, they avoided the heavy
ego involvement scenes that sometimes accompany the
earliest reviews. When they were reviewing gifts, there
wasn't even the problem of embarrassing the manager
who spent half of the department budget on the item.

In reviewing vendor code, they gained valuable
review experience, learned a few (nonproprietary) techniques, and frequently learned how poor some of the
commercially available material truly was. Their collective
egos were given a boost that carried them through reviews
of their own work, and they brought a lot of reviewing
experience to those reviews. They prevented a number
of costly but useless purchases, but even more important,
they saved themselves the trauma of maintaining some
of the systems after purchase.

What Should We Look For in Reviewing a Software Package or Tool?

You should look for the same things you look for in your own work, but you have a right to expect an even higher level of professional work and supporting materials. After all, the cost of such "extras" can be spread over *many* users, which is the fundamental justification for packaged software.

Does That Mean We Have to Go Through Specification Reviews, Design Reviews, Code Reviews, and the Whole Ball of Wax?

It's certainly a wise idea to follow the same pattern you use in your own work, but it won't be as expensive or tedious as you seem to think. If you start by reviewing the specifications of prospective purchases, you will be able to reject many candidates at that level. You're really not interested in the quality of the code in a package for which you have no use.

Of those candidates that pass specification review, many will be eliminated because their designs are not suitable for your installation—or perhaps not suitable for *any* installation. Only when you're sure that you have a well-designed and useful product do you need to examine the quality of the workmanship.

Reviews of Training Materials and Plans

Reviews of Training
Materials and Plans

SECTION
8

In What Sense Are Training Materials Reviewable?

With training materials, we have a choice between intentional and unintentional reviews. If we fail to review them intentionally, they will still be reviewed in the classroom. Though they may not realize it, students review all educational materials. Usually, they think the materials are reviewing them. Any difficulty they experience with the subject matter or presentation is considered to be a reflection on them, rather than on the training itself.

Students rarely believe anything is wrong with their materials, even though they occasionally grumble about a particularly flagrant case. One need only consider the current state of programming textbooks (as Kernighan and Plauger, 1974, did) to see how poorly most educational material is reviewed. It is, of course, to be expected that some errors will creep through even the most careful scrutiny, but in the case of most textbooks, it's hard to believe that anyone even read them for typographical errors. We won't even speak of a review of the content or of the approach.

If a textbook destined for use by 50,000 students is not carefully reviewed, what hope do we have for the materials used to train 50 or 500 operators of a software system? Yet hope we must, for numerous systems, otherwise reasonable, have foundered on the rocks of inept training. As we produce more and more systems with increased direct contact with nontechnical users, the need to review training plans, materials, and facilities will become obvious—but at what cost? If we can learn from our experience in other areas of system development, we'll realize that *training is the programming of the people parts of the system.* It's in *that* sense that all aspects of training are reviewable—just as any other form of programming.

Who Should Participate in Reviews of Training Materials?

There are three essential points of view to any review of training materials:

1. The producers, who know what is to be taught,
2. The teachers, who know what is teachable, and
3. The students, who are the ultimate test.

The producers will verify the technical accuracy of the materials, but cannot be counted upon to appreciate whether a given mode of presentation will be successful. The teachers, on the other hand, may not be sufficiently well versed in the product to separate meaningful material from chaff.

Ideally, training materials are best reviewed with the aid of test data. In this instance, test data means observations and measurements of typical students being taught by typical teachers using the materials. In many cases, however, this kind of test is not feasible, so much of the review has to be based on prior experience with similar situations.

Sometimes a test class is made in which the producers teach the teachers. In a very real sense, this class is a form of review, though it violates many of the procedures we have suggested. On the other hand, just because it is very much like a review, it may prove to be a misleading source of information concerning the materials. It errs in one direction because the materials are in the hands of inexperienced teachers. It errs in the other direction because the teachers are generally not at all representative of the prospective students. One can only hope that the two effects tend to cancel one another. If not, at the very least the "review class" will serve to improve the technical accuracy of the material.

What Should We Look For Besides Accuracy in Training Materials?

Besides accuracy, training materials should be judged for ease of use, ease of distribution, and ease of modification. If there is a change to the system function, will the instructors be notified, and will they be able to make the necessary changes to the materials? If not, is there a structure available to carry out this course maintenance function? Will the costs be reasonable and within a reasonable time frame?

What If There Are No Instructors—As in the Case of Self-Teaching Materials?

It's easy to overlook all the little, but essential, things a live instructor does. Training materials that are supposed to be used without the presence of a live instructor must be reviewed with far more care than materials that will be put in an instructor's hands. The instructor can correct in zillions of ways for tiny errors, misconceptions, or some approach that simply doesn't click with a particular stu-

dent. Without the instructor, the materials have to do all
that work on their own.

There is absolutely no way to verify the quality of
self-instructional material without the use of experiments
with actual students. The number of ways a student can
go wrong is far greater than the number of ways a program can go wrong—and we know how many that is. To
review such materials, tests must be conducted, after
which the results of those tests must be evaluated by both
trainers and producers in the light of the real environment
in which the materials will be used.

To be sure, much if not most self-instructional
material on the market today has not been subject to such
tests and reviews. If you need an unbeatable argument
for reviewing technical training material, just take one of
these nonreviewed courses!

Do You Have Other Checklists for Educational Materials?

The documentation checklist should be most useful for
any kind of written course material. Other course material
that fits the category of specifications, design, or code can
and should be reviewed just as real material is reviewed,
with the understanding that good *teaching* material sometimes has to fudge reality a little.

Checklist for Educational Examples

1. Content
    a. Does the example make one major new point?
    b. Does the example try to make too many major
       new points?
    c. Is the rest of the example consistent with what
       has already been learned?
    d. Is the entire example consistent with standards?
    e. Does the example introduce new terminology? Is
       that terminology defined *before* the example? Is
       it necessary?

     f. Could the student actually *reproduce* the example with present knowledge, or does it require special knowledge (e.g., as of operating system procedures)?

     g. Is the example correct?

     h. Is the point of the example relevant?

     i. Is the example placed in the sequence of materials?

     j. Are the major points of the example adequately and correctly reinforced?

     k. Is the entire example internally consistent?

     l. Are the major points of the example directly related to a real world need? If so, how? If not, why not?

2. Form

     a. Is the method of presentation consistent with our methods of reproduction? If color is used, do we have color reproduction facilities?

     b. Is the method of presentation consistent with our projection methods (35mm, 16mm, super 8mm, continuous film loop, one-half inch cassette video, three-fourths inch cassette video, overhead projector, filmstrip projector)?

     c. Does it make full use of the capabilities of the medium?

         1. Color?

         2. **Graphics?**

         3. *Different Type fonts?*

         4. Special characters? $\uparrow \Omega\Sigma\S \equiv \P\ell\Sigma\infty\Omega \equiv \uparrow$

     d. Does it use media capabilities just for their own sake, rather than to enhance the product?

     e. Does the notation and symbolism conform to current practices?

     f. Is it consistent with our computer systems where appropriate?

     g. Is the method of presentation consistent with the design of the materials (self-paced instruction being truly self-paced rather than scheduled)?

     h. Will the form of the product enhance or detract from its educational value?

3. Environmental
   a. Is there a correct balance between human and machine education?
   b. Are the educational facilities an appropriate environment for the method of presentation?
   c. Is the necessary equipment reliably and consistently available?
   d. Are necessary supplementary supplies and materials reliably and consistently available (e.g., cards, terminals, printer, paper, manuals, supplementary readings)?
   e. Have sufficient time and necessary facilities been allocated to exercise and problem sessions?
   f. Has sufficient time been allocated for programming problems and exercises?

What About Checking the Facilities and Equipment for a Course?

If you are an instructor or a group of instructors about to teach a course in an unfamiliar place, you may be interested in the checklist we have developed for our own business. We teach courses in all sorts of odd places, which makes it most useful to check out a few things both before we go and after we arrive.

- Video Playback Unit
     Playback unit, power cord, extension cords
     Monitor, power cord, extension cord
     Cables:
        Audio from playback unit to monitor
        Video from playback unit to monitor
     Extension cables
     Tapes
     Instruction manuals (playback unit and monitor)
     Phone number to call for assistance

- Video Recorder and Playback Unit
    Same as above with the addition of:
    Camera, power cord, extension cords
    Cables:
        Camera to recorder playback unit, audio and video
    Extension cables
    Lenses:
        Wide angle for fixed work
        Zoom for action
    Tripod
    Lights
    Microphone(s) and extension cables
    Mixer box for microphones, spare battery
    Instruction manuals for all equipment
    Phone number to call for assistance
- 35MM Slide Presentation
    Slides
    Screen
    Slide projector:
        Slide trays
        Remote control unit
        Extension cord for remote control unit
        Power cord and extension cord
        Spare bulb
        Instructions for changing bulb
        Lenses:
            Zoom for large room
            Fixed length for small room
        Clean cloth
        Phone number to call for assistance
    Forceps (tweezers) for removing jammed slides
    Small paperback books to adjust the height of the
    projector
    Handviewer for editing
    Small flashlight for reading script
- Overhead Projector Presentations
    Screen
    Overhead projector:
        Power cord and extension cords

        Spare bulb
        Instructions for changing bulb
        Clean cloth
        Phone number to call for assistance
      Foils—prepared and blank
      Foil frames
      Scotch tape
      Writing instruments—either permanent or erasable
      Erasing instrument
      Pointer (could well be one of the writing instruments)

- Flip Chart Presentations
  - Flip chart easel
  - Flip chart pads
  - Multicolored markers
  - Masking tape for hanging used flip charts
  - Large wastebasket
  - Kleenex or wash 'n dries for wiping hands when markers leak

- Blackboard Presentations
  - White and colored chalk
  - Blackboard
  - Board eraser
  - Kleenex or wash 'n dries
  - Instant camera with film, batteries, and flash for recording blackboard
  - Pointer (a yardstick is most useful for pointing and lining)

- General Room Conditions and Materials
  - Human conditions:
    - Temperature
    - Air circulation
    - Light
    - Space
  - Location of electrical switch and outlets
  - Microphone controls
  - Acoustics
  - Partitions (each partitioned part should be inspected to meet all conditions)
  - Wastebaskets

Ashtrays
Tables and chairs
Lectern
Hole punch
Scissors
Stapler and staples
Pencils and pencil sharpener
Writing pads
Available duplicating facilities

- Audio Cassette

Audio cassette presentations can be used with film strips, slides, or overhead presentations. Some units are programmable to control slide and film projectors.

Audio cassette unit
Extension cords
Power cord and cables, if necessary
Audio cassettes
Scotch tape
Instruction manual
Extra batteries
Microphone and extension cable if going to be recording
Supplementary visual material
Phone number to call for assistance

Reviews of Procedures and Standards

I Don't Understand the Need for Reviewing Procedures and Standards.

All programming installations of any size have sets of standards for program development, systems design, hardware procurement, or what have you. Naturally, these standards are supposed to be followed, but it has been our experience that most places do not follow them to any significant degree—and certainly not to the letter.

Quite often, when code reviews begin, people criticize code for not agreeing with standards. Actually, they are merely discovering the true "standard" that has been in effect since time immemorial. You don't really need reviews to discover that standards aren't being followed. You need only look at the sheer bulk of the written standards manual. The thicker the book, the fewer the people who are following standards. First of all, there are so many standards that nobody could possibly keep sufficiently aware of them. Second, the book got so thick because management thinks that the way to solve problems of standardization is to write some pages in a book, rather than to institute real organizational changes.

What's So Bad About Not Following Standards, When Most of Them Are So Bad It Would Be a Disaster If We Used Them?

If the standards are bad, it's certainly better not to follow them. But wouldn't it be even better to get rid of them or to replace them with meaningful, useful standards? One way to do this is to undertake a review or reviews of the existing standards.

Then too, we mustn't assume that *all* standards are painted with the same brush. Assuming there may be one or two good standards (possibly by accident) among the hundreds, how can you know, without reviews, whether or not they're being followed? There's no sense railing against a bad standard that everyone is ignoring or basking in self-congratulation for good standards that are receiving the same treatment.

The depth of illusion that is possible is well illustrated by a study reported in the January 1976 issue of *Software: Practice and Experience.* At General Motors, where "structured programming" in PL/I was supposedly the standard, 100,000 lines of code were reviewed to see what people were actually doing. Out of these 100,000 lines, there were only eleven DO WHILE statements—seven of them in one program! Among the IF statements, 80 percent had no ELSE clause, just as one would expect from FORTRAN programmers who never made the transition to PL/I.

Most installations would find similar surprises—if only they took the trouble to conduct a standards review of their existing code.

Isn't It Better to Look for Standards Violations When Reviewing Code, to Find Out Which Standards Need to Be Changed, Than to Have an Explicit Review of Standards?

If you can accomplish this, it would probably be better to get your existing standards reviewed as a by-product of other reviews. Several of our clients have declared a moratorium on standards issues in code reviews until the standards are revised. When standards violations are detected, they are recorded as data for eventual standards reviews, but not held against the code under review. When sufficient data concerning actual use of standards have accumulated, they are classified and considered in the review of the corresponding standards.

In any case, you'll have to have a way to review newly proposed standards, so the explicit standards review cannot be dispensed with—unless you decide that explicit standards can be dispensed with.

What Should We Look For in Reviewing Standards?

When you take the trouble to wallow through the pile of miscellaneous information some organizations call standards, you usually are rewarded with some interesting archaeological finds, such as:

1. Contradictory standards;
2. Ancient standards carried forward cumulatively from old systems no longer in use;
3. Standards resulting from political decisions by the old regime no longer in power;
4. Standards defined to incredible levels of nit-picking applied simultaneously with standards that are so broad as to be uninterpretable in a consistent way;
5. Arbitrary choices elevated to the level of gospel;
6. References to documents that no longer exist;
7. Standards applicable for a limited time, but with no date;
8. Rules that, according to their preconditions, could *never* be applied;
9. Explanations that make a seemingly clear standard obscure; and
10. Examples that don't apply to the standard under discussion.

If you are about to undertake a full-scale review of standards, start by taking a sample. Using the sample, try to develop a checklist of "standards for standards," including such items as:

1. Each standard shall be illustrated with at least two specific and relevant examples;
2. Each standard must contain a date of origin and a date beyond which it will not apply unless reviewed and reapproved;
3. Each standard must be accompanied by an explanation, in ordinary English, of *why* it is in the manual, so that when the reasons for its existence no longer apply, it can be deleted without fear of some unknown effect.

Once the checklist becomes reasonably stable, it may be used as the basis for an inspection of the remaining standards, each of which can be classified against its various strictures. The completed checklist then becomes an action list for revision of the standards—either meeting the issues head on or getting rid of the standard.

We Have a Permanent Standards Organization Consisting of Four People Full Time. Shouldn't They Be Doing This Review of Standards?

Of course they should, and if they are, your standards should be in pretty good shape. At least they should be internally consistent. But the standards organization doesn't function in a vacuum—or *shouldn't*, if it does. Standards writers must know what the actual producers are doing and not doing, which is one reason we recommend having someone from the standards group represented on at least some review committees.

By participating in reviews, the standards group can base their standards on what programmers are actually doing, rather than on what someone at a very high level thinks they are doing. Conversely, there should be plain-dirt programmers present in any reviews conducted by the standards group of their own material, to inform standards how their decisions will affect the programming process. As a by-product—or main product, if you like to think of it that way—the programmers may learn about the standards more quickly and more effectively than by waiting to read the nine-inch manual.

Operations and Maintenance Reviews

*Why Are Reviews Required of Systems Already in
Production, Since Changes There are Usually Minor in
Size and Complexity?*

It's hard to understand why many people have the impression that maintenance changes are "minor." The major expenditure in most data-processing installations is for maintenance. People involved in maintenance activity are generally less experienced than people involved in development, so even simple changes may appear complex.

Maintenance staffs are usually working with systems that were designed under older technologies. As a result, maintainability was often neglected, leading to systems that were hard to maintain from the start. Since their development, these programs have been patched, repatched, modified, enhanced, patched, tuned, repatched, simulated, patched, and are now running under emulation. The people who designed these systems are long since vanished from the scene, in many cases leaving nobody in the installation having experience with the system.

To complicate matters, these are ongoing systems. The business pressure of keeping these systems running is intense, thus increasing the chance for error. When an error does occur, the consequences can be staggering, yet errors occur in more than half of the maintenance changes—even those as small as one line of code.

We don't have to look far for the source of these difficulties, even in code that was originally well designed for maintenance. If documentation was created, it certainly wasn't maintained. Sometimes we find little more than a flow chart—not of what the program does, but of what it once may have done. The maintenance programmer daily encounters vestiges of old changes, such as labels that are never referenced, variables set to values that are never used, dummy routines that branch immediately back to the point of invocation, or huge sections of code activated by long-forgotten flags unknown to anyone and not described in any documentation.

The quality of these products often creates a morale problem. In many cases, this problem is intensified by the general knowledge that a new system is being designed, so that the maintenance programmers are responsible only for keeping this beast ambulatory for "one more month" until the last few bugs are out of the new one.

The pressure on maintenance is growing more intense every day. The severe rush on maintenance efforts rarely leaves adequate time to test a patch, let alone to explore its effects on the rest of the system. Eventually, things reach the point where each patch is more likely to create errors than correct them. Before long, the programmers realize that they are not correcting today's errors, but merely transforming them into tomorrow's more difficult errors. The very procedures and methodologies used in most maintenance efforts are creating monster systems that are becoming increasingly out of control. A sorry, sorry state—not at all what you'd call "minor" in size and complexity.

But How Can Reviews Help Out in This Situation, When We Already Lack Adequate Time to Make Maintenance Changes?

Pulling yourself out of a hole can be a problem, but maintenance reviews pay off quickly. True, you now spend time reviewing, but other times are reduced to more than compensate for review time. Time savings occur in:

1. Fewer computer runs,
2. Less analysis of bad runs,
3. Fewer changes to changes,
4. Less complicated future changes, and
5. Fewer production changes and concomitant reruns to repair files.

What Do We Look For in a Maintenance Review?

In the ordinary maintenance review, there are three fundamental questions to be asked:

1. Does the proposed change do what it's supposed to do? That is, is it *correct*?
2. Does the proposed change do things it's not supposed to? That is, is it *consolidated*?
3. Does the proposed change leave the code looking patched? In other words, is it *clean*?

Because the maintenance change is often to a small amount of code, but potentially harmful to a large amount of code, the most danger is from side effects, rather than incorrect intended effects. The walkthrough of the added code, therefore, is insufficient as a test of the change.

An excellent way to approach a maintenance review is to ask the three questions in order, using different review techniques for each:

1. *Correct?* Use a walkthrough here, comparing the test results to the specified results, which may take a relatively small part of the review.

2. *Consolidated?* Here an inspection may prove the best way to avoid overlooking some type of side effect. Make a checklist of the ways in which one change can affect existing code and documentation (see the following list for a starting point). Look for each of these side effects in order, so when the inspection is finished, you have strong assurance that nothing has been skipped.

3. *Clean?* Perhaps the best approach to cleanliness is just a generalized look at the code, or perhaps you will prefer a standards inspection. A good check is for each review committee member to show the code to an innocent bystander before the review, asking if they can locate the patch. If they can't tell which code was patched in, then it's probably clean enough to pass review.

How About a Checklist for Potential Side Effects of a Maintenance Change?

Over the years, we've accumulated a lot of cases of "side effects"—unanticipated and usually undesired effects that were triggered by changing "just one thing." We've gathered all these things in the checklist given below.

Because the list gathers material from many installations, systems, and programming languages, not all items will be applicable to your situation. To use the list, have several knowledgeable people sit down in a review, making sure that they understand each item and that inapplicable items are deleted, that applicable items are tailored to your situation, and that any omitted items are added.

Once the list has been tailored to your installation's needs, you may begin to use it in maintenance inspections.

Merely inspect the proposed change for each type of side effect in succession. If the change passes this inspection, it's very likely to work correctly the first time on the machine—and not to cause any side effects.

For convenience the side effects have been divided into four categories: code, data, documentation, and miscellaneous. Don't worry too much about classification, though. It doesn't hurt to catch the same problem under two different categories, but it sure hurts to miss it because of a jurisdictional dispute.

Code Side Effects

Generally, code side effects are the most dramatic, though for that reason they may be detected and corrected earlier. Many of these potential side effects can be caught by a good compiler, perhaps with the aid of the linkage editor and/or operating system. You'll be better off, though, to catch most of them before compiling, since maintenance changes often require huge compilations, within which error or warning messages are often missed.

1. *New Error Message.* If you do make a compilation, make sure that no new messages are issued and no old ones are changed or deleted unless that was the purpose of the change.

2. *Active Label Deleted.* The deleted portion of code may have contained a label branched to from elsewhere. Compiler or cross-reference should spot this, but it's an easy manual check to trace back all deleted labels.

3. *Active Subroutine Deleted.* The deleted portion of code may have contained a PERFORMED paragraph or a closed internal subroutine that is executed from elsewhere. Should be caught by compiler if hand check misses it.

4. *Active Macro Deleted.* The deleted portion of code may have contained a macro definition used to expand code elsewhere. Under some systems, this

would not be caught automatically if the name of the macro is a legal default name, leaving code with a valid interpretation of the unexpanded form.

5. *Active Label Changed.* Instead of deleting a label referenced elsewhere, the change may have placed the label in a slightly different position or changed the code following that label that would be executed after a branch to the label. (Note that without GOTO's these label problems can be controlled.)

6. *Active Subroutine Changed.* A closed subroutine or executed paragraph invoked from elsewhere may have been changed. The cross-reference list should be used to check for this and the label possibility (point 5).

7. *Active Macro Changed.* Any change, no matter how slight, to a macro definition can cause arbitrary amounts of trouble if that macro is used in a different context. Cross-reference listings may not identify all places the macro is invoked. A macro listing from the previous compilation might help—otherwise a hand check of the source code (before macro expansion) must be made. If this list is not available, get a straight listing of the program source code.

8. *Changed Function.* Any function whose line of execution passes through the changed statement could be changed. Walk through each different function that passes through the changed code, checking that the input and output state are as they should be in the new code.

9. *Timing Relationships.* If the speed of execution changes—either faster or slower—and there are any time-dependent operations, the change could cause you trouble. It's best not to have time-dependent code, but sometimes there's no way out. Remember that it's not just slower code that causes trouble of this type.

10. *Efficiency.* Although the code may be time independent, your budget may not be. All functions that pass through the affected code must be checked for

important speed changes that might hurt your computing budget or the performance of the entire program. Don't just check the function you're changing.

11.   *Access Arm Contention.* When timing relationships are changed, new files are added, or file characteristics are changed, the result can be increased access arm contention on movable arm disk files. The function may be exactly the same, but total elapsed processing time can be raised by huge factors—100 times or even more.

12.   *Memory Usage.* If the change requires more primary storage, it may push that part of the code over its allocated memory, resulting in an error.

13.   *Memory Layout.* Even if memory usage decreases, the change may affect the layout of other parts of the program. If the original program was correct and relocatable, this change shouldn't affect it, but the original might not have been entirely correct. For instance, a data word was uninitialized in the original, but happened to fall on a word left zero by the loader. Deleting one word earlier in the program caused the uninitialized word to be laid over a non-zero word, causing the program to fail. The error was, of course, in the original, but wasn't manifest until the "foolproof" change.

14.   *Virtual Behavior.* Any change in core layout, no matter how small, could have an effect on the paging behavior of the program, resulting in a surprising and perhaps unacceptable change in efficiency or elapsed time. For example, pushing just one instruction over a page boundary (and it need not be anywhere near the changes) can double or triple the amount of paging experienced by a program. So large an effect is rare and unpredictable, so you'd better be prepared to ask if it would be possible, and to check for it in the first executions.

15.   *Invocation Count Change.* Certain subroutines, including system subroutines for handling I/O and other system functions, keep a count of the number of

times they are invoked. This count may be used to control messages, priority, system aborts, and other functions. If you change the number of times a routine is entered—either increasing or decreasing—the invocation count will change and could cause side effects.

16. *Change of Priority.* In some operating systems, priority can be lowered and/or raised dynamically by the application program or by the operating system if the program behaves in certain ways. Such a priority change could be triggered by a small change in program size or perhaps a change in the pattern of calling some system routines, resulting in vastly altered operating times.

17. *File Opening.* By opening a file at a different point in a program, we may accidentally give a file different characteristics. For instance, in PL/I an implicit opening can be caused by many file operations, with each operation giving different attributes. Explicit opening before first use prevents this problem, but not all programs in maintenance have followed this safe practice.

18. *File Closing.* The program may cause trouble if it closes or causes to close a file that was open previously. This problem cannot be so easily prevented as the file opening problem. It depends, instead, on a discipline on each programmer to avoid any closing before the last possible use.

19. *On Unit Change.* In PL/I and other languages that provide for interrupts, a program change could change the "active ON UNIT"—that is, the action to be taken in case of a particular interrupt. Such a change could affect any following process that may expect to be interrupted.

20. *Interrupt Mask Change.* In systems with interrupts, certain interrupts can be "enabled" and "disabled" by program action. If a change modifies the "mask" governing enabling and disabling, any subsequent process can be affected. There can be an interrupt

that was previously disabled, or a previously enabled interrupt may now be "masked."

Data Side Effects

Data side effects can be very subtle and related to the actual change in the most oblique ways. Many data side effects lie unnoticed for weeks or months after a change, until some user gets a funny feeling about what's happening to the output. The savings to be gained from finding data side effects in a review before they happen are therefore potentially enormous.

1. *Flag Change.* If the change modifies the state of a flag or deletes the modification of a previously modified flag, or changes the conditions under which a flag is modified, any part of the program that accesses that flag could be affected.

2. *Condition Change.* In languages such as COBOL, which have named conditions, changing a data item's value could change a condition that doesn't seem to have any obvious relationship, according to its name. Check all conditions that are based on any data item changed by the program.

3. *Data Value Change.* Any time a data item is used in more than one place, any change to that item could cause problems with any process that accesses it. Use the cross-reference listing to indicate potentially changed processes.

4. *Changed Allocation.* When dynamic storage allocation is used, any change that allocates or deallocates storage could affect another part of the program. For instance, if an extra item is put on a stack, the stack count in other places could be out of synchronization, perhaps leaving one item unprocessed. If an item is deleted, a system error might result when the stack empties too soon. Also, the total allocation might become too large, dynamically, if additional allocations are made by the changed code.

5. *Overlay Change.* When various data areas are overlaid, the chances for side effects escalate. Avoid overlaying whenever possible. Where it must be done or has been done, check each and every name under which the same storage can be accessed or changed.

6. *Parameter Change.* If a subroutine is changed, and if that subroutine now changes some parameter passed to it by reference, the calling routine can be devastated. In FORTRAN, for instance, the called routine can even change "constants." Search out all references to parameters and eliminate such changes if possible, but be sure to check out all that can't be eliminated.

7. *File Position Change.* If a sequential file is read or written or was formerly read or written by the changed code, any change in the number of reads or writes or in any other file positioning actions could disturb the behavior of other regions of code. Even on a print file, an extra line could cause disruption of line counts or break up a previously contiguous group of output lines.

8. *Invalid Pointer.* Whenever data structures are linked together by pointers, certain operations on the pointer itself are not, of course, side effects, but operations on the referenced material may affect the pointer in nonobvious ways. If the number of items in a table is changed, the pointer to the last element may not be updated, or the table count may not reflect the change. Even moving an item within core or back and forth to a backing store can render pointers invalid.

9. *Record Layout Changes.* Expanding, contracting, or deleting a field in a record can change the definitions of other fields, which in turn can disrupt other programs that reference those fields or other parts of the same program. In higher level languages, recompilations may be required, but these do not always automatically correct the problem. In some data base systems, the change of physical record layout

is "transparent" to the user programs—except for possible efficiency considerations or bugs in the data base system.

10. *Security Alterations.* In some operating systems, files and data bases can be protected with some access control scheme. If the scheme is dynamic, any change to the security level or interlock pattern could have effects on other portions of the same program or on other programs operating in parallel.

Documentation Side Effects

Probably the most frequent side effect of maintenance changes is the corruption of the existing documentation. The programs change and yet the documentation remains the same. Even when an effort is made to update the documentation, subtle points are overlooked in the rush to production. Eventually, the accumulation of small errors in the documentation produces documents that nobody can rely on. After that, nothing short of a major effort to rewrite can restore the documentation to usefulness. Only by systematic review of the impact of each change on all documentation can we keep the documentation current and useful.

1. *New Name.* When a new data name, file name, or label is created, it must be posted to all reference lists. The newest names are the ones most likely to be sought in the documentation, yet are the least likely to be found there.

2. *Old Name Deleted.* When an old name is no longer used, it should be deleted from all appearances in the documentation. If the documents are not well indexed, it may prove difficult to locate all references. Eventually, old names accumulate in a document, cause confusion, and slow down the use of that document. An excellent practice is to create a section of the document called "formerly used names."

These names are kept in the index as well, so that anyone running across a leftover name can immediately find out that the name is no longer in use. The list of formerly used names can also be helpful in avoiding the use of names recently in use, which may prove confusing.

3. *Invalid Index.* When pages are added to or deleted from a document, the index may be rendered invalid. Without automatic production of the index that updates all later page references, such an index becomes worse than useless. It becomes misleading. One method of keeping the index valid is to use fractional page numbers for inserts. This postpones the problem of updating the index until the pages are renumbered, but then makes the job practically impossible without starting over. Also, any indexable items in the insert must be referenced—to the fractional page numbers. This kind of updating seems, at the time, to be a real pain in the neck, but if you aren't going to do it, then get rid of the document altogether.

4. *Invalid Table of Contents.* When sections are added or deleted, the table of contents becomes invalid. Usually, all this requires is a retyping of a page or two. Don't make the mistake, however, of thinking that the table of contents is the only reference list that must be updated. In general, especially for large documents, the index is a far more important starting point for information searches.

5. *New Error Message.* Of all the error messages, the newest are the ones most likely to be encountered in the use of the system, yet they are the least likely to be found in the message reference manual. "Self-documenting messages" are one solution to this problem, but few systems are willing to devote sufficient storage or time to make messages truly self-documenting. The best way to be sure that messages get into the message documentation is to have an automatic way of updating that documentation. Even

then, the reviewers need to check that the programmer has taken the trouble to activate the update.

6. *Deleted Error Message.* It's not usually too serious if we forget to delete the documentation for a deleted error message. Nevertheless, it's good to keep things tidy and to prevent the documentation from growing overly large. Also, keep a list of previous error messages so that they won't be reused. There often are old copies of documentation laying around that would give a user the wrong interpretation of the new message under the old name.

7. *Error Message Meaning Changed.* Old copies of documentation make it very difficult to "spread the word" when an existing message changes meaning, even if the master documentation is updated. The review group will want to question any change of meaning or addition of new meaning to an existing error message. Usually it's best to create a new message to handle the new case. Any cost in machine resources is quickly recovered by benefitting the otherwise puzzled users.

8. *Operator Response Changes.* All the same arguments we've given about error messages apply to operator responses. In addition, if new operator responses give the operators more power, it's usually a good idea to provide training. Otherwise, the operators tend to continue as always, ignoring the new and improved ways of doing things. The review group should ask, How will the operators learn to use these new features?

9. *Accepts New Data.* When input routines are modified to be more forgiving or to accept previously forbidden forms of input, failure to document and train can wipe out the value of the changes. The review group must once again ask, How are these new features communicated to the people who prepare the input?

10. *Rejects Old Data.* When acceptable ranges of input are narrowed, the users will ordinarily find out, even

if the changes are not documented, when they try to use previously acceptable inputs. Nevertheless, their attempts to get the system to accept these data will prove costly and annoying unless they are informed in advance of the changes.

11.   *New Data Interpretation.* When previously acceptable input is now accepted under a different interpretation, users will make costly mistakes unless they are most carefully and thoroughly prepared for the changes. It will generally be best for the review group to question a design that changes the interpretation of existing inputs, rather than incur the costs of dumping such a design on the users, no matter how carefully they are prepared.

Miscellaneous Side Effects

Rather than debating the classification of a particular side effect you encounter, add it to this list of miscellaneous side effects.

1.   *Clerical Procedures.* Take the time to review what effects will be made before and after the computer portion of the processing. For instance, incorporating more information in a report may eliminate or change clerical operations that previously had to be performed before the former report was used. Although these short cuts may seem completely advantageous, any changes in clerical procedures can initially be expected to lead to errors unless specific provision is made to retrain those people performing the operations.

2.   *Forms.* Changes may require new forms or new interpretations of old ones. In the first case, form printing may be the longest lead time item in the design—and the existence of a five-year supply of old forms may generate resistance to the new system. In both cases, the review group had better check that the system will provide some information along with the first new outputs, so that users understand the new material.

3. *Impact on Other Systems.* In one case, a maintenance change increased the amount of six-part output from an insignificant few pages to a major portion of the inventory. When it came time to run other systems using six-part paper, the stock was quickly depleted. There's no end to such subtle effects and no way to guarantee that all of them are caught in a review. It never hurts, though, for the review group to take a few minutes and brainstorm what areas may have been overlooked. Keep track of all cases that occur, and eventually you'll have a pretty effective checklist, including such items as:
    a. Use of a shared forms inventory;
    b. Shared hardware resources;
    c. Skilled personnel needed by two systems;
    d. Scheduling conflicts;
    e. Telephone or communication line loading;
    f. Exclusive use of files; and
    g. Competition for auxiliary equipment or services, such as bursters, delivery carts, and storage space.

4. *Job Control.* Many program changes require associated job control changes. Such changes are obviously part of the "side effects" of any maintenance change. Less obvious are the changes that make the job control procedures less efficient, though still valid. The review group must check that the previous job control is still the best for the modified system. Will there be inefficiencies? Will operating procedures become less convenient? Can we take advantage of the change to bring the system more in line with present operational standards or with newly available equipment?

5. *Expectations.* One of the most frequently overlooked side effects is the effect of a modification on *what people think*. The announcement of a change may make the users prepare themselves (perhaps wisely) for a rash of errors. On the other hand, the announcement of one change may lead them (foolishly) to expect that other changes will naturally accompany it or soon follow. The net result of an "improvement" is often a mob of even less satisfied users, so the review group

ought to speculate on what will happen when this change encounters the wooly world of the human psyche.

6. *Success.* In the past, maintenance has been so fraught with side effect dangers and just plain errors that success was seldom achieved. Once our maintenance reviews are in full swing, however, we have to anticipate that we will in fact succeed once in a while—and we must also anticipate what that success will bring. For instance, one error-riddled system was seldom used by its several hundred potential users, so management decided to mount an effort to have the system repaired in a systematic fashion. The resulting system was so dependable and useful that usage suddenly increased by a factor of a thousand over previous usage. This increase in transaction volume made the file design of the system completely inadequate to the daily load—which soon meant that nobody could get results fast enough to be useful. The entire problem—and so many others like it—could have been avoided if the review group had only considered that unavoidable law of nature:

Success breeds failure.

So, just when your maintenance reviews start to pay off, be prepared for the inevitable reaction. If you start making systems better, your users will want more of the same—the best side effect of all.

Our Problem Is That Our Old Code Is So Bad That It Wouldn't Pass a Maintenance Review. If We Start Reviewing It, Won't Our Maintenance Programmers Become Aware of How Bad It Really Is, Thus Leading to a Revolt?

Although management may not be aware of the sorry state of existing code, it's doubtful whether the maintenance programmers are unaware. If a revolt comes, it won't be the introduction of reviews that causes it. What the review can do is make *management* more aware of the pitiful state of code under maintenance. With this information documented in the review reports, it will be harder for the ostrich type manager's head to stay under the sand.

Suppose Management Becomes Aware of the Situation and Wants to Do Something. In What Ways Can Reviews Help Correct the Poor Situation We've Gotten Into Over Many Years of Nonreviewed Maintenance?

There are three types of review that can help alleviate the situation of poor code from the past:

1. *Simple Review of New Changes.* This review at least keeps the situation from getting worse—i.e., stops the polluting.
2. *Fix-and-Improve Review of New Changes.* This type of review provides a gradual improvement in old, bad code—i.e., removes the pollution.
3. *Separate Production and Maintenance Acceptance Reviews.* This separation of function stems the tide of non-maintainable new work coming into maintenance.

What's a Fix-and-Improve Review?

Instead of limiting the maintenance work to externally originated changes, the maintenance group undertakes to apply an old Boy Scout principle:

> **Leave the product a bit better than you found it.**

In a fix-and-improve review, we add one question to the list of (1) correct, (2) consolidated, and (3) clean (see page 399):

4. Does the proposed change leave the product easier to maintain in the future? In the words of the farmer, is it *cultivated*? Successful farmers thoroughly understand the principle of cultivation. It's not enough to take crop after crop out of the ground. If you don't actively improve the soil, it inevitably grows worse. Programs may be exactly the same as soil, in which case passive correction will lead to depletion of maintainability. Since we can't be sure that a correction is entirely clean, why not ensure cleanliness by leaving the product obviously cleaner, more cultivated, than it was before?

Each of these improvements must, of course, satisfy the other review criteria. The review committee must ask:

1. Does this change cultivate the program, leaving it better than before?
2. Does the attempt at cultivation create other problems?

If the answer to the first question is no, then the product fails the *improve* criterion of the review. But if the second answer is yes, then the *fix* requirement fails. We want positive side effects, not negative ones.

One interesting side effect of fix-and-improve reviews is the effect on the morale of the maintenance programmers. When some improvement is demanded along with the fix, the programmer can employ and demonstrate creative talents—talents that may have been long suppressed in the highly constrained maintenance environment. Thus, the fix-and-improve review not only improves a deteriorating product, but also improves a deteriorating staff.

Doesn't It Cost a Lot of Time and Effort to Make These Improvements? We Can See That the Fix-and-Improve Strategy Might Eventually Pay Off, But We Really Can't Afford to Increase Present Maintenance Costs.

It's been our experience that it costs no more to make an improvement than not to make an improvement, as long as you keep the improvement under control by reviewing it. What you may lose in extra material to review, you gain in a cleaner product to review. Just be sure that the improvers realize that the improvement should be no bigger than the requested change. It may not seem like much, but the additive effect is tremendous.

What Is Meant by a Separation of Production and Maintenance Acceptance Reviews?

As part of a program to ameliorate the maintenance situation, an obvious step is to put some maintenance programmers on reviews of new developments. (A not so obvious, but perhaps even more effective, step is to put some development programmers on maintenance reviews, so they'll better understand what's going to happen to their products.) The people currently working on previously developed systems will undoubtedly have worthwhile contributions to make from the point of view of maintainability of the product.

If you do add maintenance programmers to a production review, you may find that a program is rejected by the committee on grounds of nonmaintainability. If management didn't consider this a valid or important criticism in the past, the rejection may be disregarded in an effort to get a crucial job into production. But if management decides to accept a product that the review committee has judged unacceptable, the review process will soon become totally meaningless. Thus, a conflict arises between timely production and proper maintainability.

Before reviews, the conflict existed but was hidden. Because it was hidden, it was always resolved in favor of early production and against maintainability, which is one reason maintenance is such a morass today. For a long time, we pleaded with managers to give more weight to maintainability in this argument, but we always lost to hard-nosed short-term practicality. Then, while sitting in yet another review where the production-maintenance conflict arose, we suddenly saw the resolution in a flash.

Whenever a piece of work changes hands, there should be some kind of review, though of course there may be other reviews when the work is not changing hands but only changing from one point in its life cycle to another. What we had overlooked was that when a piece of work goes into production, there are, in certain installations, *two* changes of hands:

1. From development to operations, and
2. From development to maintenance.

Just because those two changes happen at about the same time, there is no reason why they have to be tied together! If they are tied together, it will always be maintenance that drowns! Therefore, if we want to improve the situation in maintenance, we must institute two separate reviews, with two separate decisions.

One review assures the correctness of the code or other product, from the point of view of readiness to ship or put into production. The other review is conducted largely by maintenance people. At the end of the review, if the product is accepted, the maintenance people have assumed responsibility for keeping it up and running properly forevermore. If they don't accept it, however, the development team retains responsibility until such time as they have managed to get it into acceptable shape, as certified by another review.

That Won't Work Because Our Maintenance People Will Reject All Work, Just to Make Their Jobs Easier.

In practice, this prediction doesn't come true. To begin with, the maintenance people must have reasons for their conclusions. When they state explicitly what they find unacceptable about the product, the development people have the opportunity to improve the quality in these specific areas. Second, the review committee, properly constituted, will also contain nonmaintenance people who can be expected to provide an unbiased view.

If a conflict does arise that can't be resolved by the technical people, then there is indeed an inherent conflict between the needs of development and maintenance. Such a contradiction cannot be resolved by technical people acting alone, but requires management decision. To take an analogous case, consider the purchase of any piece of capital equipment—a truck, say. If there is a choice between two trucks, the decision will rest on the relative costs of purchasing and operating the trucks. If truck A is both cheaper to buy and cheaper to maintain, then the decision over truck B is obvious. But if A is cheaper initially but costs more to keep running, then only management can decide how much present cost can be traded for how much future cost. It is not a technical decision. The role of the technical people is merely to supply accurate information on what the costs actually are, after which management must make a decision.

How Can We Tell Management What the Costs of Maintenance Are Going to Be?

Naturally, any statement about future maintenance costs will be statistical, but so will statements about additional development costs. Here are some questions we've found useful to ask in a maintenance review if there is some doubt about management's acceptance of a negative decision:

1. What is the probability that this code contains an error that will cost more than
    a. $1,000   a. 1 person-week
    b. $10,000   b. 10 person-weeks
    c. $100,000   c. 100 person-weeks
    to fix during its first three months of production running?

2. If a "typical" change in your installation takes one hundred units of maintenance work (cost), how many units would such a typical change take in the code

being reviewed? How much would a one-line change cost?

3. If a "typical" program in your installation has to be changed one hundred times in a certain time period, how many times will this program have to be changed in that time period?

From these figures, management should be able to estimate what kind of costs they are committing to by sending the work into maintenance as is.

Those Questions Seem Awfully Subjective to Me. How Much Faith Can Be Placed in the Answers the Review Committee Comes Up With?

It's true that the whole question of maintainability is harder to quantify, in advance, than some other review questions. When there is an error, there's not much controversy about its existence, but when someone says "a typical change to this program might cost 175 units," we are left with a wide margin for doubt.

Yet if you examine the statement about an error, you'll see that there's a lot of doubt there, too. Some errors cost millions if undetected, while others cost pennies or nothing at all. Consequently, a simple listing of errors contains an implicit statement that all are of equal importance—a statement that obviously isn't true. If we try to quantify the costs associated with the errors, we become just as subjective as when we try to quantify the costs associated with poorly maintainable code.

Once again, part of the problem comes from not having kept good records in the past. If we keep track of true maintenance costs in the future, we'll be able to compare them with what the reviewers predicted. Eventually, as this information feeds back into the review process, we'll find that we can make reliable estimates of code maintainability.

Should Operations People Be Involved in Maintenance Reviews?

Several questions about maintainability impinge directly on operations, so if there are qualified technical people in operations, they should be invited to the maintenance reviews. And, of course, they should participate in the review that transfers development work into operations.

What Other Roles Do Operations People Play in Reviews?

We see several important involvements of operations people in the review process:

1. Participation in operations and maintenance reviews;
2. Participation in specification and documentation reviews concerning operating procedures and instructions;
3. Gathering production history information for feedback into the review process; and
4. Initiating the review of existing products that no longer meet performance criteria.

What Sort of History Information Does Operations Feed Back Into the Review Process?

A review is, in effect, a prediction. Anything that a review predicts should be measured and fed back in against the predictions. Operations can keep track of such items as:

1. Running time,
2. Memory usage,
3. Error or trouble reports,
4. Operational difficulties,
5. Number of test runs,

6. Number of maintenance modifications,
7. Machine cost of maintenance modifications,
8. Reruns due to changes, and
9. Reruns due to original design or coding.

How Does Operations Initiate a Review of an Existing Product?

Whenever someone is at "the end of the line," problems tend to accumulate in that person's front yard. Everyone involved in the handling of a software product has to have some recourse when given a bad product by someone further up the line. That is why we institute maintenance reviews, documentation reviews, and reviews initiated by operations.

A review may be initiated when the performance of a system has deteriorated because of:

1. Changing hardware environment;
2. Changing software environment;
3. Maintenance changes; and
4. Data changes, including increased volumes.

But these are not the only reasons for operations to initiate a review. A program that was previously a good performer may become troublesome as the system becomes more heavily loaded or as the load characteristics change. Maintenance changes can cause problems, but so can changes that are not made when they should be. Carefully kept production statistics may reveal undesirable characteristics of a program that previously went unnoticed. For any of these reasons, the operating group may initiate a review of an existing system. If they are not allowed to do so, you can be sure that they will begin to feel "dumped on"—a feeling you don't want operations to get, since they can hurt you in so many ways.

A review initiated by operations is like a review initiated by a user, after having had some experience with a product. Operations is, in fact, a kind of user of every software system. These reviews are more or less like high level design reviews, but instead of being based on conjecture, they are based on actual historical data not available at the time of the design. In the design review, the problem is to prevent an activity (coding) if the product fails the review. In an operations review, the problem is to initiate an activity (redesign) if the product fails. It's very easy, therefore, for management to ignore the negative result of an operational review, since it seems to call for an immediate new expenditure. Consequently, the initiators of the review need to take special care in gathering the facts upon which the review will be based.

You Haven't Mentioned Anything About Postimplementation Reviews Except When Things Go Wrong. Can You Have Regularly Scheduled Postimplementation Reviews?

A typical pattern adopted by many of our clients is to hold a review three months after turnover to operations, regardless of what is happening. In the past, before they inaugurated formal technical reviews, this type of schedule wasn't necessary. They *always* had so many troubles with a system in the first few months that there were frequent meetings between development and operations in the first months of a system's life. But once reviews got going, there were very few excuses for development to speak to operations about a new system. Development people, being busy, lost contact with how their systems actually worked out—contact that good designers must have if they are to design well in the future. So regular reviews were instituted at the three-month mark.

Do You Continue on a Three-Month Interval?

That's possible, but after the first one, a regular six-month to one-year scheduled review is probably adequate for most systems, to keep things from slipping away. Of course, there are maintenance reviews that automatically reveal certain things about operations that you might not have seen when the system was designed, so only in rare cases will regular reviews more frequent than every six months be necessary. But don't be afraid to adjust your own circumstances or the unique circumstances of each system in your shop. The important thing is that no system ever be left with no review scheduled at *some time* in its future.

Reviews in an Academic Environment

We haven't said much in this handbook about classroom training in review procedures, partly because we doubted the ability of many academics to adapt to new methods. Therefore, we were more than a little pleased to receive the following article from two of the leading writers of programming texts, Gary B. Shelly and Thomas J. Cashman.

Because the article is so important to the subject of reviews, and because it appeared in a privately circulated newsletter not readily available to most of our readers, we asked Shelly and Cashman for permission to reprint the article here in its entirety. They generously granted permission, and Gary Shelly also gave us the following additional information:

You may be interested in some of the results of our Oklahoma Institute in terms of walkthroughs. At the Institute, we divided the classes into teams of three persons for each programming assignment, and walkthroughs were conducted for both the design of the program and coding of the program, using the methods discussed in the "Implementation" article. I have talked to six instruc-

423

tors who have returned to their schools and implemented walkthroughs for their classes. All but one claim great success. They have indicated that the students enjoy the walkthroughs and have come to insist on a walkthrough before they compile and execute their programs. In addition, the students seem to enjoy the interaction with other students and the ability to learn from and with others. In the one case where the walkthroughs have been less than successful, there was one instructor who wanted to conduct them and one (not attending the Institute) who did not, thus leaving the students with the question of "Are they necessary?" In addition, they were implemented for students who have already had a considerable number of programming classes without them; and the students apparently did not care for peer examination of their programs. It thus appears that second year programming students can exhibit much the same symptoms of possessiveness that experienced programmers can. As a whole, however, it would seem that the walkthroughs can be successfully implemented by instructors with relatively little experience in using them.

Implementation of Structured Walkthroughs in the Classroom

GARY B. SHELLY AND THOMAS J. CASHMAN

> *We do know through our experience with egoless programming that there is no particular reason why your friend cannot also be your sternest critic.* [1]

Structured walkthroughs have been implemented in industry in order to improve programmer productivity and to improve the quality of software that is produced. The purpose of the structured walkthrough is to have a "peer" review of the program design and program coding so that any errors which have been made will be caught in the early stages of the program rather than waiting until the program is in the midst of testing, where the corrections are more difficult and more expensive to make.

The prospect of implementing team concepts and structured walkthroughs in the classroom has been raised by several authorities, most notable of which is Dr. Gerald Weinberg, the author of the book

The Psychology of Computer Programming. During a speech in Atlanta in February, 1977, to community college instructors attending the SIGCSE Technical Symposium, Dr. Weinberg advocated the use of a team approach at all levels of programming instruction, not just on large projects which are typically found in the last course of instruction.

Since that time, structured walkthroughs in the classroom have been conducted both at Long Beach City College and at the Fourth Annual Institute for Business Data Processing Instructors for both introductory and advanced programming classes. In all instances, the walkthroughs have been unqualified successes. The following

---

1 Weinberg, G., *THE PSYCHOLOGY OF COMPUTER PROGRAMMING*, Van Nostrand Reinhold Company, 1971.

425

paragraphs indicate some of the advantages of these techniques, a method in which they can be implemented in the classroom, and a response to frequent objections to using structured walkthroughs.

ADVANTAGES OF STRUCTURED WALKTHROUGHS

Perhaps the most significant advantage of conducting structured walkthroughs, beginning with the first programming class, is that the student has an immediate acceptance of the idea that a program should be open to everyone; that is, a program is not a private work of art but rather is public property which is open to all for inspection. This concept has proven difficult to impart in industry, where many programmers have concealed their programs for a myriad of reasons. By presenting the philosophy that programs are public property from the first program in a student's career, the student will accept this very important concept from the beginning and ideas will not have to be changed at a later time.

Another consequence of utilizing structured walkthroughs in the classroom is that better programs are produced by the students. The programs are better in several ways: First, by having the programs reviewed by fellow students, there is "peer pressure" to make the programs as readable and understandable as possible. This is especially true if the instructor emphasizes the importance of readable programs from the beginning of the class.

Second, since errors will be detected through the use of the walkthroughs, the programs which are finally submitted for compilation and execution will be much more likely to compile and execute properly the first time they are run.

Indeed, it has been found that the "unheard of" prospect of having a program work the first time becomes the norm rather than the exception. The concept that a program must contain errors is negated by the fact that a good review of the program will, in many cases, allow the program to contain no errors when it is compiled and executed.

A third reason that programs are designed and written better is based upon the "Hawthorne Effect." Students are aware that their programs are to be reviewed by fellow students and, therefore, will take more time and effort in writing a program which will be clear to the reader and which also will be correct logically. There has been almost universal agreement among students who have been exposed to structured walkthroughs that they take more time in preparing their programs and are more conscious of whether their programs are right or wrong than would be the case if they merely coded the program and "threw" it on the computer to see what would happen.

The structured walkthroughs also provide a meaningful learning experience for the student. In the past, if a student did not understand a programming concept or instruction, he or she struggled largely on their own to correct the problem. Although an informal session with fellow students or contact with the instructor may have been used to solve the problem, in most cases this took place only after considerable time and frustration on the part of the student. Through the use of structured walkthroughs, the areas which are not understood by a student will normally be detected by fellow students. As a result, the student need not spend unproductive hours searching for a solution to a problem; instead, the solution is found early, with the result that the student will have a better understanding of the programming techniques and instructions which are being taught.

In addition, the student is exposed to more than one solution to a problem when participating in a walkthrough. Thus, the learning experience is broadened by examining new approaches to a problem. In many cases, the new approach will be equally as good as the solution developed by the student; in some cases, the new approach will be better, thus leading to additional learning. Even if the solution is worse than the one proposed by the student, learning takes place because the student must make a concerted effort to evaluate the program being reviewed and be able to justify the reasons that the program being evaluated is not as good as the program which the student had designed or coded.

Another important advantage of conducting formal structured walkthroughs is that the student becomes used to working in and with a team. Experience has shown that after several programs have been written and subjected to walkthroughs, the student will not have a desire to submit a program for compilation and execution prior to a walkthrough. Instead, the walkthrough will become as much a part of programming as the coding. Students will insist on having their programs reviewed before submitting them for compilation and execution—truly a revolutionary idea as compared to the thinking of many programmers that their program is private property to be exposed to no one.

It should be noted that a structured walkthrough is not dependent upon a particular programming language or a particular technique being used in the program development. Thus, it is as useful in an RPG II or Fortran class as it is in a Structured COBOL programming class. The whole intent is to have the program reviewed by someone who is not familiar with the method of solution or the coding within the program. Thus, every programming class, regardless of the language and regardless of whether it is an introductory class for non-majors or the final programming class for majors, should include formal structured walkthroughs.

CONDUCTING STRUCTURED WALKTHROUGHS

Although there are a number of methods which could be used for a structured walkthrough, depending upon class size, number of hours available, etc., it has been found that the following procedures are quite successful in implementing structured walkthroughs in the classroom.

1. For each programming assignment or project, divide the class into programming teams, with 3 students to each team. (Note: If there are "extra" students it is suggested that the extra students be placed on other teams, resulting in 4 member teams; however, 3 students to a team seems to be the optimum number in an academic environment).

2. After design of the program is completed, the class should meet formally and the assigned teams should review the design of one another's program. It is IMPORTANT to note that a structured walkthrough does not imply a group project. Each student MUST complete, individually, the design of the program.

3. During the structured walkthrough, the student programmer should review, together with the other members of the team, the design of the program. It is important that each design is reviewed

individually; and the members of the team, if working on the same programming assignment, should not compare their design with the design being reviewed. The primary objective of the design review is to ensure that the programmer has designed a proper solution to the problem which has been posed. Thus, the reviewing students should review the structure of the program to ensure that it is valid and logical, and also review the logic within each module of the program to ensure that the logic specified will solve the problem. It should be noted that this design walkthrough is not concerned with any particular language syntax or other formal requirements. It is concerned with the structure of the program and the logic within the program.

4. After one student's program has been reviewed and the team members are confident that the program is logically correct and will process the data properly, that program is "put away" and another team member's program is reviewed. Again, the program is reviewed on its own merits, without comparison to the manner in which another team member solved the same problem. It is reviewed to determine if it will work, not if it is the same as someone else's program. After all of the programs of the team members have been reviewed, and the teams members are confident that each program will produce the proper results when converted to code, the walkthrough is completed. The time required for a program design structured walkthrough may vary from as little as 15 minutes per program to as long as an hour per program, depending upon the complexity of the programs being reviewed.

5. During the walkthrough, if it is determined that the design of the program is entirely wrong, the team should not attempt to redesign the program; rather, the student should be directed to redesign the program and the team must then make arrangements to reconvene at a later time. It must be noted that the reason for the walkthrough is not to design the program for another member of the team, nor is it to provide the solutions to errors within the design. The function of the team members is to point out to the person whose program is being reviewed where there are potential errors in the design and logic of the program. It is up to the programmer whose program is being reviewed to either justify as correct the logic which is contained in the design of the program or to redesign the program to correct the errors which have been found. The coding of a program should never begin until the members of the team are completely satisfied that the design is sound and the program will function properly when coded.

6. In these structured walkthroughs there will be a great deal of discussion and interaction among the members of the team. During the walkthrough, the instructor should not monitor the team discussions, determine how many errors are made in the original design by individual students, or otherwise attempt to evaluate the students. The instructor should merely be available as a "chief programmer" to answer any questions which cannot be resolved by members of the team. The walkthrough is not an evaluation process; it is a process to ensure correct programs and must be treated as such in the classroom.

It is important, however, that the performance of the team as a whole be monitored and also that any students who are not actively participating in the walkthrough be identified. Therefore, it is suggested that each student submit to the instructor at the completion of the entire programming assignment a form which relates the number of errors which were detected during the walkthrough and the number of runs necessary to compile and execute the program properly. In this manner, the instructor can evaluate the efforts of the team in properly checking the design and coding of the program. The number of errors which are detected in the walkthroughs should not be a factor in determining the grade of the student for the programming assignment. Only the number of runs required should influence the grade, together with an evaluation of the program by the instructor in terms of the programming techniques used, the data names used, the clarity of the program, etc. It must always be borne in mind that the function of the walkthrough is to discover errors before the program is coded, compiled, and executed. Thus, evaluation of the student should not take place during the walkthroughs.

7. After the design walkthrough has been completed and each member of the team is satisfied that the programs of the team members will function properly, the student should code, INDIVIDUALLY, the required program. After the program is coded, it should be keypunched and an 80/80 listing of the program obtained for each member of the team. THE PROGRAM SHOULD NOT BE COMPILED OR EXECUTED AT THIS TIME. The only operation which can be performed by the programmer individually is to search for keypunch errors so that they may be removed prior to the code walkthrough.

8. After the listings have been produced, a formal time should be established for the structured walkthrough of the coding in the listing. At the code walkthrough, the team members review on a line for line basis the program statements of the listing. It is suggested that these listings be distributed to the team members at least one day in advance of the time designated for the walkthrough so that the team members have an opportunity to review the listings prior to the walkthrough. In the preliminary review before the formal structured walkthrough, team members should concentrate on detecting any syntax errors which may have been included in the program. Each syntax error which is found may be circled so that the listing can be returned to the programmer with the syntax errors indicated on the listing. The reviewing team member should also inspect the listing for the use of meaningful data names, proper indentation, correct use of comments, etc. Any examples of incorrect coding should be noted on the listing.

At the walkthrough, each team member will walk the other members through his program by explaining how his program works. In this formal walkthrough, the main intent is to ensure that the coding will accomplish the logic which was expressed in the design of the program. Any errors which are found must be pointed out to the programmer whose program is being reviewed.

As with the design walkthrough, if serious errors are found, then the programmer should recode the program and the team should meet again to review the program. Errors such as syntax errors or the use of poor data names will not normally require another walkthrough. When errors in coding are found, it is not up to the team members to rewrite the program for the programmer being reviewed; their function is to merely point out possible errors. The writing of the program is an individual effort which, after completion, is exposed to the reviewing team members. It is not the function of the team to write the program for the programmer.

After each team member's code has been reviewed, and the team is confident that all errors have been found, then the errors should be corrected by the programmer and the program should be compiled and executed. Since the program has been carefully reviewed, and each team member is confident that the program is correct, it should compile and execute properly the first time that it is placed on the machine.

PROBLEMS WITH
STRUCTURED WALKTHROUGHS

In conducting walkthroughs in an academic environment, several problems occur which have not previously been found in a programming class. These problems are addressed below.

1. Students are not ready for the walkthrough - In order for walkthroughs to be successful, team members must all be ready for their design or code walkthroughs at the appointed time; otherwise, the walkthrough cannot take place. Therefore, there is considerable pressure on the student to be ready at the time when the walkthrough is to take place. This pressure is not bad because it is only an inkling of the pressure which will occur when the student becomes a programmer in industry. If a student is not ready for the walkthrough, it is suggested that the student receive a grade of "F" for the program assignment. In this manner, it is shown to the student that it is quite important to be ready on time. For most students, this is sufficient incentive to be ready; if it is not, the student probably does not belong in a programming class.

2. Students do not participate in the walkthrough - It has been observed in the classroom that even if a student is ready for the walkthrough, he/she may not actively participate in the walkthrough; that is, little or no effort is placed in finding errors in another team member's program. This, of course, defeats the purpose of the walkthrough. To counteract this problem, it is suggested that in addition to the individual grade assigned for each student's program, a team grade be assigned based upon the success of the execution of all programs for a given team. This concept follows a common evaluation procedure in industry, where the success of any large scale programming project is dependent upon the success of the individual members of the team. The following grading scale is recommened:

INDIVIDUAL GRADING SCALE

GRADE	NUMBER OF RUNS
A	1 RUN
B	2 RUNS
C	3-4 RUNS
D	5-6 RUNS
F	7 OR MORE RUNS

TEAM GRADING SCALE
[3 MEMBER TEAMS]

GRADE	TOTAL NUMBER OF RUNS
A	3
B +	4
B	5-6
B -	7
C +	8
C	9-12
C -	13
D +	14
D	15-18
D -	19-20
F	21 or more

Using the charts above, if a student requires 2 runs to properly compile and execute a program, the individual grade of B would be assigned. If another member of the team required one run to compile and execute the program and a third member required four runs to compile and execute the program, each member of the team would be assigned a TEAM GRADE of B-. By assigning both an individual grade and a team grade, the student is encouraged to actively participate in both the design and code structured walkthroughs. Although the grading scales may seem very strict, and in fact, "impossible" (1 run for an A), if proper program design and structured walkthroughs are used, instructors will find that a large number of their students will be receiving A's.

The instructor should also reserve the right to adjust the grades downward if the program contains bad coding techniques, is not easily read, contains nondescriptive data names, etc.

3. The entire team grade suffers if one member does not care - If the grading scheme in number 2 above is used, there is the possibility that the entire team grade will suffer because one individual does not put forth a good effort. This problem is normally solved in several ways. First, it is suggested that the members of a team be changed for each programming assignment. Therefore, the student who is causing this problem will not "jeopardize" the grades of other students for an entire quarter or semester.

Secondly, it has been found that "peer pressure" will many times cause the student who is not doing a conscientious job to change his/her attitude. In most cases, after fellow students become aware of the student who is not doing all that can be done, that student will be pressured to perform adequately.

4. Personality Conflicts - In any large gathering, there are bound to be some students who have a personality conflict. If these are known in advance, then the instructor would do well to not assign those students to the same team. If these are not known in advance, the suggestion that team members be switched for each new programming assignment should keep these conflicts to a minimum.

5. Some students are less intelligent than others and do not do as good a job as others - This condition will occur in practically every classroom. As long as the student is performing up to capabilities, there is very little that can be done by the instructor in terms of motivation. However, by changing the members of a team for each new project, one group of students will not be burdened by this classmate for an entire quarter or semester.

6. Excused absences on the day of the walkthrough - This problem is one which cannot normally be solved by the instructor. Sickness and other reasons may excuse a student from the walkthrough; if this occurs, the two remaining students can conduct walkthroughs on their programs by themselves or the instructor can assign them to other teams for that day only. The student who missed the walkthrough should still have his/her program reviewed; therefore, the other members of the team will have to arrange for a time outside of normal classroom time for the walkthrough.

7. Obtaining copies of the program design and the 80/80 listing - In some instances, obtaining the material to be used in the walkthrough may present some difficulties. It has been found that one copy of the design material is normally adequate for the design walkthrough. It will be recalled, however, that it is suggested that copies of the 80/80 listing be distributed at least one day in

advance of the structured code walk-through, requiring that multiple copies be obtained. In most installations, the use of multiple part paper or a request for three copies is possible; in other instances, however, the instructor will have to deal with this problem according to the particular circumstances in the school.

8. Students compare on a line for line basis - There is a great temptation on the part of students to compare the program being reviewed on a line for line basis with their own program rather than analyzing the program being reviewed on its own merits. The instructor must guard against this happening by observing the walkthroughs and being sure that each program is reviewed on its own merits rather than on a comparison basis with other programs. The purpose of the walkthrough is to determine the correctness of the program being reviewed, not whether it compares with another program.

OBJECTIONS TO STRUCTURED WALKTHROUGHS IN THE CLASSROOM

In addition to solving the problems discussed previously, there are a number of other objections which have been voiced against the walkthroughs. Some of these objections, together with a response, are contained below.

1. There is not enough time for structured walkthroughs - It is estimated in industry that walkthroughs will consume 15%—25% of an application programmer's time. This time estimate has been a shock to many in industry and they have cried that there is not enough time. Yet, numerous studies point out that testing and debugging occupy approximately 50% of a programmer's time. Industry is now realizing that a greater emphasis on program design will substantially reduce the time spent in testing and debugging. In addition, more reliable and more maintainable programs are being produced with the increased emphasis in program design, which includes the structured walkthroughs.

In the classroom, it is not unusual for a student to require 5 runs or 7 runs (even 10 - 12 runs?) to compile and execute a relatively simple program. Almost all of this time is misspent time—the student is attempting to correct errors which should not have occurred in the first place. By conducting a structured walkthrough of the program, these errors can be eliminated before they ever occur on the machine. Therefore, instead of wasting a great deal of time trying to correct a program, the student can spend more time in educationally meaningful activities, such as learning more about program design and good program coding. In fact, it can be argued that there is not enough time in a programming class to teach the meaningful and important programming information unless structured walkthroughs ARE used.

2. The students learn from making errors - Although there may be a ring of truth to this (after all, if you touch a hot stove, you probably won't touch it again), the philosophy of telling students that they are going to make errors is all wrong. Chemistry students are not told that they are going to cause an explosion in the laboratory prior to finally getting an experiment right; engineering students are not told that the first four times they try to build a bridge it is going to collapse. Only in data processing is the idea that failure is a natural consequence of performing an activity imparted to a student. This is not the proper philosophy either in the classroom or on the job—the student must be encouraged, yea even

coerced, into making the program correct the first time it is compiled and executed. If this occurs, the student will have more time for meaningful learning rather than attempting to correct insignificant errors which should not have happened.

3. A walkthrough is the "blind leading the blind" - Although in the first programs of an introductory course the students are not well versed in a given language, it has been found that with three students on a team, what one of them does not know, the others probably do. Therefore, most errors which are made in a student's beginning programs are found in the walkthroughs. This has the added advantage that the student learns from the walkthrough and the discussion with team members much better than he would from a language diagnostic or incorrect output from his program.

4. Students do not know what to do in a walkthrough - They will know if the instructor tells them. Hopefully, this article will be of some aid; but there are a great many sources for information on walkthroughs and team programming. The classic source is Weinberg's **The Psychology of Computer Programming**; every person who has anything to do with data processing and programming should read this book several times.

5. Students do not want to be criticized - It is extremely important early in the student's programming career that he/she is able to separate a program which they have written from themselves; that is, a program is NOT an extension of the person (Weinberg calls this egoless programming). Therefore, in a walkthrough, the intent is not to criticize the person who wrote the program, but rather to aid the person who wrote the program by finding potential errors in the program. This is an extremely important

concept which structured walkthroughs will help develop in students quite early in their careers.

There may also be some fear by instructors that the motivation of the students will be lessened because of the need to go through a walkthrough. In fact, it has been found that just the opposite occurs; students tend to write better programs and take more time in preparing their programs since they are going to be reviewed by fellow students. It is a classic application of the Hawthorne Effect and will lead to better programming by the students.

6. Programming must be done individually in order for students to learn the language - It is true that students must individually write their programs, at least the programs in the introductory programming courses, in order to gain the experience of coding in the programming language. Structured walkthroughs do not contradict this; the walkthroughs are used only after the student has individually written the program. And as noted previously, it is not the function of the team members to rewrite a program with logic or syntax errors; the student who wrote the program must make the corrections to the program. Therefore, students are not deprived of the experience of writing their own programs; rather, they have the added experience of having their programs reviewed and discussed by their fellow team members.

SUMMARY

Although structured walkthroughs in the classroom present a substantially new approach to the teaching of computer programming in an academic environment, it has been shown that the use of walkthroughs provides a meaningful learning experience for students, substantially reduces the number of runs required to properly compile and execute a program, and develops within the student a "new philosophy of computer programming" in which the student approaches programming problems with the attitude that the program is expected to work the first time. This new philosophy can only lead to the production from our schools of better quality students who will be entering the data processing profession.

Bibliography

Boehm, B.W., R.K. McClean, and D.B. Urfirg

"Some Experiences with Automated Aids to the Design of Large Scale Reliable Software"

Proceedings of 1975 International Conference on Reliable Software, p. 105.

A summary of experience in analyzing sources of error in the design phases of large software projects. A large preponderance of design errors over coding errors was found to exist—both as to the number of errors and the relative time and effort required to detect and correct them. A prototype of an automated aid, the Design Assertion Consistency Checker, was developed to examine possible mismatches between input and output assertions in a large-scale design. This paper is also part of the TRW Software Series, TRW-SS-75-01.

Chumura, Louis J. & Henry F. Ledgard

Cobol With Style: Programming Proverbs

Hayden Book Co., New Jersey, 1975

This book is based upon Ledgard's Programming Proverbs, but all examples are given in COBOL. A noteworthy addition to this volume is an introduction to top-down programming.

Cohen, Gerald

A New Way To Test Writing

22nd International Technical Communications Conference, Anaheim, California, 1975

This describes the Cohen Cloudiness Count.

Crossman, Trevor D.

"Some Experiences in the Use of Inspection Teams"

Proceedings of the 15th Annual ACM Computer Personnel Research Conference, August, 1977, p. 143

A detailed account of the inspection methodologies followed by a "Development Department" of the Standard Bank of South Africa since mid-1975.

Daly, E.B.

"Management of Software Development"

IEEE Transactions on Software Engineering

Volume SE-3, Number 3, May 1977, pp. 230-242

This down-to-earth article puts various kinds of reviews into the perspective of the entire system development process, on the development of on-line systems with extremely high reliability requirements.

Edwards, N.P.

"The Effect of Certain Modular Design Principles on Testability"

Proceedings of 1975 International Conference on Reliable Software, p. 401

A general, easy to read discussion of design principles necessary to achieve testability of complex structures.

Ethnotech, Inc.

A Close Look at Team Programming, Course Notes, 1972

These notes are referenced in a number of articles on formal reviews. The review material in them is now largely incorporated in this handbook, and in the Ethnotech course on formal reviews and/or teams.

Ethnotech, Inc.

Critical Program Reading, Course Notes, 1972

These notes concern methods of code review. Their essence is contained in the IPTO Support Group report, IBM GE 19-5200, though incorrectly referenced there to The Psychology of Computer Pro-

gramming. The updated version of these notes is incorporated into Ethnotech training on reviews and terms.

Fagan, Michael E.

"Design and Code Inspection to Reduce Errors in Program Development"

IBM Systems Journal, Vol. 15, No. 3, 1976

Examination of the value of formal inspections of design and code in the achievement of substantial net improvements in program quality. A number of tables of program error data are provided. It is concluded that inspections increase productivity and improve final program quality.

Fagan, Michael E.

"Inspecting Software Design and Code"

Datamation, October 1977

This article contains much of the author's "Design and Code Inspection to Reduce Errors in Program Development" which appeared in IBM Systems Journal.

Fitzpatrick, Richard C.

"Making Documentation Painless"

Datamation, August, 1977, pp. 62-68

Of most present interest in this narration of systems and procedures for effective documentation is a checklist that may be helpful in conducting an overall documentation review of a project.

Flesch, Rudolph

How To Test Readability

Iowa University Press, Ames, Iowa, 1963

This book contains a number of measures for readability. including FLESCH'S READING EASE FORMULA.

Gerhart, Susan L. and Lawrence Yelowitz

"Observations of Fallibility in Applications of Modern Programming Methodologies"

IEEE Transactions on Software Engineering Vol. SE-2, No. 3, September 1976

An examination of a variety of published algorithms to ascertain certain common errors, inconsistencies, or confusing points. Possible causes of error are pinpointed and general guidelines formulated which may help avoid further errors. Three error classes are discussed: specification errors, systematic construction errors, and "proved program" errors.

Gilb, Tom

Software Metrics

Winthrop Publishers, Massachusetts, 1977

A comprehensive examination of methods of measuring software quality. Includes a section on inspection of the software development process and useful bibliography and index.

Gunning, Robert

The Technique of Clear Writing

McGraw-Hill, New York, 1968

This work contains many sensible ideas about clear writing. The Fog Index is a measure of readability. It does not address the quality of the content, just its readability.

Hale, R.M.

Inspections in Application Development—Introduction and Implementation Guidelines

IBM Form GC20-2000-0 (July 1977) updated by TNL GN20-3814 (August 1978). About 70 pages.

IBM's way of doing inspections—the bible for many people.

Hetzel, William C., editor

Program Test Methods

Prentice-Hall, New Jersey, 1973

This volume is based upon the proceedings of the Computer Program Test Methods Symposium held at the University of North Carolina in June, 1972. Included are papers dealing with testing concepts, designing programs for testing, and standards and measurements of program quality, among others. An extensive bibliography is also provided.

Ingrassia, Frank S.

"Combatting the '90% Complete' Syndrome"

Datamation, January 1978, pp. 171-176

This article describes the Unit Development Folder, or UDF, as used at TRW. The UDF is a repository in the form of a 3-ring notebook, for all the historical documents relating to one unit of a system, typically comprising 50-300 related source statements. The UDF is a good place to store Review Reports and Issues Lists.

IPTO Support Group (IBM)

Code Reading, Structured Walkthroughs, and Inspections

IBM Report GE-19-5200

Zoetermeer, Netherlands, 1976

A well-written compendium of information on reviews derived from a variety of sources.

Jones, Capers

"Program Quality and Programmer Productivity"

IBM Technical Report TR 02.764, 28 Jan 77

A thorough engineering study of "old" versus "new" programming, including a number of models of the role of technical reviews in defect-removal activities. Like most studies, however, it confines itself to defect-removal properties of reviews, ignoring in its approximations the defect prevention ability of reviews (because of their educational properties) and their variance-reduction properties (which contribute most to successful management).

Kernighan, Brian W. and P.J. Plauger

The Elements of Programming Style

McGraw-Hill, New York, 1974

This relatively small volume contains a large number of programs (Fortran & PL/I) which are rewritten to demonstrate possible improvements in the code. The principles of style should be of interest and value to all programmers, regardless of programming language used.

Kohli, Robert O.

"High Level Design Inspection Specification"

IBM Report TR 21.601, 21 July 1975

"This report is written to be used as a specification for the inspection of High Level design materials. The report describes in detail the process of inspecting High Level design materials against specific exit criteria."

Larson, Rodney R.

"Test Plan and Test Case Inspection Specification"

IBM Report TR 21.586, 4 April 1975

The report's abstract states: "This report addresses how to apply an inspection process to the Functional Verification Test Plan and Test Cases." It contains procedures, forms, and some checklists for these inspections.

Ledgard, Henry F.

Programming Proverbs

Hayden Book Co., New Jersey, 1975

This very small volume is an easy to read light-hearted guide to better programming. The programming examples are given in both Algol 60 and PL/I. They should provide good starting material for checklists on code reviews.

Ledgard, Henry F.

Programming Proverbs for Fortran Programmers

Hayden Book Co., New Jersey, 1975

This book is essentially the same as Legard's Programming Proverbs with the exception that programming examples are given in Fortran rather than Algol 60 and PL/I.

Lehman, John H.

"Software Engineering Techniques in Computer Systems Development"

Department of the Air Force, Report No: SM-ALC/ACD-76-04, 15 Dec 76

This is a report of lessons learned in an Air Force attempt to do programming in the modern way. For present purposes, the most important information in this report is in this quotation from page 24: "Though some problems were encountered in the procedures, or lack of procedures, followed for walk-thrus and though not all HIPOs and even less code was reviewed, the use of walk-thrus was considered, in aggregate, the most significant factor in contributing to the reduction in program bugs."

Lemos, Ronald S.

"An Implementation of Structured Walkthroughs in Teaching COBOL Programming"

CACA, June 1979, Vol. 22, No. 6, pp. 335-340

A study of reviews in an educational environment showing they produced more effective writing of programs in exams and fewer average runs to complete homework.

Macdonald, Nina H.

"The Writer's Workbench"

The Writer's Workbench is an ongoing project at Bell Labs, as of 1981, concerned with automatic aids to writers, including various measures applied to stored text which could be considered "automatic reviews". For the latest on this project, write to Bell Labs:
  Human Performance Engineering Department
  Bell Laboratories
  6 Corporate Place
  Piscataway, NJ 08854.

Mills, Harlan D.

"Software Development"

IEEE Transactions on Software Engineering, Vol. SE-2, Number 4, December 1976, pp. 265-273

One of the philosophical fathers of "modern programming" examines the underpinnings of the software development process with an eye to discovering what will ultimately be possible. Among other provocative statements: "The best debugging tool . . . is the human mind."

Meyers, Glenford J.

Software Reliability: Principles and Practices

John Wiley & Sons, New York, 1976

A comprehensive examination of possible solutions to the problem of unreliable software. Topics covered include major causes of unreliability, design of reliable software, software testing, and development of reliable software. Under the latter topic attention is given to project organization, management of programming teams, and design walkthroughs. The book also contains a very extensive bibliography of related works.

Musa, J.D.

"An Exploratory Experiment with 'Foreign' Debugging of Programs"

Proceedings of the Symposium on Computer Software Engineering, Polytechnic Institute of New York, New York, 20-22 April, 1976

In this small study, Musa shows that "educational" benefits of working with other people's programs may far outweigh any of the "direct" benefits. Foreign debugging is another way of reviewing, but one that Musa finds more motivating than other methods of reviewing. This could be a comment on the way in which other reviews are conducted.

Plum, Thomas

"Team Programming in the Small Technical Company"

Proceedings of the 15th Annual Computer Personnel Research Conference, August, 1977, p. 132

A report on six months' experience with team programming, including experience with walkthrough rules. An appendix provides a "Handbook on Structured Walkthroughs and Formal Reviews."

Scharer, Laura L.

"Improving System Testing Techniques"

Datamation, September, 1977, pp. 115-132

This report outlines standards and procedures for the system testing function, including the checklist provided in the handbook.

Shelly, Gary B. and Thomas J. Cashman

"Implementation of Structured Walkthroughs in the Classroom"

See end of bibliography for this entire article.

Shooman, M.L.

"Types, Distribution, and Test and Correction Times for Programming Errors"

Proceedings of 1975 International Conference on Reliable Software, p. 347

This paper presents the results of an experiment conducted at Bell Telephone Laboratories to investigate types and frequencies of software errors. It was found that a large percentage of errors was found manually at a much lower cost than techniques involving machine testing.

Weinberg, Gerald M.

PL/I Programming: A Manual of Style

McGraw-Hill, New York, 1971

The earliest examination of stylistic questions in the use of a particular programming language.

Weinberg, Gerald M.

The Psychology of Computer Programming

Van Nostrand Reinhold, New York, 1971

The first book to put in writing the significance of reading programs in all their stages of development, not just for defect-removal, but for its influence on all aspects of the program development process.

Weinberg, Gerald M., Stephen E. Wright, Richard Kauffman, and Martin A. Goetz

High Level COBOL Programming

Winthrop Publishers, Cambridge, Mass., 1977

A complete survey of the modern methods of programming applied to the development and maintenance of COBOL programs, including a number of procedures, checklists, and examples for applying various forms of technical review.

Yeh, R.T., editor

Special Collection on Requirement Analysis, IEEE Transactions on Software Engineering, Vol. SE-3, No. 1, January 1977

Contains seven papers and one editorial on the subject of requirements analysis. Although reviews of requirements are not the explicit topic of any one paper, anybody implementing requirements reviews will want to study this special collection.

Index